WELCOME

REAL

WORLD

WELCOME TO THE
REAL
WORLD

A Complete Guide to Job Hunting for the
Recent College Grad

John Henry Weiss

Skyhorse Publishing

Skyhorse Publishing books may be purchased in bulk at special discounts for sales promotion, corporate gifts, fund-raising, or educational purposes. Special editions can also be created to specifications. For details, contact the Special Sales Department, Skyhorse Publishing, 307 West 36th Street, 11th Floor, New York, NY 10018 or info@skyhorsepublishing.com.

Skyhorse® and Skyhorse Publishing® are registered trademarks of Skyhorse Publishing, Inc.®, a Delaware corporation.

Visit our website at www.skyhorsepublishing.com.

10 9 8 7 6 5 4 3 2 1

Library of Congress Cataloging-in-Publication Data is available on file.

ISBN: 978-1-62873-686-1

Printed in the United States

This book is dedicated to four talented, compassionate, and caring medical professionals:

Marilyn Edinburgh Baker, CNM, Robert Wood Johnson University Hospital, Hamilton, New Jersey

Jeffrey Drebin, MD and PhD, Hospital of the University of Pennsylvania, Philadelphia, Pennsylvania

Robert Mirsky, MD, St. Mary Medical Center, Langhorne, Pennsylvania

Steven Orland, MD, Capital Health Medical Center, Pennington, New Jersey

CONTENTS

Introduction ix

PART 1 Welcome to the Real World of Work 1
Chapter 1 You Have the Diploma . . . and the Invoice.
Now What?..3
Chapter 2 How to Begin Your Most Important Job Search........39
Chapter 3 Establishing a Home Office for Job Hunting 51
Chapter 4 Terms and Numbers You Absolutely Need
to Know... 61
Chapter 5 Business and Technology Certification 75
Chapter 6 Business Etiquette..81
Chapter 7 Hired! Fired! Retired! The Human Work Cycle........87

PART 2 The Place of Technology in the Workplace 97
Chapter 8 Caution! Technology Is Changing the
Workplace . . . *Fast*....................................99
Chapter 9 Social Media and Job Hunting: Be Creative!...........113

**PART 3 Finding Employers and Starting Your
Own Business 129**
Chapter 10 How to Find Employers................................ 131
Chapter 11 Where to Find Employers 149
Chapter 12 Finding Employers at Trade Shows,
Conferences, and Business Parks........................ 181
Chapter 13 Starting Your Own Business............................213
Chapter 14 Jobs for Returning Military Personnel..................225

PART 4 Written Communication: Write It Right! **245**
Chapter 15 Writing a Resume and a Career Profile.................. 247
Chapter 16 A Sample Resume and Digital Profile 267
Chapter 17 Cover Letters and Follow-Up Letters 277

PART 5 Verbal Communication: Say It Right! **283**
Chapter 18 Personal Interviews at Offices, Trade Shows,
                and Restaurants 285
Chapter 19 Phone Interviews 305
Chapter 20 How to Dress for an Interview............................ 311

PART 6 Job Descriptions, Job Offers, and Company
            Evaluations **325**
Chapter 21 How to Interpret and Respond to a Job
                Description... 327
Chapter 22 How to Evaluate and Negotiate a Job Offer 339
Chapter 23 How to Evaluate a Company 361

PART 7 Giving Back while Moving Forward in Your
            New Job **375**
Chapter 24 Work and Money: Make It Big and Give
                It Away Big.. 377
Chapter 25 Using What You Have Learned from This
                Book as You Move Forward 391

Acknowledgments **395**
Index **397**

INTRODUCTION

Welcome to the Real World addresses a continuing national crisis: more than 60 percent of recent college graduates holding associate's, bachelor's, or master's degrees have not found employment six to twelve months after receiving their diplomas. They continue to live at home, much to the distress of parents, spouses, or partners, and sit at their computers firing off resumes into space believing *that* is the way to find that all-important first job.

If you fit this description, you probably have student loans to pay off as well, and you see the debt mount each month as your job searches yield few bona fide leads despite the flurry of resumes you have sent. When the resume routine gets boring, you might turn to tweets and text messages as a last resort for finding employment. You rarely leave home to look for a job and believe that somehow the job will come to you because, after all, you are a college graduate.

Many of you truly believe the words of the speaker at your commencement exercise who may have said something to the effect of, "Congratulations, college graduates! Your college degree is your ticket to a life of happiness and job opportunities. Go forth from these hallowed halls and slay dragons, and do good things for society. You are a college graduate. You are a master of the universe."

Six months later, you begin to wonder what that diploma *really* means. You do, however, know (and so do your parents) that those nasty loans need to be paid off, and this means you had better find a job quickly. It is not a pretty picture.

Like many college graduates you probably buy into the hype about the bad economy causing the seeming lack of job opportunities. You and your colleagues blame politicians and unethical businesspeople for the high unemployment rate. "I can't find a job because there's nothing out there, and it's not my fault," many of you bellow from Boston to Seattle, from Bemidji to Miami. However, in your heart you know that is not the real reason. There is something wrong and you just cannot figure it out. There is help, however, and it is this book, *Welcome to the Real World*.

Welcome to the Real World believes that the lack of success is not due to the state of the economy or a lackluster job market; rather, it is the result of unfamiliarity with the adult world of work, its processes, and its nuances. This challenge is beyond the level of experience for you and other recent college grads, and all of you are crying out for help, along with your parents, partners, or spouses. Let's get real. For most of you, even the jargon of work is unfamiliar.

Ask most recent college grads the meaning of the term "cold call" in relation to a job search and you'll get a blank stare in return. Tell them that the best way to get a job is to knock on the doors of potential employers and they think that is "so yesterday." Tell them that communication begins with the way you dress and you get another blank stare. These are basics for those with experience in the adult world. For newly minted college graduates, like you, it is a new ball game. Your minds are truly clean slates when it comes to navigating the world of work because you have not yet played in the real world of work. There is nothing wrong with that picture. You have to begin somewhere, and I am here to help.

Adding to your confusion may be the conflicting literature about the meaning of work. Some interpret "work" as doing good things for others at home and abroad, cracking glass ceilings, or leveling the playing field for technology access. While some of that may be true, *Welcome to the Real World* believes that work is a means to self-sufficiency. When we work, we receive money in return, which enables us to provide our own food, shelter, and clothing. If a job does that and brings fulfillment in addition, that is fortuitous.

A PERSONAL NOTE TO PARENTS

Job-hunting college graduates are not the only family members feeling the stress resulting from unemployment. Parents feel the angst, too. The US Census Bureau studied the problem of children staying too long in the nest in 2012 and released some startling statistics:

1. Twenty-six-million young adults between eighteen and thirty-four were living at home with their parents.
2. Seven percent of parents with adult-age children living at home have had to alter their plans for retirement.
3. Thirteen percent of parents with adult-age children living at home have had to delay important life events, like buying or selling a house.
4. Twenty-six percent of parents with adult-age children living at home have had to take on significant debt, not only to support them while living at home, but also to repay their student loans.

There is nothing more disruptive to a family than having a diploma-holding child without a job living at home six to twelve months after graduation. Parents cringe when they hear their living-at-home college graduates whine, "There's *nothing* out there."

In a sincere attempt to help their college-educated children find a job that will put them on the road to independent living, parents often give advice of dubious value, which compounds the problem. The children shout back, "What do you know? You're twice as old as I am and your ideas are old-fashioned!" Parents shout back, "Listen to me! I've had a job for the past twenty-five years and I know how this works. If you would only do as I say, you would be working today!"

Both sides are somewhat right and somewhat wrong. To gain perspective, objectivity, and current information about the job market, parents should read *Welcome to the Real World* along with their recent college graduates. This way, the playing fields will be level, meaningful conversations will begin, and the bickering will end.

A PERSONAL NOTE TO RETURNING MILITARY PERSONNEL

I have included a bonus chapter devoted to first jobs for military personnel returning to the civilian workforce. These are the brave men and women who voluntarily gave years of their lives to keep America safe for all of us at home. Many veterans are entering the civilian job market after serving in Iraq and Afghanistan and, like recent college grads, are finding that job hunting is not for the timid.

Many of you in this category face challenging tasks, like convincing potential employers that your time spent in the military was truly a work experience. Your work experience in the military should be noted on your resume in civilian terms, and I will show you how to do just that in chapter 15. In the same chapter, I will tell you how a returning officer, Captain Kiel King, found his first civilian job after discharge. Don't miss it.

A PERSONAL NOTE TO JOB-HUNTING COLLEGE GRADS

Welcome to the Real World is a career field guide for learning the process of finding a job, and for learning how work and your personal life can live together in harmony. If you follow my advice faithfully, you *will* find that first job and make your parents, and the bank, very happy. And do not forget Grandma. After graduating, you may have learned that she kicked in $25,000 for tuition in your senior year because Mom and Dad were short on funds and the bank refused to extend your loan, which already had reached

$50,000, or maybe more. Grandma will weep with joy when she learns that you have been hired!

WHO SHOULD READ *WELCOME TO THE REAL WORLD* ... AND WHY?

Welcome to the Real World is for college graduates holding degrees at all levels who are seeking their first full-time jobs, and for their parents, partners, and spouses. It will help you navigate the confusing world of work, and help you understand that the primary function of work is to make money so that you can live independently and provide your own food, shelter, and clothing. If the job has a social mission, like teaching inner-city kids from Newark, New Jersey, how to read, that is a happy coincidence.

This book will put work in the right perspective by reviewing numbers specific to the workplace, and it will provide guidelines and even scripts for communicating with potential employers. It will provide valuable information about where to find potential employers in the flesh. It will help you chart a lifetime of meaningful work activities that dovetail with your personal life as well.

Perhaps most importantly for grads who have grown up in the digital age, *Welcome to the Real World* will tell you how to make productive use of social media to find your first job. As a millennial and digital native, you have an edge over past generations who did not have technology readily available. You have a working knowledge of every digital device on earth, and you know how to use thousands of apps. You can use social media, too, but are you using it correctly? In chapter 9 I'll tell you the cautionary tale of what happened to Miss Seattle after she used Twitter inappropriately and jeopardized her chance at proceeding to higher levels of competition. You cannot assume that LinkedIn, Facebook, Twitter, YouTube, and the various job boards will lead you to the Promised Land.

Welcome to the Real World provides real-life examples of job seekers who have been successful and those who have not. It xiv Welcome to the Real World

provides URLs that are digitally active and will give you a pathway to valuable information. A click on your iPad or an entry on your laptop or smartphone is all that it will take.

In part 4 and part 5 there are guidelines and rules for effective written and verbal communication. Worried about how to write a resume that means something, or how to communicate during an interview? You have come to the right place. To help you avoid common errors when communicating with potential employers, *Welcome to the Real World* provides basic survival tools and real-life examples. You might cry when you read about poor Patti from St. Louis, who lost a $200,000 job because of a spelling error on her resume. She learned the hard way that written communication must be precise and completely error free. If you submit a written document, print or digital, that contains spelling or grammatical errors, save your *mea culpas*. You are toast.

At the end of most chapters, you will find two bonus items. The "Chapter Takeaways" are indispensable rules that will guide your behavior as you search for that first job. The books listed under "Job Hunter's Library" will extend the chapter content and act as the backbone for your work library.

I know the challenges and problems of recent college grads. I hear you, and I'm going to help you find solutions. Read this book and frequently check out the companion website, www. firstjobsforcollegegrads.com, for the latest research on the job market, tips for making productive use of your time, and newsletters and blogs from your peers. Most importantly, I provide listings of venues, like trade shows and conferences, where you will meet hiring authorities personally. I even go so far as to list by name and website the important conference centers in each state in chapter 12.

Frequently, I provide the names and websites for companies that I consider the best of the best, and call them *Real World Faves*. These are companies like Whole Foods, Salesforce.com, Dow Chemical, and MassMutual Financial Group—all trusted names in their market niches and all sporting a worker-friendly culture.

TWO GUIDING PRINCIPLES

Welcome to the Real World provides a working set of instructions for college graduates searching for their first jobs. The two main premises of the book are:

1. Companies do not hire resumes, images, tweets, or videos. They hire living human beings who had the smarts to find them and build a personal relationship. One does that by leaving the house to seek out employers, in the flesh, at venues such as job fairs, trade shows, conferences, and even coffee shops like Starbucks. You will hear that refrain many times throughout this book because it is critically important to your success in finding your first job, or your second, third, or fourth.
2. Work is a means of becoming self-sufficient—that is, to be able to provide your own food, shelter, clothing, transportation, insurance, and any other necessities required to function independently in today's world.

ABOUT THE TITLE

The title for this book was chosen with great care by the author and publisher. It is not just another marketing ploy to sell books. *Welcome to the Real World* was chosen to reflect where you are at this point in your life. When you were in college or the military, your world was entirely different, and you played in that world with a different set of rules. You have moved on to a new reality: the adult world of work. Welcome!

Consider *Welcome to the Real World* and this website, www.firstjobsforcollegegrads.com, your career guide not only for finding your first job, but also for understanding the real world of work and for beginning the rest of your life.

PART 1

WELCOME TO THE REAL WORLD OF WORK

Chapter 1

You Have the Diploma ... and the Invoice. Now What?

You've worked hard to earn that coveted degree held by only 35 percent of the US population. "What are my options?" you might ask. "Do I look for a part-time job and continue on to graduate school? How about an MBA? Law or med school? Should I join the military or teach?" The choices are many, and you probably hadn't really thought about them until now.

CONGRATULATIONS, COLLEGE GRAD!

After the parties, the congratulatory messages from family and friends, and a few days or weeks of celebrating, you now are faced with what to do with the rest of your life. You might have assumed that looking for a job would be an easy task because you have a college diploma.

But suddenly you find yourself five or six months into this job-hunting process, and you don't even have a lead for a personal interview. That's worrisome because a bank officer has already called you three times about your late student loan payments.

Unless you had a specific vocation in mind while attending college, like being a medical professional, a teacher, or a software designer, you are faced with daunting decisions about the rest of your life, particularly those related to careers.

It's a tough road to navigate, and that is why I wrote *Welcome to the Real World* and created its supporting website, www.firstjobsforcollegegrads.com. Not only are you looking for your first job, but you are also looking at the rest of your life. What you learn in *Welcome to the Real World* will help you determine how to spend the next forty or so years in the world of work, which consists of three parts: *being hired*, *being fired*, and *being retired*.

The business of life is not difficult to understand. You are born. You die. And, in between, you work. That is the human condition, and *Welcome to the Real World* will help you through the "in between."

BREAKING THE MYTH THAT COLLEGE GRADS ALWAYS WORK IN WHITE-COLLAR JOBS

The common wisdom is that if you earned a college diploma, you must work in a white-collar job. Your rightful place is in the halls of Big Company USA, and to do anything else means you are a failure. This is just not true and reflects a pervasive disconnect between holding a diploma and employment.

You attend college not only to increase the chances of finding a job upon graduation, but also to learn how the world works and how to find your place in it. College helps you hone your verbal and written communication skills. It helps you develop an understanding and appreciation of different cultures, value systems, and points of view. It helps you develop empathy for those less fortunate and a resolve to give back to the community in proportion to your success. These attitudes and skills will be with you for the rest of your life, whether you are the president of a company or a hands-on worker in the home construction industry.

Now that you have that coveted diploma, you can do whatever you want to do in the world of work. If you have an affinity for working with your hands in an occupation like carpentry, just do it, no matter how much your parents might whine, "We sent you to college and now you want to pound nails?" Tragically, many workers go through life doing something in the corporate environment when they really want to be out working in a construction job, or producing commercials, or being an environmental photographer focusing on Alaska and the Arctic tundra (like Tom Mangelsen, www.mangelsen.com), or owning and managing a storefront business like a fast-food restaurant.

DO WHAT YOU LOVE

You've heard it said: "Do what you love and you will never work a day in your life." Guess what? It's true. Find a first job that gives you satisfaction in addition to the ability to pay the bills for food, clothing, shelter, insurance, transportation, and entertainment, and you will be a happy individual.

I can understand where you are at this point in your life because I was faced with the same decisions when I earned my undergraduate degree from DePaul University in Chicago. I can feel your anxiety as you search for answers. I think your alma mater should have given you at least one course in career choices and job hunting for the $125,000 to $250,000 you spent on tuition, room and board, books, tech hardware and apps, transportation, and all the rest, including a diploma fee. (A diploma fee? That's just ridiculous!) However, let's not waste time whining and proceed instead to the six options you have as the result of being awarded a diploma:

1. You could work for a large company or a small business.
2. You could work for the federal government or your state government.
3. You could start your own business.
4. You could continue your education.
5. You could join the Peace Corps or enlist in the military.

6. Or you could sit at home firing off resumes, tweets, and YouTube videos into space, hoping that by some miracle of technology these lame efforts will land you a job.

CHOICE NUMBER ONE: WORKING FOR A LARGE COMPANY OR A SMALL BUSINESS

You can seek work with a large corporation or a small business using this book and our website, www.firstjobsforcollegegrads.com, as major tools for securing an entry-level position. Your immediate goal is to find a job that pays enough money to make you self-sufficient. You are not looking for "fulfillment" just yet. First, you need to enter the workforce to make money to pay off your debts, like that nasty student loan, and gain experience and skills that will enable you to advance as far as your intelligence, energy, and passion will take you. If that first job happens to be one that you are passionate about, then all the better.

How Your College Major Relates to Job Opportunities

Consider your college major as you begin to explore various industries and companies within those industries. Certain majors like math and science will lead you in one direction, while business and education will take you down different roads. Arts and humanities majors will travel different paths, too. Let's consider where your major might take you.

Arts and Humanities Majors

Arts and humanities majors have a challenging task breaking into the world of work because there so many options. If you are not sure what path to follow, it is probably because you are not aware of the thousands of jobs available in many different industries. Here are some valuable resources.

Occupational Outlook Handbook, 2013–2014. This comprehensive thousand-page resource developed by the US Department of Labor can be viewed online or by purchasing the print version, which I recommend. Buy it for $19.95 from Barnes & Noble (www.barnesandnoble.com), or Amazon (www.amazon.com), or directly from the publisher, JIST Publishing (jist.emcp.com). Click now and this resource will be at your door in just a few days. Want to see it today? Go to your local library, or buy it online and download it to your digital reading device. Here is an example of how this resource works and how it could lead to your first job:

Access the *Occupational Outlook Handbook* using the JIST website at jist.emcp.com. Click on the "Career Opportunities" button under the "About JIST" menu option as I just did. I found job openings in California, Texas, Tennessee, Kentucky, West Virginia, New York City, and New Jersey. If you see a position you like and want to apply, do not send your resume to employment@emcp.com as the company requests. Call the customer service number and ask for the name and email address of the human resources director. Too bold? I did just that and the customer service rep gave me her name and email address. No questions asked. What could be easier?

Sending your cover letter and resume directly to a named person like the human resources director is the best way to establish a relationship with a key person in the organization, one who is in charge of hiring entry-level employees like you. Isn't that better than sending your resume to employment@emcp.com? Remember, companies do not hire resumes; they hire living, breathing human beings. Better yet, if you live in the Minneapolis/St. Paul area, where the company is headquartered, take your resume, go directly to the company offices, and ask to see the human resources director. In the world of work, this is known as making a "cold call" (more on this later). If she asks how you found her name, tell her how it happened and give her my regards.

Customer Service Workers. While tracking down the human resources director, I just learned about another valuable resource for information: the customer service representative. These individuals are trained to be helpful, courteous, and just plain nice. Customer service reps have many social-worker attributes and will do anything within reason to help individuals in need. If you want information about a company, always call the number listed for the customer service department, not the general company number. Alternatively, you can contact the customer service department online for help, but I recommend using the phone because it establishes a more personal relationship. When you get this person on the phone, simply state your case like this: "I'm Barbara Smith, and I want to contact your human resources director about job opportunities. Could you please give me her or his name and email address?" Enter the name, phone number, and email address of the customer service rep in your database for future reference.

The Yellow Pages.   Another overlooked resource is your local Yellow Pages directory available in either print or digital format. It lists every business in your area alphabetically and provides email addresses, phone numbers, and even the names of owners of small businesses. I recommend the print version for using the flip method to scan for businesses and industries that interest you. In chapter 11, I will tell you how one person found a great job using the Yellow Pages.

Certain arts majors have a greater challenge entering the corporate world of work. Let's assume for a moment that you majored in English but have no idea about what to do next. One path is to explore a career in the communications industry working in an editorial position with publishers like McGraw-Hill, Pearson, the *New York Times*, Skyhorse Publishing, the *Chicago Tribune*, the *Wall Street Journal*, *Forbes*, *Sports Illustrated*, the *Los Angeles Times*, *Travel and Leisure*, and the *Detroit Free Press*, just to name a few. Where will this entry-level position take you twenty-five years from now? What can an English major really accomplish? Well, how about becoming governor of Massachusetts? Mitt Romney, who was CEO of Bain Capital, CEO of the 2002 Winter Olympics Committee, and a 2012 presidential candidate, started out as an English major.

Business Majors

In years past, business majors had a relatively easy time finding entry-level jobs, but today that is not the case. Business majors may know how to read a balance sheet and know the meaning of acronyms like EBITDA, but employers are looking for more than that. Business majors need to add more bullet points to their resumes, like exceptional written and verbal communication skills.

Having a working knowledge of business relationships is vital because every job involves dealing with customers. Why? Because every product and service produced by a company is sold to customers. How many times have I been stunned by MBAs who know nothing about their customers? A lot. Once you consider the human factor, business operations take on a completely new meaning.

Business majors with knowledge of the human side of business are marked for success. You might consider bypassing traditional jobs in accounting and finance and opt for a job in sales, marketing, or business development. These are exciting places because jobs of this type involve dealing with people outside of the office, namely, the customer. The next time you see a sales, marketing, or business development job, explore it. You may uncover an entirely new way of looking at the business world.

By the way, business majors, if you are thinking about pursuing an MBA, note that admissions directors do not accept every Tina, Tom, and Tamara who submits an application. Now, one of the most important factors in assessing MBA candidates is potential employability. Your candidacy will be assessed not only by the admissions staff, but also by the career counseling staff. They will want to know if your career goals are reasonable and coordinate with your undergraduate degree and your future MBA. This is important because graduate schools of business are judged by the employment rate for their MBA graduates. If you walk in for an interview knowing little or nothing about the job market, your chances of gaining admission are greatly reduced. Therefore, everything I talk about in the following pages is important for you to know. In today's world, MBA candidates should consider the admissions process comparable to the process for securing a job with a private-sector employer.

One thing you might do to enhance your chances for admission is to earn your business and technology certification from an organization like HigherNext (see chapter 5).

There are many career choices for business majors, ranging from an accounting job with a local entrepreneurial employer in your neighborhood, to employment as a financial analyst with Wall Street behemoths like Goldman Sachs, JPMorgan Chase, Wells Fargo, or Bank of America. Exercise due diligence evaluating these companies, however, and look closely at their ethical behavior in recent years in addition to their performance records. The last thing you want is to be part of a company that manipulates the numbers for the benefit of a handful of executives or a select list of clients. Here's an example of one such company:

Despite its big name, Barclays is somewhere you might not want to work. This multinational financial company with revenues in the billions of dollars was caught in an unlawful and unethical scheme to fix interest rates. The company admitted to this charge and agreed to pay a fine of $453 million to the US Justice Department and the UK Financial Services Authority in 2012. The last thing you want to do is cast your lot with a company with an unsavory past.

Real World Faves   **Upstanding Financial Institutions to Work For**

There are many upstanding regional banks and financial institutions to explore for your first job. The banks listed here are frequently cited by financial rating firms as being the best of breed. I'm giving you their URLs so you can review their career pages as you read this book. If you like the feel, smell, and look of money, you may find the Promised Land with one of the following companies:

1. *Sun Trust Banks,* www.suntrust.com, Atlanta, Georgia. This company traces its roots back to 1811, operates in all Southern states and Washington DC, and employs 30,000 workers.
2. *Regions Financial Corporation,* www.regions.com, Birmingham, Alabama. This bank has 1,700 branches operating across sixteen states in the South, the Midwest, and Texas, and employs close to 30,000 workers.
3. *Fifth Third Bank,* www.53.com, Cincinnati, Ohio. Its history extends back to 1858. The company has more than 1,200 full-service banking centers and operates in the South, the Midwest, and Pennsylvania.
4. *US Bancorp,* www.usbank.com, Minneapolis, Minnesota. This is the country's fifth largest bank and employs approximately 60,000 workers. The company operates in twenty-five Midwestern and Western states. Interestingly, US Bancorp financed Charles Lindbergh's history-making flight across the Atlantic Ocean. This bank has an excellent reputation for hiring women into what was once exclusively a man's world and has been cited frequently for its quality service to its customers.
5. *First Niagara Bank,* www.firstniagara.com, Buffalo, New York. First Niagara was founded in 1870 as Farmers and Mechanics Savings Bank. Its footprint covers New York, the Mid-Atlantic states, and New England. The company posts many of its job openings on LinkedIn.
6. *Columbia Bank,* www.columbiabank.com, Tacoma, Washington. This bank operates 157 branches in Washington and Oregon and employs 1,200 workers. It was founded in 1988.
7. *Frost Bank,* www.frostbank.com, San Antonio, Texas. Frost was founded and chartered in 1868 and operates 110 service centers across Texas. Frost employs more than 4,000 workers and is noted for its involvement in community affairs. It

likes to be known as a good neighbor serving the community. Frost has seven human resources offices across Texas, and if you go on its website, you will find the locations *and* the phone numbers. All you need to do is call, ask for the name of the human resources director, and begin to build a relationship. Hey, Texans, get on this one … Now.

Education Majors

Finding a teaching position is not as easy today as it was just a few years ago. Budget cuts at the state and local levels have resulted in local school districts reducing staff or consolidating. For example, the Philadelphia school district cut more than 3,000 teaching positions going into the 2014 school year and closed twenty-seven schools. You will need to follow the same instructions as arts, business, and STEM (science, technology, engineering, and mathematics) majors.

Most likely, you received help finding teaching opportunities from your college career counselors and education advisors, but unfortunately, many of you still do not have a full-time teaching job six to twelve months after receiving your diploma. Many education majors take substitute teaching jobs as they look for permanent assignments, and I believe that is a good way to get your foot into the world of school employment.

Nancy from North Carolina. I attended an education industry conference recently in Baltimore and met a vice president for sales with an educational technology company. I was evaluating his candidacy for a position, and in the course of our conversation, he mentioned that his daughter Nancy had just found a teaching job in a very interesting way. She put aside her digital gadgets and began calling on individual elementary schools during the summer months.

Her plan was to meet school principals personally instead of just making a phone call or sending a resume.

She drove to Washington School, parked her car in the empty parking lot, and made her way toward the building. Unbeknownst to her, the school principal was looking out the window, saw her walking toward the building, and commented to his administrative assistant about how unusual it was to see a well-dressed young woman coming to the building. When Nancy arrived at his office, she received a warm welcome and learned that a job was available because a teacher had recently resigned due to pregnancy. The principal was so impressed with her demeanor and dress that he hired her on the spot after reviewing her resume and teaching credentials. How did Nancy's father know this? The principal told him this story when he was visiting the school on parent's night to see his daughter's classroom.

Your search activities should begin with a personal visit to your county or district superintendent's office of education. Dress appropriately; this means no jeans, sneakers, sweatshirts, or other casual dress. You are looking for a job and the unwritten rules of conduct apply to teachers as well as corporate workers. The story about Nancy from North Carolina illustrates my point.

Recruiters for Education Majors

Another source for finding teaching positions is to contact recruiters who specialize in placing teachers. Conduct an Internet search for education recruiters in your area and check out the following as well:

CalWest Educators Placement, www.calwesteducators.com, (800-390-4737). This recruiter is located in Encino, California, and places teachers in California and the West.

Carney, Sandoe & Associates, www.carneysandoe.com, (617-542-0260). This Boston-based company places teachers in the US and abroad.

The Education Group, www.educationgroup.com, (800-369-9102). The Education Group is based in Dallas and places teachers and administrators in Texas and across the entire US.

Educational Directions Incorporated, www.edu-directions.com, (800-647-2794). This firm is located in Portsmouth, Rhode Island, and places teachers across the US and internationally. It specializes in placement for independent (or private) schools.

Educator's Ally, www.educatorsally.com, (914-666-6323). Educator's Ally was founded in 1975 and is located in Bedford Hills, New York. This firm places teachers and administrators in private and public schools.

Social Networking for Educators. The premier social networking site for educators is EdWeb, www.edweb.net. This is a professional online community. EdWeb not only will keep you updated on the latest trends and research in education, but also will provide leads for teaching and administrative positions in education, especially in the Mid-Atlantic area. In addition, you can participate in frequent webinars at a great price ... Free. There is no charge to sign up for EdWeb. Do it now.

What Else for Education Majors?

As an alternative to teaching, education majors might consider pursuing a corporate job. Human resources directors always like candidates with a degree in education because workers attracted to the teaching profession usually have a good sense of values and mission. Follow the general rules in this book and opportunities will come your way. As a former teacher from Chicago, I can tell you how highly my candidacy was respected when I decided to change my career path and seek employment in the corporate world. I targeted educational publishing companies for positions in sales, and after only three months into my search, I was offered sales, positions with three major publishers.

The Education Industry

If you want to work in the broadly defined field of education but are not keen on being a classroom teacher, there are many jobs with companies that produce instructional materials and provide services for grades K–12 and higher education.

A recent Association of Education Publishers (AEP) newsletter lists four good reasons for pursuing a career on the corporate side of education. Here they are:

1. You believe that literacy and learning is the birthright of every child.
2. You have a passion for providing the educational tools that will help today's students fully develop their creative and intellectual potential to become tomorrow's productive, engaged citizens.
3. You believe that there is an urgent need to develop effective learning solutions in all subject areas for students of all talents, skills, and ability levels, and that these solutions must motivate them to be lifelong learners so that they can adapt and compete in a global economy.
4. You view the digital transformation as an opportunity to equalize education for all students and to support teachers in meeting the classroom challenges of the future.

Common Core Standards and NCLB

All education majors need to be familiar with the Common Core Standards and NCLB, the No Child Left Behind Act, the latter a set of accountability standards passed by the federal government in 2001. It was a bipartisan piece of legislation written and promoted by President George W. Bush and Senator Edward Kennedy. This bipartisan legislation is an example of what can be accomplished when both parties come together to do something good for America.

Employers, whether they're from a school district, a state department of education, or a company in the education industry, will require that you have a working knowledge of the Common Core Standards and the No Child Left Behind Act, which you can learn more about by clicking on www.nea.org, one of many sites that will give you the history and content of this landmark piece of legislation. Do not go into an interview without first doing your research on NCLB.

The same should be said for Common Core Standards, which were designed to reform and unify instruction for English/language arts and mathematics education across the country. Common Core is not a federal program, and as such, adoption of these standards rests with each individual state's Department of Education (DOE). So far, almost all states have signed on. To learn about Common Core generally, once again click on www.nea.org. To learn about Common Core in your state specifically, go to your state's Department of Education website. For example, if you are in Florida, click on www.fldoe.org.

Education majors, do not sell yourselves short. You bring much to the table and employers will respect your candidacy, regardless of industry. You are off to a good start, and I am confident you will find your place in the world of work and have a rewarding career. When you find your first job, please access my website and tell me about your success story. Click here and tell me the good news, which I will share with your colleagues: www.firstjobsforcollegegrads.com.

Science, Technology, Engineering, and Mathematics Majors

If you have a degree in one of the STEM majors (science, technology, engineering, and mathematics), your career path is already focused, but you, too, will profit from the advice in this book. The process of finding an entry-level position is the same for all college graduates, regardless of major.

STEM majors are usually filled with boundless energy and are always thinking ahead. Do you want to be president of a company?

When you get that first job as an assistant mechanical engineering technician, do you look forward twenty-five years and envision your business card reading, "Joe Smith, President, the Boeing Company"? All company presidents began their careers with an entry-level position. Aim high and you will get there.

The US provides jobs for 155 million workers. More than half of these workers are employed in STEM-related positions. Huge manufacturing companies like General Motors, Ford, Chrysler, Boeing, John Deere, and Caterpillar are waiting for you with a variety of jobs located all across the US and abroad.

Luckily, manufacturing is still alive and well in the US and accounts for about 12 percent of our GDP. Do not buy into the hype, "The US is a service economy. We are no longer a manufacturing country." It's just not true. For example, two of America's premier heavy equipment and farming implement manufacturers are Caterpillar and John Deere, and both companies employ hundreds of thousands of workers.

Recently, I saw an interview on CNBC with the CEO of the Peoria, Illinois-based company Caterpillar. He was begging for STEM majors to apply for jobs. His company employs more than 125,000 workers worldwide. Review the website to see what's available for you. Just click here to get started: www.caterpillar.com. Go to "Careers" and you will see a multitude of jobs not only in the US but in other countries as well.

Next, take a look at John Deere at www.deere.com. Click on "Our Company" and you will get to the career pages. You will be surprised at what this great American icon has to offer. I like the way Deere discloses the fundamental points about working there, including information about their culture. Deere was founded in 1837, is based in Moline, Illinois, and employs close to 60,000 workers.

For Every Major: Find Your Passion

So what interests you? There *is* something that you must like better than anything else, but it may be buried deep in your psyche. How do you reach down and discover what this is? A starting point is to read the latest edition of the ***Occupational Outlook Handbook*** because it lists every job by title in every industry in the US, *and* provides salary information, job requirements, and projections for job growth in a particular field.

The first chapter in this handbook is titled, "Green Occupations," which includes some intriguing niche industries like biomass, geothermal, hydroelectric, wind, and solar energy production, as well as weatherization installation, environmental restoration, water resource management, industrial ecology, and more. Many jobs in the green industry require hands-on technical work, but many others include specialties like finance, marketing, sales, human resources, customer service, and project management, all positions that do not require a STEM major.

CHOICE NUMBER TWO: WORKING IN A FEDERAL, STATE OR LOCAL GOVERNMENT JOB

Contrary to what you might think, the largest employer in the United States is not Google, Microsoft, Apple, or General Motors. It's the government. At the end of 2012, the total number of federal, state, and local government employees was approximately twenty-two million. Of that number, the federal government alone employs approximately sixteen million workers. These numbers are based on data from the Bureau of Labor Statistics and the Census Bureau.

There is much confusion about government jobs. The common perception is that these are positions that come and go with elections. However, there are many jobs that exist regardless of the political party in power. These jobs keep the wheels of government turning and frequently carry attractive salaries and excellent benefits. Federal, state, and local websites post these jobs, and you apply for them in the same way that you would apply for a non-government job. Check out all government websites to see what's available. Here are a few to get you started:

US Department of Health and Human Services, www.hhs.gov

US Department of Education, www.ed.gov

US Department of Labor, www.dol.gov

Many government jobs offer significant job satisfaction plus attractive income. In addition, jobs in local, state, and federal education give you the opportunity to make a significant social impact. Government is something that touches every citizen, college graduate or not, and your participation in the process is a significant responsibility. The process of government in a country with a population of 315 million, like the United States, is complex but offers the opportunity to do something meaningful and long lasting. Yes, one person can make a difference. It's not all partisan politics.

Here's an example of what one person did that affects all of us living in the United States. It happened because she applied her intelligence, energy, and passion to get the job done, and it flies in the face of the media gurus who have nothing but criticism for our elected officials.

Congresswoman Patricia "Pat" Schroeder from Colorado. Mrs. Patricia Schroeder was a mother of two young children when she decided to make a difference and run for political office in Colorado. She had no family history in politics, no one to pave the way for her through political connections, and no family money to pay for her election campaign. After a hard-fought campaign, she was elected to the United States House of Representatives and went on to serve twelve two-year terms.

During her tenure in the House, she became the Dean of Congressional Women, co-chaired the Congressional Caucus on Women's Issues for ten years, and served on the House Judiciary Committee, the Post Office and Civil

Service Committee, and was the first woman to serve on the House Armed Services Committee. As chair of the House Select Committee on Children, Youth, and Families from 1991 to 1993, Mrs. Schroeder guided the Family and Medical Leave Act and the National Institutes of Health Revitalization Act to enactment in 1993, a fitting legislative achievement for her lifetime of work on behalf of women's and family issues. In addition, she was active on many military issues, expediting the National Security Committee's vote to allow women to fly combat missions in 1991, and working to improve the situation of military families through passage of her Military Family Act in 1985.

So what's the big deal about the Family and Medical Leave Act (FMLA)? Here's a summary of this act from the US Department of Labor:

The FMLA entitles eligible employees of covered employers to take unpaid, job-protected leave for specified family and medical reasons with continuation of group health insurance coverage under the same terms and conditions as if the employee had not taken leave. Eligible employees are entitled to twelve workweeks of leave in a twelve-month period for the following reasons:

- the birth of a child and the care for the newborn child within one year of birth;
- the placement with the employee of a child for adoption or foster care and the care for the newly placed child within one year of placement;
- the care for the employee's spouse, child, or parent who has a serious health condition;
- a serious health condition that makes the employee

> unable to perform the essential functions of his or
> her job;
>
> - any qualifying exigency arising out of the fact that
>   the employee's spouse, son, daughter, or parent is a
>   covered military member on covered active duty;
> - Twenty-six workweeks of leave during a single
>   twelve-month period to care for a covered service
>   member with a serious injury or illness if the eligible
>   employee is the service member's spouse, son, daugh-
>   ter, parent, or next of kin (military caregiver leave).

Prior to FMLA, unscrupulous employers frequently fired women who had a child and took more than a week or two off from work.

Mrs. Schroeder is the author of *Champion of the Great American Family* and *24 Years of House Work ... and the Place Is Still a Mess.* She is in the National Women's Hall of Fame and the Colorado Women's Hall of Fame. She was presented the 2008 Winn Newman Lifetime Achievement Award from the Americans for Democratic Action. Also, she served as CEO of AAP and was the Board Chair of the English-Speaking Union, a New York City-based nonprofit dedicated to promoting scholarship and educational opportunities for its members in the US and in other English-speaking nations.

When you are in need, and the FMLA comes to your support, think of Congresswoman Schroeder and give thanks that she had the courage, intelligence, energy, and passion to do something good for all Americans. Her story proves that one person can make a difference. If she did it, *so can you*, as an elected politician.

CHOICE NUMBER THREE: STARTING YOUR OWN BUSINESS

If working for a company or the government is not appealing to you, a good alternate is to start your own business, working as a single proprietor or in partnership with a trusted colleague. Can you really be successful this way? Well, once there were two people who dropped out of college and began working on their dream in a garage located in a place we now call Silicon Valley, California. Their names were Steve Jobs and Steve Wozniak. You know the rest of the story. Apple. And do not forget a Harvard dropout who started his own business in the middle of a recession. His name? Bill Gates. His company? Microsoft. And how about another Harvard dropout, Mark Zuckerberg, Facebook founder and CEO?

Most people who start their own businesses have neither the inclination nor interest in establishing a technology company like those mentioned above, but are satisfied with something like a window-washing business or a wood flooring company. Both are terrific businesses that could deliver a six-figure income. In chapter 13, you will read about Gary Schultz, who said "forget it" to corporate work and now has a six-figure income from his window-washing business in the Philadelphia suburbs.

CHOICE NUMBER FOUR: CONTINUING YOUR EDUCATION

Your fourth choice is to continue your education by enrolling in graduate level courses in a field you find interesting. Of course, this presupposes that you have the money to pay the tuition, or that you are willing to take a student loan to cover this cost. Even if you have no interest in a graduate degree at this time, I suggest that you continue your education even as you seek your first job.

Going forward, you will need to update your skills continuously to remain competitive in the job market. In chapter 22, I will tell you how to negotiate company-paid education and professional development into your benefits package. Make no mistake about it—you will need to continue your education to remain self-sufficient during your work cycle, and it is your own responsibility to do so. If your company will not contribute to your continuing education, you must do this on your own.

Nobody owes you anything in this world. This is your ball game, so get with the program. By the way, potential employers will be impressed when they learn that you are continuing your education . . . on your own dime.

Hola, Amigos! Habla Español?

Updating your technology skills is imperative, but knowing a foreign language, like Spanish, will be a very big plus for your candidacy throughout the work cycle. According to the Pew Research Center, 86 percent of the population growth in the US between now and 2050 will come from immigration, primarily from Asian and Hispanic countries. It's estimated that Hispanics will comprise 29 percent of the US population then, by far the largest ethnic group in our country.

The reason for learning Spanish is *not* because the US is destined to become a bilingual country. As American companies increase business activities in Central America and South America, workers who speak Spanish will have a decided advantage over those who do not. For example, if you are director of marketing for a domestic solar energy company and are dealing with a company in Buenos Aires, Argentina, at their home office, you will need to speak Spanish to communicate effectively.

You will gain a decided advantage over your peers who speak only English by learning Spanish in your spare time. It's inexpensive, it's fun, and it will open doors to jobs and social contacts that you never imagined. And you don't need to attend a brick-and-mortar school to get started. Here are two online sources for learning Spanish: Rosetta Stone, www.rosettastone.com, and Berlitz, www.berlitz.com. Click now and learn how to speak and write in Spanish quickly and inexpensively. Also, check your local community colleges for foreign language instruction courses. Usually these courses are inexpensive and will get you started in the right direction.

Business and Technology Certification

To improve your technology and business skills I recommend that you take the business and technology certification course from HigherNext, a Philadelphia-based company. Their model is nothing short of brilliant. The program is called the Certified Business Laureate Program (CBL). Earning this online certification degree will give you a decided advantage over job candidates holding only a bachelor's or master's degree. Check out their website and take this reasonably priced course. Enter this URL in your smartphone, iPad, or tablet, or just click on this active link: www.highernext.com. At $79, this is the best money you will ever spend. Can you imagine walking in for an interview and presenting not only your resume, but also your CBL degree to the hiring manager? You cannot afford to miss this one! For more, go to chapter 5.

CHOICE NUMBER FIVE: JOIN THE PEACE CORPS OR THE MILITARY

Consider giving back to the country by joining the Peace Corps or enlisting in the military. Both offer exciting opportunities for personal growth and acquiring skill sets that will last throughout your work cycle.

The Peace Corps

The Peace Corps (www.peacecorps.gov) no longer means working in rice paddies in Cambodia or building houses in rural Kenya. Today, college grads volunteering for the Peace Corps work in foreign countries on initiatives that involve education, economic development, health education, health care, agriculture, and environmental programs, just to name a few. The Peace Corps offers a comprehensive list of benefits, including deferment of your student loan, opportunities for graduate level education, full medical and dental insurance, lengthy vacation periods, free travel, and living and housing expenses. Review the website for more information and instructions for submitting your application.

Going forward after leaving the Peace Corps, you will find that employers consider this experience valuable and will move your candidacy to the front of the pack.

Joining the Military

Join the military and you will embark on an exciting career serving the nation in one of five service branches: the army, the navy, the marine corps, the air force, and the coast guard. Serving in the military is more than fighting in foreign countries. In fact, most military personnel never see combat. They work behind the scenes in jobs that require a college level education and leadership skills.

Joining the military does not mean a lifelong stint in the service branch of your choice. You enlist for a certain number of years after which you can leave the military or reenlist for another specified time period. While serving, you will have opportunities for graduate level education and learning leadership skills that will serve you well when you return to the civilian work force.

What's your choice? The air force, where you could find yourself piloting an F-16? The army, where you could be working in an engineering position? The navy, where you might be working on a nuclear submarine or nuclear aircraft carrier? These are exciting careers, and you can learn more about them by reviewing these websites:

Today's Military, www.todaysmilitary.com. This is an official Department of Defense website that will walk you through each branch of service and tell you the processes for enlisting. In addition, it will provide links to each branch of service so that you can explore your area of interest in detail.

Join the Military, www.military.com. This site provides all you need to know about each step in the enlisting process in non-military language. It will tell you specific requirements for enlisting, how to contact a military recruiter, how to move through the process, what's involved in basic training, and more.

Joining the military today is not a slam dunk for just anyone who contacts a recruiter. The military does not accept everyone. You must meet a rigid set of requirements before being considered to serve. But once accepted in the service branch of your choice, you can rest assured that this will be an unforgettable experience.

CHOICE NUMBER SIX: SITTING AT HOME AND FIRING OFF RESUMES

A sixth choice after receiving your diploma is to sit at a computer and fire off resumes and tweets to places like Job Box 29, Position #127, Employment Counselor, Planet Mars, and the like. Here's an example of what could happen if you choose that route:

Recently, I saw a three-minute segment about the job market on CNN. The spot focused on job hunting by recent college graduates. A highlight of this clip was a recent college grad named Bob who sat in front of a desktop computer and said to the camera, "I've been looking for a job for over six months with no luck. I have a BS in Business Administration and have sent out several hundred resumes and I have not connected. It's really discouraging." I felt sorry for Bob. I really did. Nobody at his alma mater had told him that firing off resumes to an entity without a name was no way to find a job. And nobody told Bob that using digital media exclusively to find a job has a success rate of only 10 percent. However, I must compliment Bob because at least he had established a home office just as I instruct in chapter 8.

Don't Be a Bum

Sending a resume or a candidate profile to *something* rather than *someone* is, in a word, "dumb." If you continue on this route, you are well on your way to becoming a bum.

If you choose this route, let me know. I'll toss a couple of bucks in your pot when I see you panhandling at Fisherman's Wharf in San Francisco. If I do not find you there, I'll look for you at Penn Station in New York City, where you might be strumming a guitar and wondering how all of those commuters hustling to catch the 5:45 train to Trenton found their first jobs. I'll buy you a coffee and a couple of Krispy Kreme doughnuts. What do you like, chocolate-glazed or plain? Take a coffee break, my compliments, and think about it.

But wait a minute! Maybe you can turn the coffee break into a job. While munching on your chocolate-glazed, put down the guitar, take out your iPad, and click on www.krispykreme.com for information about a franchise. The last time I checked, I found that franchises were available in Chicago; Houston; Buffalo and Rochester, New York; and Harrisburg/Lancaster/York, Pennsylvania. Owning and operating a doughnut business is a sweet job. Check it out while you are taking a break from begging!

Finding your first job means leaving the house and building personal relationships instead of sitting at home and firing off resumes into space. I'll tell you how in upcoming chapters, so stay tuned.

LEAD, FOLLOW, OR GET OUT OF THE WAY

Finding your spot in the world of work is one thing, but what you do after you find that spot will determine how you will spend the next forty or more years of your life. Let's assume Ford Motors hired you for an entry-level marketing position and your title is assistant to the marketing manager for Ford Fusion, a hybrid that has become a bestseller. It is a nice job and entitles you to a discount on a new car in addition to a competitive salary, bonus, and benefits. Life is good. Now that you have arrived, what's next? Do you want to remain an assistant for the next forty years, or do you want to move up the ladder to a position of greater responsibility and authority?

If you are happy with this level position, that is fine. You can perform needed tasks that will benefit the company as a whole by generating revenue, which in turn can be used to expand the business and create more jobs. You can support your boss, the marketing manager, by offering loyalty and carrying out the mission of your job in every respect. You can participate in company outreach efforts to do good things for people in need because Ford is very community conscious. That is a brief description of a good follower, and every company needs workers like that.

However, you might not be entirely happy in an assistant or associate position and have your sights set on being the next marketing manager, and after that, marketing director, and after that, vice president of marketing, or even president. You have always been an ambitious person, dating back to your high school years, when you were senior-class vice president and wrote an environmental column for the school newspaper. In college, you were the president of the Spanish club, where you decided on the community outreach initiatives for the group. You derived much satisfaction from taking a leadership role. You liked to create and implement plans by directing the activities of others and mentoring new members.

If this is your profile and you envision yourself in a management position, ask your boss to mentor you and lead you in the right direction so that you can move into a position of greater responsibility when the opportunity arises. Being a leader is a serious responsibility because the workers you manage will depend on you for direction, mentoring, inspiration, and leadership.

Both leader and follower are important roles for workers to play. One is not more important than the other is. Both have meaning. Both have value. Leaders cannot function without loyal followers to accomplish the mission. Followers will not have a productive work experience without competent leaders. If you are neither a good leader nor a good follower, you might as well get out of the way.

RESOURCES FOR FINDING A CORPORATE JOB OR STARTING YOUR OWN BUSINESS

President Calvin Coolidge, in his 1925 Address to the American Society of Newspaper Editors, said, "The business of America is business." That is as true today as it was then. The majority of college graduates will work in the business world, and therefore, you should know how the business of America works.

There are many resources to help you navigate the world of work. They will save you time, build your knowledge of the business world, and steer you in the right direction. Let's review some of these easily accessible resources.

Venture for America

This organization recruits the best and brightest college graduates to work in entrepreneurial businesses located in cities throughout the country. It describes itself as "a program for young, talented grads to spend two years in the trenches of a start-up with the goal that these graduates will become socialized and mobilized as entrepreneurs moving forward."

Venture "fellows" are recruited each year and are paid a salary and benefits while honing work skills over a two-year period with entrepreneurial businesses, working in cities across the country. The goal of VFA is to recruit 100,000 college graduates by 2025. Applicants are required to have a bachelor's degree from an accredited college or university, a minimum cumulative GPA of 3.0, and be a citizen of the US.

The program provides training and company placement at the conclusion of the two-year period. The training begins with a five-week residency for orientation and training at a college or university close to cities where the candidate will be working. For example, in 2013 candidates will spend five weeks during the summer at Brown University. VFA is supported by some of America's largest corporations, like Bank of America, and is staffed by professionals from the business world and academia.

VFA is truly a hidden gem that you need to explore because what the organization offers recent college graduates is unique. You can begin exploring Venture for America by clicking on www.ventureforamerica.org. Do not pass up this exciting opportunity.

Occupational Outlook Handbook, 2013–2014

This is one of the best resources you will ever find, available in print for just $19.95, which is the cost of a couple of beers or margaritas. Its summary of the "100 Best Jobs" is fascinating. Here are ten of them in ranked order:

1. Software Developer. Annual Earnings, $92,000. Annual openings, 36,590
2. Network and Computer System Administrators. Annual Earnings, $70,970. Annual Openings, 15,530
3. Plumbers, Pipefitters, Steamfitters. Annual Earnings, $47,750. Annual Openings, 68,640
4. Accountants and Auditors. Annual Earnings, $62,850. Annual Openings, 135,630
5. Architects. Annual Earnings, $73,340. Annual Openings, 5,090
6. Instructional Coordinators. Annual Earnings, $59,280. Annual Openings, 11,620
7. Administrative Services Managers. Annual Earnings, $79,540. Annual Openings, 9,980
8. Surveyors. Annual Earnings, $55,590. Annual Openings, 4,840
9. Health Educators. Annual Earnings, $47,940. Annual Openings, 3,690
10. Electrical and Electronic Engineers. Annual Earnings, $88,540. Annual Openings, 12,900

Here are the ten top jobs in the "100 Best Jobs" category, by income:

1. Dentists
2. Architectural and Engineering Managers
3. Computer and Information Systems Managers
4. Natural Science Managers
5. Pharmacists
6. Lawyers
7. Advertising, etc
8. Financial Managers
9. Top Executives
10. Sales Managers

Here are the top five jobs in the "100 Best Jobs" by the number of annual openings:

1. Registered Nurses, 965,920
2. Home Health and Personal Care Aids, 151,270
3. Accountants and Auditors, 135,680
4. Carpenters, 122,490
5. Sales Representatives, 87,930

Business and Career Publications

The following publishers specialize in business books and periodicals. Go online or to Barnes & Noble to explore these publishers and their business offerings. For single-topic career books, see the McGraw-Hill Dummies series list of titles. Here you will find a host of titles pertaining to careers and job seeking. A click on the following links will open valuable resources to help you find that first job.

McGraw-Hill, www.mcgraw-hill.com

John Wiley & Sons, www.wiley.com

JIST Publishing, jist.emcp.com

Ten Speed Press, www.tenspeed.com

Wall Street Journal, www.wallstreetjournal.com

Forbes, www.forbes.com

Inc. Magazine, www.inc.com. You are going to like this online magazine. It provides a wide range of articles about the economy in general and job hunting specifically. When you are on this website, look up Jeff Haden's articles. You don't need an MBA to read them.

Television Programs

Because you will be spending the next forty-plus years of your life in the work cycle, educate yourself on how business works by viewing these channels and programs.

CNBC. This channel produces business news live daily, from 6 a.m. to 10 p.m. Among the programs you should check out is *Squawk Box*, hosted by Becky Quick, Joe Kernan, and Andrew Ross Sorkin. Also, tune in to see Maria Bartiromo every day at 3 p.m. EST. (By the way, Maria was not a business major. She majored in sociology. Her verbal communication skills are phenomenal.) And you cannot afford to miss *Mad Money* with Jim Cramer. CNBC frequently features live interviews with business leaders, including CEOs from America's largest companies.

BLOOMBERG. This channel telecasts daily business news live, twenty-four hours a day.

FBN. Fox Business News telecasts business programs daily from 6 a.m. to 10 p.m. EST. Every Tuesday, Fox has a five-minute spot called *Fox Jobs Reports*, which highlights five companies that are hiring. Tune in each Tuesday at 8 a.m. and go to the website, www.fox.com, to get the latest inside job information from Cheryl Casone, a Texas native with a broad and deep knowledge of business and finance focused on the consumer and employment. If you watch Cheryl each Tuesday, at the end of the month you will have discovered twenty new companies to explore for job opportunities.

Job Boards

It seems that a new job board comes into existence every day. I urge caution because research indicates that the exclusive use of job boards is one of the least successful methods of securing a job. The success rate for finding a job using online job boards is about 10 percent, and those are not good odds. Here are some of the most productive boards:

Career Builder, www.careerbuilder.com. This was one of the first job boards to come online. One of the disadvantages in using Career Builder is that you cannot send a resume for an advertised job to a named person. All you can do is send your resume to Career Builder, who will forward it to the company that posted the position. However, I have noticed that Career Builder is beginning to post the name of the company along with the position description, especially for jobs in Puerto Rico. Do not spend much time on this board because you know that the way to get a job is to communicate with a living, breathing person who has a name and a title.

Monster, www.monster.com. This is *the* original board, and like all other boards, you are at the mercy of the system. When you apply for the posted position, Monster links you directly to the named company. You send your resume to the company, not to a person in the company with a name and title. You and I know this is not productive. What you can do, however, is call the company customer service department and ask for the name, email address, and phone number of the human resources director. Send your resume and cover letter to that person. Never send your resume to a something. Send it only to a person with a name and a title who works for a particular company.

The Ladders, www.theladders.com. Ladders began as a board handling jobs with compensation packages of more than $100,000, but in 2011, it opened the compensation range to include jobs paying $40,000 to $250,000. I consider Ladders to be one of the best, and it has won many prestigious awards. There are five membership levels ranging from free to $149 per year. Each succeeding level provides access to a greater number of jobs. I suggest that you take the free membership now. If you like what you see you can upgrade to the next level for $25 per month, which will give you unlimited access to all posted jobs.

LinkedIn, www.linkedin.com. Some call this a job board, but it is much more than that. It is really a social networking site for making business connections at every level and in all industries. Access is free, but there is an upgrade path for those seeking positions that require experience in a particular field. I will talk more about LinkedIn in chapter 6. This site boasts having 200 million members and has been quite successful. Sign up now and you will not be sorry.

Craigslist, www.craigslist.com. Craigslist is a good resource for finding job openings by city or state. Be sure to investigate any jobs on Craigslist before you apply because, unfortunately, the site has been a target for scams in some locations. To avoid these scams, apply one of my cardinal rules of resume submission: send your resume only to a named person who is employed by the advertised company.

FirstJob, www.firstjob.com. This is a very useful site because it posts entry-level jobs for recent college grads. It provides the name of the company, the job location, and a description of the company. This site has been running since 2011 and is one of the best for recent college grads. Be sure to check it out.

There are many other job boards that you might want to review. Just Google "job boards" and go from there. Remember, reliable research indicates that the success rate for finding positions using only job boards is less than 10 percent. Your job hunting time can be spent more productively using other methods, which I will address in later chapters.

Recruiters

Most recruiting firms work with companies to conduct searches for workers at the managerial level and up. Some recruiters, however, do handle entry-level jobs, so you should make every effort to connect with them. You can find the entry-level recruiters online. In addition, you can find them on LinkedIn (conduct a LinkedIn search by entering "recruiters," and you should find a number of listings). Some recruiters write monthly newsletters to keep you updated on current job openings and provide useful information about the economy. Take this information seriously, because recruiters are in touch with the job market every day. Finding qualified candidates for corporate clients is their business, and their view of the job market is about as current as you can get. For example, here is what the recruiting firm Executive Net has to say about jobs that will be available in 2013 and beyond:

Top Jobs by Industry

1. Healthcare, including hospitals, clinics, managed care, pharmaceuticals, biotech, and medicine
2. Technology
3. Pharmaceuticals
4. Manufacturing
5. Energy/Utilities

Top Job Functions That Will Lead to Executive-Level Jobs

1. Business Development
2. Sales
3. Engineering
4. Operations Management
5. General Management
6. Marketing

Connect with recruiters even if they do not handle entry-level jobs. As you gain work experience, you always need to remain alert to new job opportunities, and recruiters can help you do that. One day you will need all the help you can get because the odds indicate you will be fired from your job, your company will go out of business, or it will be sold, which could result in your being terminated. Today, no job lasts a lifetime.

As you check out the various recruiting firms, you will learn that most specialize in jobs for specific industries like education, insurance, medicine, finance, automobile manufacturing, etc. Some recruiters cut across industry lines and specialize by job functions, such as marketing, sales, accounting, and human resources. To find recruiters who specialize in your field of interest, conduct an Internet search. For example, if you search for "sales recruiters," you will find companies such as the Porter Group, www.portergroup.com, which is located in New York and recruits sales reps and managers in the Mid-Atlantic area. Check out their website and review their free sales certification program.

Here are recruiters you should explore:

ExecutiveNet, www.execunet.com. This is a unique company in that it works both sides of the employment process for candidates *and* companies. Sign up for their newsletters and you will find valuable information about the job market.

Heidrick & Struggles, www.heidrick.com. This is a highly respected worldwide recruiting firm that was founded in 1953. It has an excellent reputation across all industries worldwide. It is headquartered in Chicago and operates regional offices in many cities in the US and around the world. Its stock is listed on the NASDAQ stock exchange as HSII.

Korn Ferry, www.kornferry.com. This general recruiting firm is based in Los Angeles and has eighty offices in forty countries. The company has an excellent reputation in both domestic and international recruiting for all types of jobs.

Professional Healthcare Recruiters, www.professionalhealthcarerecruiters.com. This company is based in Sarasota, Florida, and specializes in placing physical therapists, occupational therapists, nurses, and technologists.

MarketPro, www.marketproinc.com. This Atlanta-based firm specializes in placing marketing workers nationwide. The company is one of a number of recruiters working in this specialty and has offices in most major cities.

Belcan TechServices, www.belcantechnicalstaffing.com. This Cincinnati-based company specializes in recruiting engineers and technical workers nationwide. Their recruiting staff places workers in both temporary and permanent positions. STEM majors, be sure to check this out.

Robert Half, www.roberthalf.com. This company is the worldwide leader in placing workers in accounting and finance jobs. It has 350 offices worldwide and recruits for many of the leading finance and accounting companies, like the *Wall Street Journal. Fortune* magazine ranks this as one of the world's most admired companies. When you review the website, remember to check out the salary guide and other useful tools.

Career Confidential, www.careerconfidential.com. This online company provides interesting webinars and advice for job seekers in addition to general recruiting services.

There are recruiting firms for every industry and every job function in every city throughout the US. Find a recruiter in your location that specializes in your field of interest by conducting an Internet search. Recruiters can be your best friend during the course of your work cycle. Build those relationships by contacting them by name and by visiting them personally. Follow the same rules as you would for working with a company directly, and you will not be sorry.

YOUR LIFE, YOUR BUSINESS

The *old* paradigm of work is that you are beholden to a company that pays you money in return for your labor. It sounds nice, but what happens when your boss calls you into the office and says, "You're fired." The model breaks down quickly because you permitted someone else to be in charge of your life. You must take control of your work life. You *are* your own business. You are your own CEO. Think of yourself as James Jones, Inc. Take control of this business. Tune out the background noise, the noise that says you must work for a corporation because you have a college degree. There are other choices.

GOING FORWARD

Frequently, college graduates believe they have arrived once they receive that diploma, but that is a misguided assumption. When you believe that you have arrived, you stop growing. An educated person, a growing person, is always in a state of becoming. Receiving a diploma, or finding that first job, is not arriving. It is only the beginning.

CHAPTER TAKEAWAYS

- *Companies do not hire resumes, tweets, or YouTube videos. They hire living, breathing human beings who invested their time and effort to learn the names and titles of hiring managers, and then contacted them personally.*
- *You are not obligated to seek a corporate job because you have a college diploma. Tune out the background noise and do what you love to do.*
- *Educated people are always in a state of becoming. When you stop learning, you stop growing.*

JOB HUNTER'S LIBRARY

US Department of Labor, *Occupational Outlook Handbook*, JIST, 2013.

Malcolm Gladwell, *Outliers*, Little, Brown and Company, 2008.

Robert Kiyosaki, *Why "A" Students Work for "C" Students and "B" Students Work for the Government*, Plata Publishing, 2013.

Suze Orman, *Women & Money*, Spiegel & Grau, 2010.

Richard Walsh, *The Start Your Own Business Bible*, Adams Media, 2011.

Chapter 2

How to Begin Your Most Important Job Search

America employs in excess of 155 million workers, making our workforce alone equivalent to the seventh largest country in the world. In fact, the United States is the number one destination for immigrants, legal and illegal, from all over the planet because we have more job opportunities than any other country.

Now it is time to get away from the desk and contact employers personally, because when you leave the house, you never know where the fun will end, or when an employer will say, "You're hired!" But first, you must establish a written work plan to begin the most important job search of your life.

BEGINNING YOUR JOB SEARCH

Many college graduates leave campus without the slightest idea about what they are going to do next. The prevailing wisdom is that once you have that diploma, a job will automatically fall into your lap. With that in mind, college grads begin looking for a job with no plan whatsoever. They believe that tweets and texts from friends, a survey of the job boards, and a lot of Facebook chatter will miraculously result in job offers and life will be happy. That is not the way it happens.

Ed's Bungled Search

Recently, I watched a *Sixty Minutes* episode that devoted thirty minutes to job hunting and focused on recently fired and laid-off candidates. What I saw was startling and bore a close resemblance to what first-time job hunters do. The program portrayed experienced corporate workers, all college graduates, whining, "There's nothing out there. I've been at my computer every day for two years and can't find anything." A man named Ed said that he had only three interviews over the course of a year.

These people should have known that you do not get a job sitting at a computer. You find work by leaving the house and meeting hiring managers at conferences, job fairs, and industry trade shows, or by cold-calling them at their offices in industrial parks. Nobody is going to hire a resume and nobody is going to knock at your door and offer you a job. That is not how the world works.

Looking for a job is a job in itself, and job hunters must have a written plan that takes them out of the house. Writing an objective is the first step, and it may read something like this:

> *Objective: a full-time job with a reputable employer in the insurance industry that will provide enough money to pay off my student loan and provide me with food, shelter, clothing, transportation, insurance, and recreation.*

JOB-HUNTING PREP

Now that you have established a bona fide objective, the next step is to create a plan to accomplish that objective. Here are nine steps to take in preparation:

1. ***Establish a Home Office.*** This is an important but often overlooked part of the job-hunting process. You will need

more than the kitchen table with a smartphone, more than a table at Starbucks and your iPad. You need a designated place where you have peace and quiet and the tools to get the job done. A job search is not a helter-skelter activity but a course of action that requires concentration and a place to call, "home sweet home," or, in this case, "office sweet office." We consider this so important that we devoted chapter 3 to the process.

2. ***Find Your Passion.*** A job is a major commitment of time and energy, not something that you do when you feel like it. It's not something that will make you smile or feel fulfilled every day. In fact, much of the work can be boring but necessary to accomplish valid objectives. When it comes to the details of a job search, boring is good. A key factor is finding what you really like to do, what gives meaning to your life.

How do you find your passion? It's not rocket science. It does not take days or weeks completing personality inventories to determine what you like. Let's keep it simple. Do you have a sheet of paper and a pen, or a tablet, or a smartphone?

Make a list of things that interest you. Sports? Food? Clothing? Housing? Government? Political parties? Charitable foundations? Cars? Airplanes? Boats? Teaching? Art? Music? Web design? Digital marketing? Medicine? Make a list of what you like in ranked order.

Let's assume that your top three preferences are music, cars, and housing. The next step is to learn about jobs in these fields of interest. How? First, go to the latest edition of the *Occupational Outlook Handbook* to find pertinent information about jobs in your fields of interest. Look at the compensation levels, types of jobs related to each industry, and the outlook for employment over the next ten years. It's all there in the *Handbook*.

Next, go to the Internet and Google each category. I entered "entry-level jobs in the music industry" and received an interesting array of hits, including one from LinkedIn. This one entry gave me a days' worth of information to explore jobs in the music industry.

3. ***Find the Companies Specializing in Your Passion.*** Let's continue with the music industry theme. I entered "companies in the music industry" and came back with another day of research. To learn how productive this process is, take your digital device and click here for a list of these companies in this business: www.ranker.com/list/music-industry-companies/reference.

I found a professional organization called the National Academy of Recording Arts and Sciences. This organization listed a number of both talent and business jobs, one of which was for "extra" actors in various locations. It is not the top of the food chain in the entertainment industry, but one day an extra, the next day a star!

Repeat the process for your top three fields of interest and see what you get. Before you do, however, be prepared to spend the next several hours or days online, because you will learn much about yourself and about jobs that not only may satisfy your passion but also allow you to make enough money to become self-sufficient.

4. ***Search Job Boards for Your "Passion" Industry.*** Search the various job boards for companies catering to your passion. Assuming it's music, go to LinkedIn, and under the "companies" menu, enter "music." I did just that and found Universal Music Group, which listed a number of job openings for marketing and sales people across the US.

5. ***Make a Target List of Twenty Potential Employers.*** This is an important part of the plan because it will focus your efforts on companies that interest you. After making a list

of twenty companies, rank them using you own criteria for evaluation to supplement what you find online. Also, use the information found in chapter 23.

6. *Distinguish Yourself from the Rest of the Crowd.* The most common mistake job hunters make is spending days or weeks constructing the *perfect* resume. Some of you may have paid good money to have a professional resume writer construct your resume. Guess what? Thousands of recent college graduates have done the same thing. The result? Thousands of resumes will look just like yours, or like Tammie's from Topeka, Jose's from San Diego, and Rebecca's from Boston. Submitting a look-alike resume is outdated. You need to distinguish yourself by constructing a personal career profile package where your resume is only one of several documents. Go to chapter 15 to learn how to package yourself for employment.

7. *Learn from Online Resources.* The Internet is filled with thousands of sources for job hunters of every stripe. Some of these resources are very good and others are mediocre. One of the best sites we have found for entry-level job hunters is Career Confidential. This Texas-based company provides webinars on all aspects of job hunting from resume writing to phone interviews. In addition, the company provides online or phone coaching—for a charge, of course. However, most of its webinars are free, and podcasts are available for a nominal charge. Check it out at www.careerconfidential.com.

8. *Join Professional Organizations.* To match every passion, there is a professional organization. If, for example, you are planning to teach K–12 mathematics, join NCTM, the National Council of Teachers of Mathematics. The website is www.nctm.org. Professional organizations will keep you updated on industry trends and practices and post job opportunities. How can you lose?

9. **Make a Written Plan.** Assuming you have completed steps 1 through 8, is it finally time to leave the house? Not really. What you need first is something that every business pro needs: a written plan, like the one John Hirsch constructed. It put his company on the map.

John Hirsch from Minnesota. John is a very successful car dealer in suburban Minneapolis. After earning a bachelor's degree in history, he started an automobile dealership in Cambridge, Minnesota, called John Hirsch Cambridge Motors. The business grew to include dealerships for Chevrolet, Buick, Chrysler, Dodge, and Jeep. Can you imagine owning five automobile dealerships in a major metropolitan area like Minneapolis-St. Paul, Minnesota? What did John do right? What was the one thing that propelled his business to the top of the pack? Well, I hope you're sitting down, because the answer will knock you off your feet, it's so obvious.

John attributes his success to a firmly held belief that before you do anything in the business world you must take time to construct a written plan. His mantra is "Plan your work. Work your plan." How incredibly simple, yet how insightful. It does not require an MBA to get the message.

You cannot run a business without a plan, and that piece of advice applies to finding a job as well. You cannot run a job search without a plan. When you land your first job, you will quickly learn that companies do not make it up every morning. They do not delete everything on the server at 5 p.m. and reprogram the following morning. Companies plan two to five years out, and everyone follows the plan each day. Let's follow John's road to success and write a job-hunting plan that will take you to the Promised Land of employment.

PLAN YOUR WORK. WORK YOUR PLAN.

Let's assume that you have decided to seek a position in the insurance industry, and that you are interested in sales, where you can make a fortune and have a life of your own. Alternatively, you want to explore marketing positions for insurance companies because that field may provide more opportunities for entry-level positions.

Your next step includes a number of proactive initiatives. You have looked in the Yellow Pages directory for insurance companies in your local area, within a ninety-minute drive of your house. You found twenty listings for home offices, regional offices, or offices of insurance salespeople. (Do not expect job locations to be a few blocks from home. Sometimes they will be across town or seventy-five miles away. According to the US Census Bureau, the average commuting time to work is approximately 25 minutes. In urban areas like New York City and Chicago, it is longer than it is in North Dakota or Idaho.) In addition, you have looked on the Internet for convention centers in your area. You found six trade shows and conferences, three of which you would like to attend. Smart college grad that you are, you believe that personal meetings are the best way to find a job, so your thoughtful plan includes face-to-face visits with workers in the insurance industry to seek their advice for landing your first job. In fact, you have decided to visit your parent's insurance agent for auto, homeowner's, life, and health insurance to seek her advice.

Constructing Your Job-Hunting Plan

This is a good beginning, but let's take it a step further and put it in writing. Here is a step-by-step activity plan to follow.

1. Access the calendar on your computer or construct a paper calendar for the next three months. Make sure the calendar provides writing space for each day of the month. You are

going to plan one month in advance. In the last week of that plan, you are going to make another plan for the following three months. If you connect with a job during the first three months, you can say good-bye to the second quarterly plan. Remember to visit www.firstjobsforcollegegrads.com and tell me about your first job. I will share it with your colleagues, and you will receive congratulations from across the US.

2. In the space for each day, write the activities you will perform. Fill in all of the blanks for each day for the next three months. You cannot make your plan at 7 a.m. each morning because that is the time you will be leaving the house. Your plan for the first week should look something like this:

Job Search Plan for the Week of August 4, 2014

Monday: 8 a.m. to 5 p.m.

- 8 a.m. to 10 a.m. Visit ABC Auto Insurance Company regional office to see the marketing director for an interview.
- 10 a.m. to 11:30 a.m. Visit Prudential Life Insurance Company home office. Learn the name and contact information for the human resources director, and ask for an interview.
- 11:30 a.m. to 1 p.m. Lunch. Have a sandwich and review what happened during your morning calls. Record your plans for follow up emails or personal notes when you get home.
- 1:30 p.m. to 2:30 p.m. Visit local insurance agent whose name you found in the Yellow Pages.
- 3 p.m. to 4:30 p.m. Visit United Health Insurance district offices. Learn the name and contact

information for the director of sales, and ask for an interview.

- 5 p.m. to 6 p.m. Return home and send follow-up emails or write personal notes to people you saw or did not see today.

Tuesday: 8 a.m. to 5 p.m. Work at home office.

- Conduct research on insurance companies.
- Review job boards for leads.
- Send career profiles to human resources directors in response to three job leads from company websites.
- Email or text thank you notes to the people you saw yesterday.

Wednesday: 8 a.m. to 5 p.m. Attend insurance trade show at McCormick Place, Chicago.

Thursday: 9 a.m. to 4 p.m. Work at home office conducting trade show follow-up and research.

Friday: 8 a.m. to 4 p.m.

- 8 a.m. to 9 a.m. Coffee at Starbucks with your father's car insurance agent. Informational interview.
- 9:30 a.m. to 11:30 a.m. Appointment with human resources director at Ajax Life Insurance Co. Bring career profile package.
- 11:30 a.m. to 1 p.m. Lunch. Make notes about your meeting at Ajax.
- 1:30 p.m. to 3 p.m. Cold-call an Allstate auto insurance district office. Learn name and contact information for the district sales manager. Request an interview.

> • 4 p.m. Return home to write follow-up emails and personal notes.
>
> **Saturday and Sunday:** Take the weekend off unless there is a trade show, conference, or job fair to attend. Don't miss an opportunity to meet potential employers personally, even if the show falls on a weekend.
> This was a loaded week! Who said finding a job would be easy?

Next, construct a written work plan for the next three weeks just as you did for the week above. At the end of week three, construct your work plan for the following month, and in the third week of that month do the same for the next month. What you will have done is constructed a quarterly work plan, just like the big guys do in corporate America. Welcome to the real world of work!

THE PAYOFF: YOUR QUARTERLY NUMBERS

Let's review the results of your work plan, which covered three months, assuming the following:

- You have attended two trade shows, conferences, or job fairs each month. That's six in one quarter.
- You have made an average of five personal calls to potential employers each week. That's twenty in one month, sixty in one quarter.
- You have spoken to one referral contact each week, as you did on Friday when you had coffee at Starbucks with your father's insurance agent. That's four in one month, twelve in one quarter.

Here's what you will have accomplished in one three-month period, or as they say in the corporate world, in one quarter:

1. Six trade shows and/or job fairs attended. Spoke with representatives of more than 300 potential employers.
2. Sixty personal meetings with information sources or hiring authorities, apart from trade shows, conferences, or job fairs.
3. Twelve personal referral meetings for coffee or lunch.

The number of people you spoke with personally could go up considerably depending upon the number of people you saw at trade shows, conferences, and job fairs. My experience has been that if you attend a medium to large show where there are anywhere from fifty to 400 exhibitors, you will average approximately twenty-five meaningful personal contacts per conference. If you multiply that by the six trade shows you attended in one quarter, you will have spoken with 150 potential employers. Making that many personal contacts in one quarter could never have happened if you sat at home all day firing off resumes to Job Box 29 or sending tweets to your friends complaining about how lousy the job market is.

This is a good show for one quarter and should yield positive results.

PERSONAL MEETINGS: THE PATH TO YOUR FIRST JOB

Isn't it remarkable that by planning your work and working your plan you can make hundreds of personal contacts in just one quarter? Remember what we learned in the earlier chapters of this book. Companies do not hire resumes; they hire living human beings. You have the intelligence, energy, and passion to find them. By working your plan, you see hundreds of people, and one of them could soon be your boss. Are you grateful for this gem of knowledge that just translated into a business plan? If you are, say thank you to John in Minneapolis. Better yet, if you live in the Minneapolis area, go to one of his dealerships, and tell John you are seeking employment and that your referral source was this book. Before you leave, ask John for a good deal on a new or used car. You will not be sorry!

CHAPTER TAKEAWAYS

- *Plan your work. Work your plan.*
- *Construct a career profile package to distinguish yourself from the rest of the crowd. Presenting yourself as a job candidate by submitting only a resume is a surefire recipe for long-term unemployment.*
- *Use your home office creatively.*
- *Follow your interests and your passion.*
- *Personal meetings with hiring managers and human resources directors result in job offers.*

JOB HUNTER'S LIBRARY

Stephen Covey, *The 7 Habits of Highly Effective People*, Free Press, 2004.

Chapter 3

Establishing a Home Office for Job Hunting

Finding a job is a job in itself, and you will need a work space to organize your search. This is an important and necessary requirement, and you should make it a priority. Job hunting is a detailed and time-consuming process and requires a dedicated space and tools to make your work productive. Getting out of bed and going to the kitchen table to make a couple of calls, or to send a few resumes into space while you have a cup of coffee is not the most productive way to go about it.

Establishing a home office will serve another purpose as well. During the course of your career, many workers will be conducting business from their homes instead of going to an office each day. Even today, many companies encourage working from home, especially for those who can conduct their work without needing constant communication with their coworkers. For example, programmers, digital designers, editors, salespeople, and researchers can accomplish their work objectives remotely. Learning how to work from a home office now will be good preparation for working remotely in the future.

Every job seeker needs an office. It makes no difference if you are seeking a corporate job, a construction job, or starting your own business. You need to have your own space while conducting your search.

DISCIPLINE

Working from home requires discipline and planning, and you cannot cheat. To believe that productive job hunting entails spending a few hours a week making phone calls, sending tweets, and firing off resumes from the kitchen table is pure folly. It will not work. But establishing a home office is just the first part of a job-seeking plan. You will use your office primarily for planning, follow-up, and research. Real job hunting begins when you leave the office to see hiring managers personally.

If you cannot work from home because there are unavoidable distractions, find another space, like a college career center or public library, where you have Internet access and a quiet space to make calls and conduct your research. However, before taking this route try your best to carve out a space in your residence. It could be a desk in your room or a corner of the basement—some place that is quiet and where there are minimal distractions.

SEVEN EASY STEPS FOR ESTABLISHING YOUR HOME OFFICE

Setting up a home office is not rocket science. To get you started in the right direction, here's a list of items you will need to be productive:

1. *A quiet work space.* Your office should be large enough to hold a desk or small table, a bookcase or file cabinet, and a chair. You will make this a friendlier place if you have a table lamp. Make sure there are no barking dogs or crying babies in the background. The quickest way to disqualify yourself from a potential job is to have your dog barking in the background while you are speaking with a recruiter, a human resources director, or a hiring manager on the phone. Don't think the people on the other end of the line can't hear the barking. They can. I have disqualified

job candidates who were clearly distracted by a shouting kid, barking dog, or traffic noise when they called me for a phone interview.

2. *Computer and printer.* Without these two items, you will be dead in the water. Don't have a printer? Go to Staples or Office Depot and buy an ink jet printer for less than $100. Alternatively, go online to find the best deal and make sure that shipping is free.

3. *Office work tools.* Your office life will be easier if you have items like notepads, pens, a stapler, paper clips, printer paper, postage stamps, envelopes, and a bulletin board to hang on the wall to post reminder notes. Don't forget the small bookcase, which you can buy at Staples for about $35. You will need this to store your growing collection of books and magazines pertaining to work. Contrary to the hype, print and paper are not yet dead.

4. *A cell phone or landline phone.* If you are using a smartphone, make sure reception is strong enough to talk in a conversational tone and without background noise. If not, use a landline for all outgoing and incoming calls. The real world of work is not like college living. This is a new ball game, and you must play by the rules. Continuous background noise will be a poor reflection on you and a breach of corporate courtesy. The world of work is not a training ground; it's a place where you earn money to pay for food, shelter, clothing, transportation, insurance, entertainment, and medical care, and to repay your student loan.

5. *Clean up your act.* This is a good time to clean up your voice mail message. Remember that hiring managers and others involved in the job-hunting process will be calling you. This simple fact of business etiquette is ignored more often than you would think. I recently made a call to a person who graduated *cum laude* two years ago and is now working for a prominent Washington, DC, company.

Her smartphone voice mail message sounded like it was recorded by a witch. What might an executive recruiter or human resources director think about that?

"Hi, Dude! This is Godzilla. Call me back when I'm awake," might have been funny when you were a sophomore, but now you are dealing with adults, and you must play by the rules. If you want a brief, acceptable, universal voice mail message, try something like this: *"This is Bob Jones at 215-825-1290. Please leave your name, phone number, and a brief message, if you wish, and I'll return your call promptly. Thank you for calling."* Do not under any circumstances disguise your voice or say something cute. In the adult world of work, remember this rule: Nobody likes a smart-ass (NLSA). Also, do not have another person record your message. A hiring manager will interpret this as too cute and surmise that you do not have the maturity or confidence to act appropriately.

6. *A record-keeping book, a planning book, or a computer app.* You can buy a daily or monthly planning book at Staples or at Office Depot for a few dollars. Better yet, use a digital database like Sage ACT or Microsoft Outlook, a part of Microsoft Office. You will need to record all of your company contacts, references, and networking sources. When you are attending conferences and talking with hundreds of people over a two-day period, you will need to record names and contact information, including email addresses, phone numbers, and social media handles.

In chapter 9, I will provide a daily planning guide to help you get started.

7. *A briefcase to carry important documents.* Purchase a briefcase to store and transport important documents like your resume and career profile to interviews and trade shows. Backpacks are not acceptable. You can buy a reasonably priced, attractive faux-leather briefcase at Staples

(www.staples.com) for about $30. Alternatively, you might consider the combination laptop-briefcase for about $45, also at Staples. If you have a few extra dollars, buy a leather one, and it will last for the next ten years or more and give an impressive appearance.

8. *Business calling cards.* Calling cards are a necessity for job-hunting activities. You will need something to establish your identity, even though you might not have a job. For example, when you meet a hiring manager or networking contact, how are you going to present your contact information? Scribbled on the back of a napkin or scrap of paper? That is not professional. You need something to leave behind, and that is a business card. And no . . . not everyone uses a smartphone to record data.

You can purchase business cards from a number of places, like Staples, or you can buy them online at a steep discount from Vistaprint, which is what I recommend. Go to www.vistaprint.com and select a design from one of hundreds of samples. You can customize your cards and order sizable quantities at the lowest prices possible, like $10 for 250 cards. Frequently, Vistaprint will have free promotions for your first order of 250 cards. I suggest that you order at least 500 cards because you will distribute hundreds when you attend trade shows and conferences.

Select a conservative card with no more than two colors. Do not get cute and order cards with bizarre designs. When you go to the website, select a design from the collection titled, "Conservative." The business card reflects your persona, and you need to make a good first impression. This is business, not entertainment.

Be sure to include the following data on your card: name, address, cell phone number, landline number, if you have one, email address, and Twitter and Facebook handles. You do not need to identify yourself as a job candidate, or an English major, or a Stanford graduate. Just your name will suffice. In addition to distributing your cards to people you meet personally, you will attach them to documents you send from your home office to potential employers by mail or FedEx. There will be occasions when a potential employer will request that you send certain documents in hard copy. Always attach a business card to these documents.

UNPLUG

Working from your home office requires focus and attention, and the best way to avoid distractions is to unplug—that is to turn off your smartphone, and silence your email, so it will not beep or chirp every time a new message arrives. Constantly looking at your smartphone to see the latest tweet or Facebook message, or constantly scanning your email for the latest round of personal messages from friends is a great way to get nothing accomplished.

We live in a digital world, and it is difficult to put the smartphone away. But who is in charge, you or a digital device? Think about it. Do you want a smartphone or tablet to control your life? Instead, allot a certain number of minutes for scanning your smartphone, tablet, and computer each day.

I recommend using the final ten minutes of each hour to interact with your digital tools. Place yourself in control, and your job-hunting day will be productive. Please note that I am not recommending that you toss away your digital tools and social media apps, like Twitter and Facebook. Most likely, both are loaded with personal stuff that you would not like a hiring manager to see, but getting rid of this stuff is a problem. The solution? Open new Twitter and Facebook accounts to use exclusively for your job search and professional life. Alternatively, go to Twitter and subscribe to only one category: business. Then, check off companies and organizations that will be beneficial to your job search, like the *Wall Street Journal*, *Forbes*, *Fortune*, the *New York Times*, Cramer, and CNBC.

A RECORD-KEEPING TEMPLATE

You must store job-hunting information in your office using a commercial app or one that you craft yourself. If you do not want to bother with a database like ACT or Windows Contacts, then create your own using index cards. It should look something like this:

A Sample Record-Keeping File

Company Name: Ford Motors
Company Website: www.ford.com
Company Address: 1234 Ford Blvd., Worcester, MA 17760
Contact Name and Position: Bob Murphy, Human Resources Director
Cell phone: 701-234-5634
Office phone: 617-456-9876
Email Address: B.Murphy@ford.com
Date and Purpose of Last Message: On 1/12/2014, received email from Bob; he received my resume and cover letter. We scheduled personal interview for 2/18/2014, at 9 a.m. at his office. Bring resume, transcript, and reference letters.
Follow-Up: 1/13/2014, emailed appointment confirmation to Bob.
Other Ford Contacts: Bob's admin is Ted Thomas; T.Thomas@ford.com.
Notes: Learned that Bob was quarterback at Michigan State. Admires Picasso's art.

That is all you will need for your record-keeping file. It's a necessary part of your job search now and forever. A database you establish now and store in your home office will be an integral part of your working life.

By the way, did you click on the Ford website? Do it now and then click on "More Ford." When you pull down this menu, click on "Careers" and you will find this category: "Students & Recent Graduates." You can do the rest. Who knows, next month you might be working at Ford and qualify for a discount on a new hybrid Ford Fusion, which gets 47 MPG, city and highway. If you connect, contact me on my website, www.firstjobsforcollegegrads.com, and tell me what happened.

While you're on the Ford website, click on "Auto Shows" at the bottom of the "Careers" page to learn where the next convention is being held. If the next show is within driving distance, you must attend because there you will find Ford hiring managers who can tell you about available jobs and about the corporate culture at this great American company.

In chapters 12 and 13, I'll provide more information about attending trade shows, conferences, and conventions.

HOW MUCH TIME SHOULD YOU SPEND IN YOUR HOME OFFICE?

The easy answer is this: as much time as you need. However, if you do not control your schedule, you will always find something else to do, like visiting your friends, shopping, surfing the Internet, or attending a sporting event. Schedule at least five hours per day working in your office once or twice a week. The other days you will be job hunting away from home, making cold calls to potential employers, attending trade shows, conventions, and job fairs, or interviewing on-site. Your home office is the place where you conduct research, collect information, make and answer calls, send resumes to a living person (not a job number), and conduct follow-up. It is not a place where you tweet friends about the latest gossip, or drool over Aunt Addy's new recipe for pierogi.

CHAPTER TAKEAWAYS

- *You are dealing with the adult world of work, where nobody likes a smart-ass. Observe the rules of corporate etiquette, and remember . . . NLSA!*
- *A home office is necessary for serious job hunting.*

JOB HUNTER'S LIBRARY

Go to www.inc.com. This source provides advice and tips about establishing a home office.

Chapter 4

Terms and Numbers You Absolutely Need to Know

In order to understand the workplace in America you need to know the meaning of frequently used numbers and terms like the *unemployment rate*. What do we mean by the *rate of employment*? Where does this number originate? Is there really such a thing as *underemployment*? How is this frequently used term measured? Who does these calculations? Are they valid or do they support a particular media or political agenda? Do the numbers tell the whole truth and nothing but the truth?

This may be one of the most important chapters in this book because finding your first job is just the beginning of a lifelong venture into the world of work. From now until the day you take your last breath, you will be involved in the work cycle. To navigate it effectively, you will need to know the meaning of significant terms and numbers.

DISTINGUISHING FACT FROM FICTION

In this chapter, we will explore terms and numbers that have a significant impact on your knowledge about the workplace in general. Specifically, we will learn how the numbers enable you to assess the job market and act accordingly. This information will affect your attitude about how robust the job market is, or is not, at any given time. Attitudes, which are based on information, determine behavior, so it is important to get it right. For example, if you take your information from the popular media and political speeches, you will most likely believe that it is impossible to get a job when the unemployment rate hovers around 9 percent.

The fact of the matter is that jobs are always available in America because companies need employees in order to function. Jobs are available even during a recession, when you hear the media and the unemployed shouting, "There's nothing out there!" That is not the reality. Jobs are always available because people leave companies at any phase of the economic cycle for a variety of reasons and need to be replaced.

WHY COMPANIES ARE ALWAYS HIRING

Jobs are always available for a variety of reasons. Workers quit their jobs or are fired and need to be replaced. Workers retire and need to be replaced. And, unfortunately, workers die and need to be replaced. Jobs may be harder to find during a recession, but they *are* there, and it is up to you to find them. Remember, companies are not going to knock on your door and offer you a job. It is up to you to find the hiring managers and present your candidacy in a personal interview.

THE SEVENTH LARGEST "COUNTRY" IN THE WORLD: THE AMERICAN WORKFORCE

Let's zero in on the number of workers, commonly referred to as the workforce, in the United States. The American job market employs more than 155,000,000 workers. All those zeroes aren't typos. It really is 155 *million.* If you compare our workforce to the total populations of the largest countries on the planet, it would make our workforce *alone* the seventh largest country in the world.

The following chart tells it all:

Country	Population
1. China	1.3 billion
2. India	1.2 billion
3. Indonesia	237 million
4. Brazil	194 million
5. Pakistan	182 million
6. Nigeria	166 million
7. *The American Workforce*	*155 million*
8. Bangladesh	143 million
9. Russia	142 million
10. Japan	128 million

The size of the American workforce has ramifications that touch all of us, entry-level candidate or veteran. Understanding what they are will help us navigate the world of work.

THE UNEMPLOYMENT RATE

Some believe that the unemployment rate released by the Bureau of Labor Statistics (BLS) on a monthly basis *truly* reflects what is happening in our workforce of 155 million individuals, but let's take a closer look.

The *rate of change* in the employment numbers, up or down, depends upon the size of the labor force and reflects the state of the economic cycle at any given time. The larger the workforce, the longer it takes for the rate of employment to change, particularly as an economy emerges from a recession or depression.

The deeper the recession, the longer it takes for the rate of employment to increase. In fact, in the US, it takes a minimum of nine to twelve months following the bottom of a recession (considered by economists to be the second consecutive quarter of growth in GDP, the Gross Domestic Product, which is the total of all goods and services produced at any given time) for the rate of employment to begin rising. In a very severe recession, such as the one we experienced beginning in 2007 and ending in 2009, the rate of acceleration in the employment numbers took even longer. Turning around a labor force of 155 million is a task not completed quickly.

Remember, the beginning and end of a recession are measured *not by the unemployment rate,* but by the rate of positive or negative growth in GDP. Check out the GDP and unemployment rate numbers now by going to www.bls.gov (Bureau of Labor Statistics).

The National Bureau of Economic Research (NBER), www.nber.org, is the government entity that defines the beginning and end of a recession. When we have two consecutive quarters of negative GDP, we are at the beginning of a recession. Two consecutive quarters of growth in GDP heralds the end of a recession. When a recession begins the unemployment rate always goes up, and when a recession has ended the unemployment rate always goes down.

It is interesting to note that the unemployment rate is the most lagging indicator. In other words, employment is the last metric to show positive gains. When we come out of a recession, numbers like consumer spending and municipal permits for constructing new homes and commercial buildings always increase before the employment numbers make their charge upward.

WHAT DOES FULL EMPLOYMENT REALLY MEAN?

Full employment does not mean that 100 percent of the workforce is employed. In the US and most other developed countries as well, there has never been a zero percent unemployment rate. Some members of the workforce will always be unemployed regardless of fiscal or monetary policy, and regardless of how robustly the private sector is functioning.

SEASONAL UNEMPLOYMENT AND STRUCTURAL UNEMPLOYMENT

Two main factors account for unemployment at any given time. First is *seasonal unemployment*, which occurs when workers are laid off because of weather or holiday-related factors. For example, in the northern latitudes, outdoor construction workers face unemployment during severe winter weather. There is nothing that can be done by the construction industry or the government to prevent that occurrence.

Structural unemployment is caused by the introduction of new technology to perform tasks that ordinarily would be accomplished by workers. For example, computers and word processing programs eliminated the need for most secretaries, whose major responsibility was to type documents for managers and executives on typewriters like the IBM Selectric that you see in movies from the 1970s.

Likewise for people who did manual tracking of inventory. That required workers to go into a business, like a pharmacy, and count all of the items displayed on the shelves. That method of inventory tracking employed many workers. Now it's done using RFID (radio frequency identification) tagging, which eliminates manual tracking of inventory. Technology has taken over this task, resulting in the elimination of thousands of jobs, which are *never* coming back. Neither the private sector nor the government can prevent structural unemployment from occurring. As technology continues its forward march, more hands-on jobs will be eliminated.

THE CONSTANT RATE OF UNEMPLOYMENT

The constant rate of unemployment in the US caused by all factors since the Great Depression averages approximately 6 percent. We might interpret that to mean that an employment rate of 94 percent is truly full employment. Since 1970, our lowest rate of unemployment was 4 percent in 2000, and the highest was 10 percent in 2009.

If we consider 94 percent to be full employment at all phases of the economic cycle, an unemployment rate of 10 percent can be interpreted to mean that the true rate of unemployment caused by a recession is 4 percent, which is not that bad, considering that the US workforce numbers 155 million. However, a 4 percent unemployment rate means that six million people are unemployed while an unemployment rate of 10 percent means that more than fifteen million people are out of work. That number has serious repercussions on our economy. It affects the amount of money not spent on consumer goods, and it increases the amount of money that the government spends on related safety-net entitlements like unemployment compensation, food stamps, and Section 8 housing.

Do not buy into the media and political hype. We will never have an unemployment rate of zero percent. It is just not possible.

UNDEREMPLOYMENT

Frequently, the media and politicians use the term "underemployment." This term means that people are not able to find jobs equal in compensation and rank to what they had before being fired or laid off. Does this make any sense? Who said that once you reach a certain level of income, say $150,000 per year as a vice president of marketing, that you are entitled to remain at that income number and rank for the rest of your life? That is not the way it works in America. Let's illustrate our point with an example of what happens in the real world of work.

After missing his sales revenue goal for three straight years, Joe gets fired from his job as vice president for sales at International Coconut Inc. Joe had slacked off and assumed his sales team would carry the load for him. Life had been good for Joe. He was making a base salary of $150,000 and another $100,000 in bonuses, plus benefits.

Now Joe is looking for another position at the same rate of compensation, but all he can find is a district sales manager position with United Antelope Meat Processing Inc. with a base salary of $125,000. If Joe reaches his revenue goal, his total compensation would be $150,000, which isn't too bad for an Antelope district sales manager, or any worker, for that matter. But Joe rejects the offer from United Antelope because it is below where he was in both rank and compensation at his previous job. He rejects other job offers, too, because they are below the rank and compensation of his job at International Coconut. Soon Joe begins to whine, "There's nothing out there." What's wrong with this picture?

For starters, who said that once you are employed as a vice president at $250,000 per year, you are entitled to that rank and compensation for the rest of your working career? The Constitution? The president? Congress? Twitter? YouTube? CNN? Your mother?

So where does that leave Joe? Collecting unemployment compensation, which comes out of everyone's pocket in the form of taxes. Enjoy the coconuts, Joe, because that will be your steady diet until you wake up and smell the coffee, which smart workers flavor with cream instead of coconut milk. You could have been making $150,000 this past year, and life would have been good for you, your wife, and your two kids.

THE UPS AND DOWNS OF RANK AND COMPENSATION

It is unrealistic to believe that your job rank and compensation at any time in the work cycle will continue to go up. Here's a real-life example of how it works and what you can expect as you navigate the work cycle.

Carol from Philadelphia. On a cold January morning, a job candidate came to my office and related that she was laid off from a computer hardware company because of a reorganization necessitated by the declining business climate. Carol was a sales representative covering three Mid-Atlantic states and had a total compensation package of $220,000 per year plus benefits. Some years she made over $300,000, placing her in the top 2 percent of all wage earners in America.

She was intelligent, energetic, and passionate about the use of technology. I told her that in a business climate heading into a possible recession, her chances of finding a comparable position and compensation were slim. She scoffed and said that is what she is worth and would not consider a job that paid any less. I tried to reason with Carol, but to no avail. She declined several jobs I offered because of the compensation. In a fit of self-righteousness, Carol told me that I just did not have the right connections and said good-bye.

Fast forward twelve months to December of that same year. Carol, still unemployed, returned to my office telling me that potential employers just did not realize how good she was. She was worth the $220,000 in base salary plus bonuses. Period. I felt sorry for Carol and wished her well as she headed out of my office.

Carol's problem was that she believed in the underemployment fallacy: once you have made a certain amount of money, you are entitled to making that or more for the rest of your life. Wake up, Carol! Job rank and compensation are not entitlements in America.

TAKE WHAT THE MARKET WILL DELIVER

In our economy, you take what you can get in order to be self-sufficient. That's our system, and it has served us well for the past three hundred years. Careers do not always progress in an upward spiral until one becomes CEO or president. Rank and compensation fluctuate according to one's abilities and the economic cycle. In other words, America is not a work entitlement economy. If you think that is unfair, then you might consider relocating to Greece, Italy, Spain, Portugal, France, or Nigeria. Happy landing because wages there are a fraction of what you will find in America, and you will be faced with unemployment rates in those countries reaching 25 percent. My advice? Try your luck first in the US.

WHO'S HIRING?

Let's revisit the critically important reason to know what is behind the numbers. Information forms attitudes, which in turn guide behavior. Understanding this important concept early in your career will help you over the bumps in the work cycle that you are sure to encounter.

Some workers consider an unemployment rate above 6 percent so egregious that they become discouraged about the prospect of remaining employed or finding new opportunities. As a result, they just sit waiting for "something" to happen while they tweet friends about the bad economy or collect unemployment compensation checks. How many times have we heard job seekers whine, "There's nothing out there"? True, jobs during a recession are fewer in number, but there is always someone hiring. The trick is to find out who is.

Frequently, when a Fortune 500 company like General Electric announces that it has dismissed several thousand employees on a given day, most likely it has hired several hundred workers that very same day, but you will rarely hear that reported. Why? Because it is bad news that makes headlines, not good news. "Five thousand laid off at General Electric" gets more attention than "GE hires three hundred workers in the home appliance division." (By the way, I'm not picking on good, old General Electric. It is one of the world's best companies, employing over 300,000 workers worldwide.

Check out the website to learn more about a true American icon and to review job postings that look right for you. Click on www.ge.com. When I checked just recently, there were 5,000 jobs open worldwide. Did you click?)

PLEASE LEAVE THE HOUSE!

Companies large and small always need workers, which is why you need to call on companies in person every day until you hit pay dirt. The human resources director, who told you at her office on Monday that there is nothing available, could very well call you on Thursday and say, "Unfortunately, Linda, our assistant director of marketing, was hit by a truck on Wednesday and didn't make it. Come in on Friday and we will talk more about that job. Linda needs to be replaced." Too bad for Linda, but good for you because you may be hired. Give yourself a pat on the back because you had the sense to pull yourself away from the iPad and call on potential employers personally. Unlike many recent college graduates who sit at home firing off resumes to Job #27, or Position #236, or Hiring Manager, or The Second Ring of Saturn, you had the brains to get out of the house and hunt for employers in the flesh. You were not intimidated by the unemployment rate and media gurus telling you there are no jobs available. Congratulations!

CAN I REALLY FIND MY FIRST JOB WHEN THE UNEMPLOYMENT RATE IS OVER 6 PERCENT?

That is a marvelous question, and the answer is a resounding yes! It may take longer when the unemployment rate is above 6 percent, but there will still be many jobs available. They may not fall into the "ideal" job category, but all work has dignity and value, no matter what the job title or compensation. America is still the best country in the world to find work, regardless of where we are in the economic cycle, and the people who know that best are immigrants. In fact, a recent Gallup poll found that 150 million people worldwide would immigrate to America if they had the opportunity to do so.

IMMIGRANTS UNDERSTAND THE NUMBERS

The overwhelming majority of immigrants come to America for one reason: *jobs*. According to the Center for Immigration Studies, from 2000 to 2010, approximately 1.4 million people immigrated to the US *each year*. Factor in illegal immigrants, and the number is even higher. Some brought with them skills sorely needed in our workforce, such as technology expertise, but others came looking for any job. They knew that America has a workforce of 155 million, and that surely, some kind of work would be available.

America continues to be the breadbasket for the world, which is why the immigrant drift to America continues unabated. If you, a college graduate, cannot find work in America, I guess it's fair to say it's your fault.

HOPE FOR RECENT COLLEGE GRADS

Is there hope for college graduates who have been sitting at a computer firing off hundreds of resumes to Job Box 29, or to the human resources director, or to some other entity without a name? Yes, there is hope for you because you are already in America, and if you apply your intelligence, energy, and passion, *you will find that first job*. All you need is a little help, a nudge in the right direction, a few nuggets of wisdom about job hunting, a quick course in how to navigate the world of work, and some easily accessible resources.

Survival Statistics for Job Hunters
As you prepare to find that first job, keep abreast of what is happening in the economy generally so you can discuss business matters intelligently during interviews. Here are sources of information you need not only to survive, but also to get your first job. The following sources will keep you updated on

all employment matters and provide the numbers you absolutely need to know.

Important Information Sources for Job Hunters

Bureau of Labor Statistics, www.bls.gov

Pew Research Center, www.pewresearch.org

National Labor Relations Board, www.nlrb.gov

ADP, www.adp.com. Automatic Data Processing is a company that tracks employment data. This company releases employment numbers each Thursday at 8 a.m.

Heidrick & Struggles, www.heidrickandstruggles.com. This is one of the largest executive search firms in the world. On the company website, you will find pertinent employment data. Many large companies use this firm to recruit high-level executives.

CNBC, www.cnbc.com. This channel produces financial TV programs that air from 6 a.m. to 11 p.m., Monday through Friday. Check it out frequently for information about the economy and to view interviews with executives of major companies, government officials, and economists. When you wake up, make this the first program to watch. You will not be sorry. Bye-bye ABC, CBS, NBC, and CNN.

Wall Street Journal, www.wsj.com. This newspaper, available in print or online, is the gold standard for obtaining information about the economy generally and the stock market specifically. The *Journal* has no political agenda. It is in business to help people make money. The Thursday edition has an entire section devoted to employment and the job market.

Occupational Outlook Handbook, 2013–2014, www.bls.gov. This 1,018-page book produced by the US Department of Labor is a necessary read for all workers. It details everything you need to know about the job market. For example, on page 173 of the current handbook, you will find information about the position titled Market Research Analyst. The median compensation for this position is $60,250 per year, and the number of workers employed in this position in 2012 was 282,700. The job outlook for this position from 2012 to 2020 calls for an increase of 41 percent, resulting in an additional 116,000 jobs for market research analysts. The usual entry-level requirement is a bachelor's degree. A major in math or business will be advantageous, but degrees in one of the social sciences will get you there, too.

Interested in jobs such as meeting, convention, and event planning? In 2011, the median pay for event planners was $46,020, and there were 71,600 workers employed in this field. The 2013–2020 outlook for this position calls for a 44 percent increase in employment. Education requirements include a bachelor's degree in marketing, business, communications, or other academic disciplines.

JIST Publishing publishes this book. If you are reading this on your iPad or tablet, click here for more information: jist.emcp.com. The book retails for $19.95. Do not hesitate to order it now by clicking on www.amazon.com.

LifeBound, www.lifebound.com. This helpful website founded and hosted by career coach Carol Carter is a site you do not want to miss. Carol gives practical advice about job hunting and financial management for young adults. In addition, she has published several books that you may find useful. While you are on LifeBound, click on "Career Blogger" for information about job hunting for candidates new to the world of work.

Ready for more—like where you can find potential employers by clicking on some URLs? Stick around because I'm about to provide more practical information about where the job market is headed in the next chapter.

GOING FORWARD

The unemployment rate always decreases as the GDP grows. If the annualized GDP is growing, it means that consumers and businesses are increasing their spending for goods and services. If first-time unemployment claims have been steadily decreasing and nonfarm private sector employment is increasing, more jobs will be available.

However, while slow but sustained increases in the GDP bode well for the economy, this will not precipitate a rapid increase in employment. The job market will continue to show positive gains as the GDP increases. When will we return to "full employment" (that is, an unemployment rate of 6 percent)? Hard to tell. The rate of growth in employment will reflect what happens in the private sector, and in that political land mine called Washington, DC.

CHAPTER TAKEAWAYS

- *The numbers tell the truth about work and the economy. Don't buy the hype. Tune out the many political agendas on TV, on the radio, on Twitter, on Facebook, on You-Tube, on blogs, and in newspapers. Make your judgments about work and careers based on the numbers and reliable sources.*

JOB HUNTER'S LIBRARY

Troy Adair, PhD, *Corporate Finance Demystified*, McGraw-Hill, 2011.

Chapter 5

Business and Technology Certification

In our world of work, technology skills and business knowledge are necessary components for an attention-getting career profile. Business majors are at an advantage when it comes to both technology and business skills for obvious reasons. However, many college graduates may need to update their skills, and this can be done easily by completing online courses.

There are hundreds of online courses for business and technology certification. Some of them are inexpensive or even free; others are very costly. Many providers are no-name organizations, and others are well-known entities like Microsoft and Cisco. Completion of specialized courses may take one or two years. Rudimentary or introductory courses may take only several weeks.

BUSINESS AND TECHNOLOGY SKILLS YOU SHOULD HAVE

There are general technology skills that everyone must have to conduct ordinary business. These include a working knowledge of word processing, databases, spreadsheets, and online research. Some of the common apps for business use are Microsoft Office Suite, PowerPoint, Adobe Creative Suite (especially if you are in marketing or design), and Adobe Muse, which is used for HTML design.

Apple users can install any number of basic or advanced apps at Apple retail stores for the OS and IOS operating systems.

Social media sites are finding their way into business, making it imperative that you know how to navigate Twitter, Facebook, LinkedIn, and others. Companies are increasingly using these products in their marketing initiatives.

WHERE TO GO FOR TRAINING AND CERTIFICATION

There are many options for training and certification, but I suggest that you first go online to find courses that fit your needs. Remember, too, that your employer (or potential employer) may offer its own proprietary business and technology courses. They may be mandatory or optional. If optional, always take advantage of these opportunities.

From the many options available, I've identified several online sources that you may want to explore:

HigherNext, www.highernext.com. This Philadelphia-based company offers a flagship product described as the Certified Business Laureate (CBL). This is a standardized business skills exam, which enables entry-level job applicants to demonstrate their business and technology skills in uniform and measurable ways to employers. Upon successful completion of this online course, HigherNext awards a written certification called the CBL Degree. It's an impressive document to present to a prospective employer as part of your career profile package (see chapter 15). The cost for the CBL certification is less than $100—a real bargain for a valuable job-hunting tool.

In addition to the CBL, HigherNext offers a Microsoft Excel certification package costing less than $25. Here's how the HigherNext certification courses work:

1. Each test is taken online and proctored through your webcam.
2. Certification bundles are generated upon completion.
3. Testing time is fifteen minutes for each course.

Coursera, www.coursera.org. This online company offers courses spanning many curriculum areas, including business and technology, at attractive prices. However, it does charge a small fee for a written certification of course completion. It describes itself as, "An education company that partners with the top universities and organizations in the world to offer courses online for anyone to take, for free. Our technology enables our partners to teach millions of students rather than hundreds."

In late 2013, Coursera boasted having 3.8 million users and offering 389 courses. This California-based company was founded in 2012 by Daphne Koller, a professor in the computer science department at Stanford University, and Andrew Ng, Associate Professor of Computer Science at Stanford. Its advisory board consists of chancellors and provosts from major universities across the US, such as Princeton, Duke, and the University of Michigan.

The wide range of courses includes:

- Creative Programming for Digital Media and Social Apps
- Computer Networks
- Foundations of Business Strategy
- An Introduction to Financial Accounting
- Introduction to Data Science
- Internet History, Technology, and Security

Alison, www.alison.com. This online company offers courses and certification free of charge. Its many courses are listed under major categories such as these:

- Digital Literacy and Skills
- Business and Enterprise Skills
- Information Technology
- Entrepreneurial Skills
- Presentation Skills

American Society for Training and Development (ASTD), www. astd.org. This professional organization offers a business certification degree. Here's what it says on its website about its certification course: "The ASTD Certified Professional in Learning and Performance Certification (CPLP) equips you with the tools to be the best in the field and lets employers know that you have real world, practical expertise that can be readily applied to the current work environment. CPLP gives you the capability, credibility, and confidence to be a high-performing contributor in your organization."

Download the CPLP candidate brochure to find out more. Also, check the many conferences that ASTD hosts across the country, and attend one in your area to meet influential workers in a variety of industries.

REQUIRED CERTIFICATIONS FOR NON-BUSINESS POSITIONS

There are certifications required for workers holding positions in the building trades, medicine, food services, and other industries. State and/or federal law requires certifications and licenses for some positions, because they involve public health and safety. If you are exploring these careers, learn about the requirements first. Make sure that the school you attend is qualified to issue the certifications you need.

Some positions require taking an examination for licensure as well. For example, lawyers and medical personnel must pass a state-issued exam in order to obtain a license to practice law or medicine in that state.

You can easily check online for the certifications and licenses required in your state.

BUSINESS AND TECHNOLOGY CERTIFICATIONS WILL SET YOU APART FROM THE CROWD

Potential employers will assess your business and technology skills. Candidates who can prove they have these skills by presenting a written certification will gain a distinct advantage over those who present only a resume. When you are competing with hundreds of other candidates for the same position, you need to use every tool at your disposal to win the game. Presenting a written certification as part of your career profile will make you stand out from the rest of the pack.

CHAPTER TAKEAWAYS

- *Technology skills are a requirement in today's world of work.*
- *Written certification documents will enhance your candidacy.*

JOB HUNTER'S LIBRARY

Lisa Guerin, JD and Amy DelPo, JD, *The Essential Guide to Federal Employment Laws*, Nolo, 2013.

Chapter 6

Business Etiquette

People across America are talking about it, but no one seems to know what to do about it. The increasing lack of corporate courtesy has reached a crisis point in the US. Employees and prospective employees complain about it constantly. Employers, hiring authorities, and candidates are asking what's happened to simple trust and decency. One would think that executives running corporate America would be above the fray, but sadly, that is not the case. It may be too late to retrain our present generation of corporate leaders.

IT IS YOUR GAME TO CORRECT

Recent college graduates have an opportunity to restore common courtesy and decency to American business. Your generation will be running the show in a few years, and it is your responsibility to get us back on track. Your responsibilities include not only making the bottom line profitable, but also making the workplace a decent environment for all workers.

Everyone has a story about the breakdown in human decency, and here are a few examples from my experience in the executive search business, the real world of work.

Harry from Chicago. Harry, a candidate for a $250,000 job, went for an interview with the president of a communications company. After the perfunctory greetings, the president said he had not had time to read Harry's resume and asked for fifteen minutes to review it before getting down to business. The meeting had been scheduled a week prior, and Harry had taken a half day off from his job for the interview. What's wrong with this picture? The president knew about the interview well in advance but was not respectful of Harry's time, which was just as valuable as his own. Someone's rank or position does not excuse him or her from showing respect and exercising basic courtesy.

Mary from San Francisco. Mary was a vice president of sales with an educational technology company and was recruited by a competitor for an executive vice president position. The CEO had scheduled a 4 p.m. interview at his company's corporate offices. Mary was on her way to another appointment halfway across the country but rescheduled her flight to make the interview. She arrived promptly but had to wait in the reception area for forty-five minutes before the CEO called her in. He then proceeded to tell Mary that he had just skimmed her resume before she came in and issued no apologies for this. He proceeded on to a Q&A session that was not only challenging but also hostile. One hour later, Mary left the interview and withdrew her candidacy, which is the smart thing to do when a company executive does not show respect to prospective employees.

Larry from Philadelphia. Larry was a vice president of technology with a well-known American company. He was victim to a corporate downsizing and was exploring new opportunities that would provide more time to be with his family. Five days a week away from home for the past five years was taking a toll on his personal life, and he was ready to change that picture. A foreign company making an entry to the American market was looking for a vice president for business development, so I presented Larry's candidacy to the company president and submitted not only his resume and references, but also a sample business plan Larry had created. After Larry had been screened over the phone, the company president requested a personal interview with him. Larry gave a half day of his time to meet with the president, whose first remark was, "I don't know why you are here. Obviously you are overqualified for this position." The interview went nowhere and Larry withdrew his candidacy. A half day of Larry's time was gone with nothing to show for it. Shame on the corporate president!

Melody from Minneapolis. Melody responded to a call from a human resources director who requested her resume. Melody complied but never received a response. The human resources director did not even send Melody a perfunctory acknowledgment that she had received the resume. Needless to say, that company's reputation was diminished as word spread throughout Melody's professional network.

Juanita from New York. Juanita's story is a common one. The costs for her interview with a hiring manager in another state included airfare, hotel bills, parking, and meals, totaling $1,200. The company promised prompt reimbursement, but sixty days later, she was still waiting. After ninety days, I went to the CEO on her behalf. Thirty days later, she received a reimbursement check. The company delayed payment of legitimate expenses for four months and gave Juanita no explanation or apology.

Sadly, executives in corporate America have created a lack of trust between employer and employee. However, I am confident that recent college graduates who will be leading corporate America in the near future can reverse it. Adherence to the basic rules of engagement will go a long way to restoring common corporate etiquette. What's at stake has manifold consequences for employers and workers, so let's begin with a set of rules that is profound in its simplicity:

TEN RULES TO IMPROVE CORPORATE ETIQUETTE

1. Respond promptly to all written correspondence and voice mails addressed to you personally. Failure to do so reflects an arrogant and uncaring attitude.
2. Remember that your colleague's time is just as valuable as yours is. The time of a field account executive is just as valuable as that of the CEO or president.
3. Follow through on promises. If you promise to act by a certain date, remember to do so. If an unforeseen conflict surfaces in the interim, reschedule that action item personally.
4. Rank does not confer superiority and the right to act imprudently or abusively. All workers deserve respect.
5. Put all phone calls on hold during personal meetings in offices, at trade shows, or at restaurants. Turn off cell phones when meeting one-on-one or with a group. Place your tablet or iPad in your briefcase as well.
6. All persons who are being fired or laid off for any reason should be treated with respect. Separations are traumatic for the employee and should be handled personally and in private. Workers should be given an explanation for the termination.
7. Everyone is busy. Give hiring managers, and/or subordinates, ample time to comply with requests.
8. Maintain confidentiality in all personal matters, especially those matters regarding employment.

9. Be punctual. Time is of the essence in all business matters.
10. Always say thank you. Always say please.

WHAT OTHERS ARE SAYING

The crisis in corporate courtesy has been recognized across the country, and a simple Internet search will yield enough hits to keep you reading for the next two weeks. I especially like what these sources have to say:

Columbia University for Career Education, www.careereducation.columbia.edu. Columbia has one of the best career counseling programs in the US. It includes advice for job hunting and rules of engagement in the world of work.

Royale Scuderi, Business Consultant, www.lifehack.org. This consultant offers sage advice for workers and employers. Follow her blogs and tweets for sound advice about navigating the world of work . . . and life itself. Royale has fifteen very good tips for business etiquette, which you can review on her website.

Robert Half, www.roberthalf.com/business-etiquette. Robert Half is the world's largest recruiting firm in the accounting field. Its business etiquette website has information about rules for using social media, and in particular, Twitter. I especially like its video titled, "Business Etiquette: The New Rules in a Digital Age." Check it out now.

CHAPTER TAKEAWAYS

- *The rules of business etiquette are indispensable for a satisfying and productive work experience.*
- *The rules of business etiquette apply to both company personnel and job candidates.*
- *Do not work for a company that displays a lack of respect, honesty, and courtesy.*

Chapter 7

Hired! Fired! Retired! The Human Work Cycle

In its most basic form, life is quite easy to understand. You are born. You die. And, in between, you work. Many books have been written about the meaning and purpose of work, and I have often wondered why. It is simple. You work to provide that which you need to survive: food, shelter, and clothing. It has been that way from the beginning of time. But in addition to making money to survive, all workers seek job satisfaction as well.

Until just recently, in anthropological time, all people needed to survive were food, shelter, and clothing. In the twenty-first century, our notions of what is needed for survival have changed as our lives have become more complex. As this list increases, so does the need for more money to pay for these "necessities," and this, in turn, changes the work paradigm.

EDUCATION AND WORK

So how does this thing called *work* actually work? It begins when someone completes a certain level of education. For about 65 percent of the population, work begins upon receiving a diploma from high shool or a GED certificate. For the remaining 35 percent of the population, the work cycle begins after receiving a college diploma.

Yes, that's right, *only 35 percent* of the US population goes to college and receives a diploma. We refer to this elite group of individuals as "college grads."

You might recall someone telling you that earning a college degree guarantees a job. "Really?" you might ask. "Then why can't I find a job nine months after receiving my diploma?" That is a valid question, and presumably, that's why you (or your parents) are reading this book, which aims to demystify the job-seeking process and help you find a job that pays enough money to provide for your basic needs. In other words, a job that will provide sufficient remuneration for your services so that you may become independent and self-sufficient.

But what about fulfillment, job satisfaction, and helping those in need? First, make sure that you earn enough money to take care of your own needs so *you* do not become a drag on the economy yourself. Then you can donate your off-work time and a portion of your earnings to help those in need.

DEFINING THE HUMAN WORK CYCLE

Here are the three phases of the work cycle:

1. Being Hired
2. Being Fired or Laid Off
3. Being Retired

I'm going to focus on the first part of the work cycle, being hired. However, I will evaluate what happens in the other two parts of the cycle so that you will know how to deal with them when they arrive.

"Fired? Retired? Me? I'm in the hiring phase of the cycle, so why should I worry?" you might ask. Think again. It's safe to assume that many workers will be fired or laid off at some point during their working years, and all workers will retire and then look for something to do in their twilight years, like finding an encore career.

BEING HIRED

Being hired is the most exciting part of the work cycle because it is a time of exploration, discovery, dreaming, learning about who you are, and breaking out on your own. Being hired is more than just landing a job; it is the beginning of the rest of your life as a self-sufficient human being. However, it can be frustrating when after six months of firing off resumes you still do not have a job.

Throughout this book, I will help you find a way to the Promised Land of employment by providing you with information, instruction, encouragement, and advice that you will not find anywhere else. I will not talk in the abstract. I will cite real-life examples that I encounter every day in my recruiting business.

Finding that first job can be challenging. It has been that way from the beginning of time, but there are methods to short-circuit the process. Although this search may be difficult, it will not be impossible if you follow the rules of the adult world of work, which I will talk about throughout this book.

Landing your first job will enable you to make money to become self-sufficient while paying off your student loans, and it will provide money you need to make charitable contributions and plan for retirement. This will be an exciting adventure for you, and it will make Mom, Dad, Grandma, and Aunt Juniper in Biloxi very happy, too.

BEING FIRED

Being fired is always traumatic, but you must be prepared to meet that challenge when it arrives. It could be only months after you are hired that you will be laid off through no fault of your own. The words *fired* or *laid off* are used when a person is asked by an employer to leave the premises.

Let's distinguish between *being fired* and *being laid off*. There are multiple definitions for the two terms, but let's cut through the hype.

Being fired means that you have been told by your employer that you can no longer continue working there because of something that you did, or something that you did not do but should have been doing. The cause may be for missing your assigned goals or violating company rules and regulations. An example of not meeting goals would be a salesperson who did not attain the assigned revenue number. Let's assume your sales revenue goal for 2015 is $2 million and you generate only $1 million in sales. That could be a valid reason for being fired. It happens every day.

Being laid off means that you are told by your employer to leave the premises for reasons other than your performance. For example, if the company is preparing to be acquired, to make the numbers look more attractive to potential buyers, it embarks on cost-cutting measures. The most expeditious way to reduce expenses is to lay off workers. That happens every day, too. Nobody is immune.

Workers in a free economy, such as ours, are always at risk of losing their jobs for any number of reasons. Some people lose their jobs because of poor performance and others because of fluctuations in the business cycle. In the recession beginning in 2007 and ending in 2009, approximately fifteen million workers were out of work. That's a whopping 10 percent of our workforce!

As an example of what can happen at any given time in the economic cycle, I will pick on Bank of America (BOA), one of the largest banks in the world and headquartered here in the US. At the beginning of 2012, BOA employed 247,000 workers. In the course of that calendar year, the company fired and laid off 14,000 workers for a variety of reasons. This happened to workers who believed their jobs were secure, because after all, they were employed by an American icon in the financial industry. It could not happen to them!

Workers in any industry can meet the same fate, and you must be prepared to face it. The odds are that at some time in your work cycle you, too, will be fired or laid off. In fact, I would say it is inevitable this will happen. Here's a real-life story that illustrates this situation faced by many.

Dick from San Antonio. One morning, I received a call from Dick, who lived in San Antonio, Texas, and was employed as a sales representative by one of the world's largest educational publishers. He had three continuous years of employment selling instructional materials to K–12 schools in a three-state territory and was averaging $150,000 per year plus expenses, benefits, and stock options. Life was good for Dick; in fact, it could not get any better. He did not have to report to an office because his job required seeing customers face-to-face to present his various texts and digital products. When he had office work to complete, he did that from his home in an office he had set up in a spare room.

Dick's flexible work schedule allowed him to participate in community outreach programs, take his kids to soccer games on Saturdays, and enjoy an active social life with his wife. Life could not get any better. Then, one Monday morning Dick received a phone call at 6 a.m. from the company president. The call went something like this: "Dick, I have to tell you that we are downsizing. Today is your last day with the company, and we wish you the best. The human resources director will be in touch with you later in the day about your severance and other separation matters." Dick was devastated.

He had been a loyal, dedicated employee who met his revenue goals and had received awards for excellent performance.

When Dick told me his story, I was sympathetic and comforting, but I was not surprised. You see, I had known that his company was going to be sold and that it was cutting expenses to make the bottom line look better. It happens all the time. Dick could have learned ahead of time what his company was doing by keeping tuned in to the industry underground network. I told Dick not to take this personally because that very same day the same fate was going to hit other workers in his company. That is part of the world of work, and you must be prepared to deal with it.

How *You* Could Be Laid Off

You are employed by Company XYZ, have been on the job for two years, and have already received a promotion from assistant marketing manager to associate marketing manager, a nice bump upward that includes an increase in salary and benefits. You have made a big dent in repaying that student loan. Life is good. You go to work every day at 7:30 a.m. after picking up an early morning latte at Starbucks, and return home at about 8 p.m. after a margarita at the local watering hole, followed by a salad at Chipotle. Here's what might happen next.

Late one Friday afternoon, your boss calls you into the office of the human resources director and tells you that the company is downsizing because the last quarter's revenue was down 20 percent. "We're sorry, but we have to let you go. We're cutting expenses, and besides, we are not entirely happy with your performance. If you recall, you missed several deadlines during the last quarter. This is your last day working here." Like it or not, you have just been fired. You feel rotten, really rotten, and you take it personally. You are angry, in a state of panic, and believe that the company unfairly picked on you. But guess what? Thousands of others have been fired today, and they, like you, did not see it coming. There is nothing more devastating than being fired when you had no hint that it was going to happen.

During the two years working for Company XYZ, you have already come to identify yourself not just as Harry Jones, but as Harry Jones, Associate Marketing Manager. When you are separated from the company, you are just plain Harry again. For many workers, this is a devastating experience, and they begin asking themselves, "Who am I?" The Rx is always to think of yourself as an independent human being, not as an associate something, a manager of this, or a director of that. Those are accidental titles that define your role and responsibilities in one particular organization. When you are hired, lifetime employment is not guaranteed. It never has been and it never will be.

When you envision your life's career path, remember this: you are not going to work in one job at one company until you retire. You will have a succession of jobs, probably five or more, and most likely, you will change industries and job focus, too. Your first job might be as assistant event planning manager for Johnson & Johnson Pharmaceuticals, but twenty years from now, you might be Mary Jones, the vice president of sales for Microsoft, or Carlos Smith, a physical therapist.

Being fired or laid off has negative connotations because the implication is that you did not meet the job requirements or you did something that violated company rules and regulations. When employees are dismissed because the company was sold, has missed its revenue goal, or is going bankrupt, it is usually called being laid off, downsized, rightsized, reorged out (short for reorganized out), or put on permanent leave. Whatever the term used, the effect is the same: you no longer have a job, which means that you will not have money to provide for the basics, and that is a serious problem.

Some call this a life-shattering experience, and many workers go into a deep depression when they are fired or laid off. In fact, during the course of my executive search career, I have witnessed that event so many times that I wrote a newsletter for my website offering first aid to the "walking wounded." Go to my website, www.weissandassociates.net, and read the newsletter titled, *Fired! An Opportunity to Rebuild Your Character.* The article will give you instructions on how to survive this traumatic event and move on to new opportunities.

The good news is that being fired can be a positive experience because it provides an opportunity for self-examination and an opportunity to rebuild your character. If you follow the instructions in this book, soon you will have another job and probably have better pay and a better working environment. You have survived being fired, and once again, you are hired.

Nobody Is Immune

In today's world, workers at every level must continuously update their information sources so they are not blindsided like Dick. What happened to him happens to many workers, even those working in sacred cow positions, like union jobs in the public sector. You say it can't happen to a union teacher in a nice state like Wisconsin? Well, read about what Governor Walker had to do in 2012 to prevent his state from going bankrupt.

Today, nobody is immune. What about age, gender, and race, the holy trinity of job security? Forget it. That is outdated. There are no more untouchables in today's world of work. However, what about presidents, CEOs, vice presidents, directors, managers, COOs, and CTOs? They are fired, too, unfortunately. I see it happen every day.

BEING RETIRED

Since receiving that college diploma, you have been hired, and unfortunately, you may have been fired. What's next? The business of work becomes a bit more complicated when we add chronology to the picture. As you grow older, your energy level and mental capacities decrease usually by the time you reach the sixty-five to seventy-five age bracket. It seems a long way off, but ask any sixty-five-year-old how quickly time passes. It will happen to you, so why not give it some thought now. This will be a very happy time in your work cycle if you prepare for it.

Encore Careers

Retirement is an important and inevitable part of the work cycle, and today it is much different than it was in previous generations. People no longer work for one company for thirty years, receive a gold watch and a retirement dinner as a reward, and ride off into the sunset happy as an iPad on the beach in Cancún. It is not too early to think about retirement because it is part of the work cycle that you will encounter.

Ten thousand a day, according to the Pew Research Center. That is the number of workers who are retiring. But are ten thousand people each day *really* retiring and hitting the rocking chair, or golf course, or whatever it is that retired people used to do?

Today it is a new ball game for retirees. When people retire nowadays, they frequently pursue what some call an "encore career" instead of just living a life of leisure until they die.

The average life span today for all Americans is approximately eighty-three years. Assuming that a worker retires at age sixty-five, that leaves eighteen more years of life on earth to do something. What that something is will determine how productive and happy your twilight years will be.

Even though your encore is far into the future, it is prudent to think about retirement in broad terms and to plan accordingly. Your strategy should include two items:

1. Start investing for your retirement by enrolling in a Roth IRA as soon as you get your first job. This should be one of your first priorities, no matter how much it hurts to have something taken from your paycheck. Failure to plan accordingly could make your twilight years miserable.

2. Begin thinking about what you really like to do in your spare time and about how you could turn that interest into your encore career.

GOING FORWARD

Now that I have defined the work cycle as having three distinct parts, *being hired, being fired,* and *being retired,* I'm ready to move ahead and concentrate in detail on the first part of the cycle.

But before I move on, let's remember two of the most important features of this book: the "Chapter Takeaways" and the "Job Hunter's Library." The takeaways are basic rules for playing the game, and books listed expand on the content of each chapter.

CHAPTER TAKEAWAYS

- *Define who you are independent of a job title. Don't permit a job to define your character and persona.*
- *Work is not (at least not at first) about fulfillment, breaking glass ceilings, leveling the playing field for technology access, or feeding the poor. Those are admirable objectives, and you can work to meet them in your off-work hours.*

JOB HUNTER'S LIBRARY

Phil DeMuth, PhD, *The Affluent Investor*, Barron's Educational Services, 2013. This timely book will tell you how to accumulate wealth safely and on your own terms. You will find advice about how to invest your Roth IRA retirement dollars.

PART 2

THE PLACE OF TECHNOLOGY IN THE WORKPLACE

Chapter 8

Caution! Technology Is Changing the Workplace . . . *Fast!*

Okay, so traditional work goes something like this. You get up in the morning, eat breakfast, and then report to a building where you do something called work for the next eight to ten hours. You report to someone called a boss who defines the tasks you perform and how you are to do them. You are given time off for a morning and afternoon break, and for lunch. At the appointed hour, somewhere between 5 p.m. and 6 p.m., you stop working, say good-bye to your boss and coworkers, and head out the door to go home. Some days you might stop at a local pub for a drink with your friends, or you might go shopping. Some of you might go directly from work to perform some sort of community outreach for which you are not paid.

Work is structured for you and your coworkers. Whether your job is entry-level or managerial, if you work in an office environment, it will be structured until the day you retire. Even for workers whose jobs take them outside of an office environment, like jobs in sales or marketing, work will be structured if you work for someone else. That's the way work is today, but as you read this book, changes are taking place below the radarscope, changes that will alter the traditional work paradigm. The main driver of workplace change?

Technology. Caution! Technology may steal your traditional job and change the traditional workplace as well.

WORK LOCATION: HOME OR OFFICE?

This is an exciting time to be a worker in America because your workplace guarantees one thing, and that's change. Your job today will not look the same five years from now because technology is changing the way tasks are accomplished. For example, the data you access and generate are stored on company servers located on company premises. That's now. Already, servers on-site are disappearing as companies store and access data from the cloud.

Companies like Salesforce.com (www.salesforce.com) store data for companies on *their* servers, which may be located thousands of miles away. If what pops up on your monitor is coming from a server thousands of miles away, why do you need to report to a certain location every day? Couldn't you perform your assigned tasks working from *your* location, your home? The answer is obvious and this will change the nature of work as we know it today. But who currently works from home? Let's look.

Are There More Home Workers in the Private or Public Sector?

According to the Census Bureau, home-based workers are more likely to be employed in the private sector than are workers in government jobs. Also, people working in finance, sales, and STEM positions (that is, positions in science, technology, engineering, and mathematics) are more likely to work from home. As for worker productivity and job satisfaction, a study by Cisco Systems found that employees working from home experienced an increase in both production and quality of life. Contributing to greater life satisfaction is the elimination of the commute from home to work. If you work at home, the savings in time increases greatly, and the stress and cost of commuting are eliminated.

Before we move on, did you open the hyperlink to Salesforce.com and check out the "Career" pages? This company is in hiring mode for all kinds of jobs, so review it now.

BYE-BYE PEOPLE KENNELS

There is no reason why most corporate workers should spend their time in cubicles, or as I call them, "people kennels." There really is no good reason why you need to come into the office every day to complete your work. In your lifetime, the transition to working at home will take place gradually. Multi-story office buildings will become grain silos, or maybe call centers as offshore work returns to America. For the most part, today's office environments are depressing and contribute to worker dissatisfaction and low productivity. Let me give you an example.

The New York Den of Depression. Not long ago I was visiting one of my clients (a CEO) in New York City, and, after the usual pleasantries in his beautiful corner office with a magnificent view of the city, he offered to give me a tour of where his workers, mostly editors and designers, put in their eight to twelve hours. We began the tour on the first level by walking from one side of a huge, open room to the other, down one aisle and up the other. Overhead, in the middle of each aisle, was a continuous line of fluorescent lighting, reminding me of a factory environment. On either side of the aisle was row after row of people kennels, each containing one living worker hunched over a small metal desk, banging away at a computer.

Crowded into the kennel were a chair, a small metal bookcase, a phone, and a wastebasket. On top of some desks were small table lamps, which made the kennel look slightly more inviting. This was a quiet environment, but every now and then I heard a phone ring, and every so often I heard keyboards being pummeled by tired fingers. Some workers had cups of coffee on their small desks; some had open cans of Coke; others were munching on a candy bar or a piece of fruit. I did not witness any human interaction, except for a muffled voice talking into a phone—a landline, because this company had not yet made the conversion to cellular.

After this depressing tour of level one, we moved up a floor and it was the same thing. And the third floor? Also the same. After returning to the CEO's office, I thanked him for the tour, quickly left the building, and headed for the nearest bar. This, my friends, is what it means to work in corporate America. That is, until you become the president or CEO and win that coveted corner office, with floor-to-ceiling windows, a polished wood desk, and carpeting on the floor.

This company, a school publishing company, is typical of corporate America, but fortunately, change is taking place.

Some companies, mostly technology companies, have recreated the work environment to make a more productive working space. Google is a good example of what a company can do to make the work environment more pleasant and productive. There you will find open work spaces side by side with refreshment kiosks, workout rooms, recreational devices, and the like. The movie *The Internship* depicts the Google workplace. Google "Google work space" and you will find pictures of this environment. Does it look like fun instead of work? Don't be fooled. Employees at Google are held strictly accountable for meeting their job objectives. Too many cappuccinos and Ping-Pong games will get you a nice, pink slip saying, "You're fired."

Other companies have redesigned the work space by lowering cubicle walls and eliminating private offices all in the hopes of increasing human interaction, which some employment experts claim increases productivity. However, in an article published in the September 11, 2013, issue of the *Wall Street Journal*, Sue Shellenbarger claims the opposite effect has been generated. Sue's research says that more open space results in frequent interruptions and distractions, which decrease productivity. It takes on average nearly half an hour to resume a task after an interruption. In fact, the interruption problem has become so acute that workers in the open environment wear signs saying, "Do Not Disturb."

However, most companies still cling to the traditional depressing work space, and they lose productivity every day because executives are hesitant to change. Here is what I witnessed on one of my business trips to visit a client's company.

Control Freaks in Chicago. While I was visiting the executive vice president at a Chicago-based technology company, I asked him why all of the workers in the kennels needed to be there. Some were programmers; others were digital product developers, web designers, and digital marketing workers. Most were working in solitary spaces with no human interaction, and there seemed to be no reason why they could not work from home.

His response was illuminating. He said that if you permitted people to work from home, productivity would go down because most workers could not be trusted to work without the boss on-site. In addition, there were too many distractions at home. I have since heard the same from other corporate executives and have concluded that it all comes down to a matter of control . . . and trust. I believe that once the digital natives, like you, take over the executive-level positions, we will see people kennels disappear as workers are permitted, encouraged, and *required* to work from home.

Get used to the new paradigm because you will see it in your work cycle. Before you start thinking about an encore career, you will most likely be performing your work from home. Change, however, is painful and comes in fits and starts as I noticed recently at one of our iconic technology companies.

Yahoo Bucks the Trend

In February 2013, Marissa Mayer, the new CEO of Yahoo, issued an edict requiring all home workers to report to an office. This was 10 percent of Yahoo's workforce, and Mayer's order was met with stiff resistance. She said that having the entire team in one location made for better communication, and increased loyalty and productivity. Yahoo reportedly had been in a state of dysfunction before she took over as CEO in 2012, but was working from home the root cause of it? You will need to keep track of where this is going. Click on the website to get the latest, and while you are there, check to see if any jobs are open at Yahoo: www.yahoo.com.

EXPLOSIVE INNOVATION IN TECHNOLOGY

As a digital native and millennial, you know that technology is playing a more prominent role in all aspects of our lives. The world of work is no exception. As the use of technology expands and replaces human workers, there will be serious disruptions to the workplace. Many jobs will be eliminated, causing widespread structural unemployment in some industries, but new employment opportunities in other industries. As you are reading this book, someone is being laid off because that person's job was eliminated by a new app. However, as one person was terminated, another was hired to work in the cloud with Salesforce.com. As you read these pages, someone is designing new technology products that will influence what you do in your work cycle. Just listen to what Peter Diamandis has to say about all this.

Peter Diamandis is chairman of the X PRIZE Foundation, www.xprize.org, a nonprofit company that awards large prizes to foster technological innovations. X PRIZE partners with organizations like the Bill & Melinda Gates Foundation, the thirty-five-billion-dollar nonprofit founded and funded by Bill Gates, founder of Microsoft. Diamandis predicts eight significant breakthroughs that will change the world of work for everyone. You will experience all of them in your work cycle, so listen carefully. Your job five years from now could be influenced by what you read in the next few paragraphs. Here are the "explosive eight" as reported in the January 22, 2013, issue of the *Wall Street Journal*:

1. Bacteriology. Biologists are making rapid progress thinking of life in terms of a programming language like Java, C, or Perl 5. This will result in the creation of many new billion-dollar companies.
2. Computational Systems. This technology gives us the ability to model almost anything, resulting in many new industries requiring many new workers.
3. Networks and Sensors. This technology will give us large amounts of data that will enable us to do anything data-related, such as earthquake forecasting, in fractions of a second.
4. Artificial intelligence. This is the stuff from which science fiction is made. AI will transform every industry in your work cycle.
5. Robotics. This exciting technology is one that all entry-level workers should explore for job opportunities. Robotics will create many new jobs during your work cycle and may even change how you perform your work. Soon robotics may replace everyone's most dreaded job: cleaning the house. Can you envision your own business called "Terry's Robotic House Cleaning Service?" It's coming, so stay tuned, or get ahead of the curve and think about a business you can create using robotic technology.

6. Digital Manufacturing. It's here already in the form of advanced barcoding techniques and 3-D printing. Think about how exciting this will be in the world of clothing design and manufacturing.

7. Medicine. Remote medical diagnosis is already on the scene but in rudimentary form. Within five years, there will be handheld devices that will record and transmit data about your body functions directly to your physician. This technology could very well take the place of an annual routine visit to your physician. After reading your data, your doctor may call and say, "Joe, get in here ASAP. You have elevated T1 and TSH readings, indicating you have a thyroid problem. I have to treat it now."

8. Nanotechnology. It works at the atomic and molecular level and has widespread applications, one being increased battery energy and storage capacities. Most interesting is the use of DNA to replace traditional technology storage devices. In your lifetime, there is no doubt that you will look back upon the cloud as primitive. Nanotechnology companies are springing up like mushrooms across America and the world. Google "nanotechnology" for a look at the present, and the future, and importantly . . . job opportunities.

A CLOSER LOOK AT THREE GAME CHANGERS

Robots. It's fascinating to explore the use of robots, particularly in manufacturing and medicine. The best way to see how this works is to visit a manufacturing company such as Ford or General Motors to learn firsthand how automobiles are really made.

Another example is the increasing use of robotic surgery, where the surgeon sits at a computer console a few feet away from the patient and manipulates probes that have been inserted into the patient through very small incisions. The result is a better outcome for the patient and new jobs for the professional nursing staff.

Traditional scalpel surgery causes significant bleeding and requires nurses to use retractors to hold open the incision and suction away the blood while surgeons perform their work. This process carries many risks, such as infection.

On the Internet, you will find a number of videos showing robotic surgery using something called a da Vinci Surgical System, which consists of various technology devices like probes, miniature cameras, computer consoles, and computer apps.

RFID Technology and 3-D Barcodes. The lowly barcode is eliminating thousands of jobs previously done by hand. For example, retail companies, like Walmart, need to take a physical count of every item on the shelf in every store for inventory purposes. With thousands of stores worldwide, this is a huge undertaking requiring thousands of workers working thousands of hours. At least, that's the way it used to be.

Now, inventory workers have been replaced by technology called Radio-Frequency Identification, or RFID, a system using 3-D barcodes to track inventory. The system tracks each individual product from the time it is manufactured until the time it leaves the store. When you buy a product, it is removed from the store's inventory automatically. When the inventory for that specific product reaches a certain level, an order for additional products is sent to the manufacturer.

Before this technology came on the scene, workers physically counted each item on a shelf and recorded that number in a notebook. It was a laborious, error-ridden process costing the company millions of dollars in human labor. RFID will continue to change the way we live and will eliminate many more jobs. How does this technology work? At the heart of it is the 3-D barcode.

These 3-D barcodes are small squares filled in with what appears to be a black-on-white scattered gram pattern. They can hold much more information than their predecessor, the 2-D barcode, which consists of a series of strips of different thicknesses.

This relatively new technology is now used to access information of all kinds, and to eliminate tedious tasks like airplane ticketing. Importantly, this technology is being used in the manufacturing process and saving money for both companies and customers. You have probably seen the 3-D barcode on your smartphone or tablet.

In your work cycle, there is no doubt this technology will affect you in some personal way, either by providing new job opportunities or eliminating others. New jobs will be created for programmers, designers, and security app engineers, just to mention a few.

Better Apples. In early 2013, Apple announced a new product that did not get too much attention because it was designed for business rather than personal use—a change in strategy for one of the largest companies in the world. We are talking about the 128 GB iPad that came on the market at a hefty price: $799 for the Wi-Fi only version, and $929 for a more robust version. This new product will replace many laptops and desktop computers used for business purposes. In your work cycle you will likely use this new iPad, or a similar product, for much of your own personal productivity and work productivity.

Continue to check for new apps such as iWork, which was released in 2010. It's the touch-friendly version of Apple's office suite and is already in its seventh revision. The iPad or tablet on which you are reading this book will be a pleasant memory five years from now. It's necessary that you update your technology knowledge and skills to remain a productive worker. Do this and you will never hear your boss shout, "You're fired!"

Learn more about these three game changers so that you will be able to discuss intelligently the future of technology with hiring authorities. Let them know that you are a forward-thinking worker who can add to the company bottom line using the latest technology.

A SHOT ACROSS THE BOW AT ALL COLLEGE GRADUATES

Going forward technology will play a more prominent role in every industry and every job. You must have updated technology skills in addition to whatever degree you have. It makes no difference if you are going to teach in a third grade classroom or work in investment banking with Goldman Sachs. Teachers are now grappling with the switch from print instructional materials to sophisticated digital products. Bankers are using *big data* to better serve their customers and improve the bottom line.

I'm not talking here about ho-hum technology skills like knowing how to use Excel and PowerPoint. Neither am I talking about your prowess with social media. Who cares if you can whack out twenty tweets a minute? Your world of work will require more, much more than that. Here is what Kirk McDonald, a former digital president for Time Inc. had to say in an op-ed he wrote for the *Wall Street Journal* in 2013:

> Dear college graduates: The next month is going to be thrilling as you cross this major milestone in your education. Enjoy the pomp and circumstance, the congratulations, and the parties. But when it's all over and you're ready to go out into the world, you'd probably like to meet me, or others like me—I'm your next potential dream boss. I run a cool, rapidly growing company in the digital field, where the work is interesting and rewarding. But I've got to be honest about some unfortunate news: I'm probably not going to hire you.

Citing recent stats from the Bureau of Labor Statistics, McDonald believes that the economy over the next decade will create 120,000 new computing jobs. Unfortunately, most recent college graduates won't be qualified to handle most of them. This should be a wake-up call to all recent college grads, regardless of major. The workplace today is changing rapidly as we speak. You need to update your technology skills constantly.

WHAT KINDS OF TECHNOLOGY JOBS ARE OUT THERE?

Here's an example of what you can expect to see as you continue to look for that first job. This is real life in today's world of work.

LinkedIn. I am part of a LinkedIn group called the Education Sales & Marketing Network and receive daily updates on industry trends, career matters, and job openings. A recent posting included the following nine job openings:

1. Marketing Manager, Online and End-User Marketing
2. Digital Analytics Manager
3. Senior Enterprise Technology Products Sales Executive
4. Senior Account Manager for Higher Education Technology Products
5. Senior Solutions Engineer I
6. Senior Solutions Engineer II
7. Systems Analyst
8. Search-and-Display Group Manager
9. Pre-Sales Senior Solutions Engineer

Look closely at this list. All nine positions are technology-related. That's where the job market is heading, and you must be prepared to meet it by constantly upgrading your technology skills, and by acquiring new skills, like web programming. Do you get the picture?

GOING FORWARD

A technology worker that I highly respect, Eric Schmidt, CEO of Google, says it better than anyone else in his new book, *The New*

Digital Age: Reshaping the Future of People, Nations and Business: "Soon everyone on Earth will be connected. With five billion more people set to join the virtual world, the boom in digital connectivity will bring gains in productivity, health, education, quality of life, and myriad other avenues in the physical world."

Need I say anymore about what technology will do in your work cycle? Listen to Eric.

CHAPTER TAKEAWAYS

- *Technology moves at lightning speed. Before an interview, search the Internet for the latest technology innovations and learn how they will impact the workplace.*
- *Speaking intelligently about technology with a hiring manager is a must.*
- *Continuously update your technology skills by taking online courses or classroom courses at your local college.*

JOB HUNTER'S LIBRARY

Maynard Webb and Carlye Adler, *Rebooting Work*, Jossey-Bass/Wiley, 2013. This timely book explores how technology can be used to be more successful in the workplace.

Eric Schmidt and Jared Cohen, *The New Digital Age*, Knopf, 2013.

Chapter 9

Social Media and Job Hunting: Be Creative!

Digital natives, like you, have come to rely on the use of digital devices for every purpose under the sun. The destination of choice for everyone seems to be social media, including Twitter, Facebook, YouTube, LinkedIn, Pinterest, and the *media du jour*.

Now that you have a diploma and are seeking that first job, you naturally turn to your digital device, your special apps, and social media. It worked to conduct research for your final term paper and to establish a personal network across the country. Why not use social media to find a job? It seems to make good sense . . . Or does it?

WHAT THE EXPERTS ARE SAYING

The *Wall Street Journal* published an article on April 24, 2013, in its Careers section that really caught my attention. The headline was JOB HUNTING MOVES TO MOBILE DEVICES. This cleverly written article used several examples of workers who found job leads by accessing job boards and social media on digital mobile devices like tablets and iPhones. Finding job leads on job boards is nothing new. It has been going on ever since job boards and desktop computers came together long ago. So what's causing all the media hype?

GOOD-BYE DESKTOPS?

The big difference is that college-grad job hunters are now accessing the job boards using a smartphone, tablet, or other mobile device. Today's college graduates are no longer tied to a desk and a desktop computer.

There is an increasing amount of media attention on the use of social media and digital devices for job hunting. It's a hot topic, and while reporters are always looking for a good story, they frequently ignore the *rest of this story*. Sure, you use digital devices to find job opportunities. But what happens after you find that lead is something else entirely? Your smartphone may have been instrumental in finding the job lead for the customer service position at AT&T, but that is just the beginning. As you move along the employment process, it becomes more personal, like knowing the name of a hiring authority inside of a company and then establishing a personal relationship.

Previously, your use of email, texting, Twitter, Facebook, YouTube, and other media revolved around your experience as a student, not as a job candidate. Now the wheels have turned and you are in competition to find a way to make money to become self-sufficient. This requires that you learn to use those digital devices and social media in a more creative way.

COMPANY USE OF SOCIAL MEDIA IN THE HIRING PROCESS

I've been witnessing the growing use of social media by recruiting firms and companies for posting job opportunities and for taking job applications, which saves time and money. In fact, many companies are *requiring* job applicants to use online application forms as the first step in the hiring process. Digital technology moves fast. Keep updated or you may be left behind.

GOING FORWARD IN THE DIGITAL WORLD OF WORK

So what's next, digital native? Let's figure out how to use social media to find your first job. Can Twitter lead you to the Promised

Land? And Facebook? I'll begin by relating something that happened while I was having breakfast at a local restaurant.

Breakfast at Fred's Restaurant in New Hope, Pennsylvania. I was sitting at the counter, and a man in his mid-twenties dressed in jeans, a purple T-shirt, and sneakers soon occupied the empty seat next to me. His natural red hair was very long but becoming, and his beard was full but attractive. He reminded me of a young Zeus. He placed his iPhone on the counter, and not to be outdone, I placed my Droid 4G Razor beside my plate. He ordered an omelet complete with bacon and rye toast, and I had my favorite: blueberry pancakes and sausages. After a few bites we began talking about the use of technology, and what he told me was fascinating.

"Zeus" told me his name was Peter and that he was a software developer for a small local company. He used various social media but in a very controlled way for both personal use and work productivity. He had two technology jobs since winning his bachelor's degree in computer technology two years ago. When I asked how he secured his first job, he said he had used LinkedIn, Twitter, and Facebook extensively. But those media did not lead him to employment. He found employment through personal networking, especially through meeting live people at trade shows and conferences. Twitter and Facebook played no role in landing a job, but LinkedIn provided networking opportunities. Peter said that for job hunting, you should use only one site, LinkedIn. He went on to say, with conviction, that the only way to find a job is through meeting people personally, and the best way to find hiring managers is to attend conferences and trade shows.

There you have it—a real-life story from a recent college graduate in his mid-twenties working in technology and familiar with all of the social media. I agree with Peter. You need to contact living human beings with names and titles. Peter will go a long way in his career because he knows how to navigate the world of work.

The point of this story is this: even though you digital natives are married to various social media and use it throughout the day, it is not the universal answer to finding a job. Using social media creatively as a tool in your plan for securing employment places it in the proper perspective.

CLEAN UP YOUR ACT

All of us have done some interesting, funny, and stupid things using social media. Remember that picture you posted on Facebook of you and your friends slugging down some Bud Lites and cheap wine on the beach during spring break? And how about that picture of you with your hair dyed green, marching in a green parade for global warming awareness? Or the YouTube video that you made your sophomore year? You know, the one of you and some friends having a food fight at Mickey D's.

The thing to remember is this. Images and text that may have been hilarious just a few years ago are not viewed the same way in the adult world of work, even at a company like Google or Facebook. The corporate world is a serious place, so you must get into the game and follow the rules of business, including proper and creative use of digital devices and social media. Play this game according to the rules of business, not according to the rules of life on campus. To illustrate the point, let me tell you about a recent encounter with a college senior who was about to receive her bachelor's degree.

Fiona of Florida. I was evaluating Fiona's candidacy and was impressed with both her resume and LinkedIn profile. She did a superlative job on both. Grammar and spelling? Perfect. Consistency? Perfect. Style and formatting? Perfect.

Then I went to Twitter and found a picture that made Fiona look like a sophomore or even a high school kid. When I advised her to get rid of it, she countered with, "The business world has become more informal. Pictures of candidates in crazy poses and saying something funny is just the way the world is. It's okay to be informal because that's the way work is today." Are you sure, Fiona? Tell that to a hiring manager and you will receive in return a pleasant smile and a polite dismissal. Enjoy the sand in Cancún. You will be spending a lot of time there instead of working to become self-sufficient and paying off your student loan.

In all fairness to Fiona, we can understand how this well-qualified candidate could have become confused about the adult world of work. Recently, I reviewed Google's website and saw pictures of young workers dressed very informally and having what appeared to be a good time while on the job. In fact, some were playing games in the corporate rec room. While that may be the way it is at Google for entry-level and low-level managerial workers, that is not the way you should present yourself to a hiring manager when applying for a job. After you are hired, you can dress the way the corporate culture allows. When you are presenting yourself as a job candidate, however, play by the rules, not by what you see on social media sites.

FIRST STEP IN USING SOCIAL MEDIA

Before you submit a resume or talk with a potential employer, delete every picture and message on your social media that could be perceived as immature. Do it now because hiring authorities vetting your candidacy are looking at Facebook, Twitter, YouTube, and other social media accounts to learn who you *really* are. Even if you use Facebook for private dissemination, get rid of the bad stuff. If you do not, you are putting your chances of finding your first job, or any job, in jeopardy. Failure to take this first step might be the reason why so many recent college graduates are whining nine months after graduation, "There's nothing out there."

The primary use of social media is to locate potential employers by name and title, so you can correspond and meet with them personally. The objective is to reach the hiring manager or human resources director personally. You can click away on your digital devices 24/7, but nothing happens until you see the hiring manager face-to-face. Make that part of your work plan.

Let's get specific and examine social media sites by name, remembering that digital mobile technology moves fast, and changes are always in the works. Keep yourself updated because the creative use of social media could get you where you need to go—that is, the personal interview with a hiring manager who has the authority to say, "You're hired!"

A GUIDE TO USEFUL SOCIAL MEDIA SITES FOR JOB HUNTING

The various media sites have different characteristics and are used in different ways for job hunting. I'm limiting our discussion to sites that I believe are most useful for job-hunting purposes.

Google and Bing

Google and Bing are not just search engines but also powerful sites for learning where the jobs are. Some pundits liken them to social media. Creative use of Google and Bing can lead to niche job boards, hiring authorities by name, and company job postings. Begin by experimenting with various search strings until you find your target.

Google and Bing are tools for employers, too. When human resources directors are vetting your candidacy, the first thing they will do is enter your name on Google or Bing. Up comes your profile on a number of different sites. Next step? They go to LinkedIn, Twitter, Facebook, YouTube, Pinterest, and others. It seems that you cannot hide your images, videos, and tweets anywhere these days.

Twitter

For all the hype it receives, one would think that Twitter is the god of social media. It seems that everyone is using Twitter, from your former roommate to the talking heads on CNN, Fox, CBS, NBC, and ABC, and the celebrity du jour. But how many people really use Twitter every day? According to statistics released by the Pew Research Center, only 8 percent of American adults who use the Internet use Twitter. That's a wake-up call for job seekers who think that *everyone* is on Twitter, even hiring authorities at Fortune 500 companies. The hype is greater than the reality.

Here's an example of the importance of cleaning up your tweets:

Ms. Seattle. Jean-Sun Hannah Ahn was twenty-two years old when she was crowned Miss Seattle in 2012. Following the crowning ceremony, she made some nasty postings on Twitter, such as "I seriously am hating Seattle right now" and "Ugh can't stand cold, rainy Seattle and the annoying people." The media latched on to these tweets immediately, and despite her sincere apologies, the damage did not go away. It jeopardized her chances for winning future pageant competitions and job opportunities.

Twitter in its Proper Perspective. Messages on Twitter are limited to 140 characters, just enough to tell your friend in San Diego, "I've responded to 400 tweets and sent out 300 resumes but I still don't have a job. There's nothing out there!" The communication medium used most frequently by adults in the world of work is email, and the number one medium for gathering information is still the good, old-fashioned Internet, like with Google and Bing. Twitter's use for job searching by candidates is limited, but companies have found it an important tool for marketing and customer service.

Twitter may be a topic of conversation during interviews, so learn all you can about its function as a marketing tool in business. You might even want to show how current you are by telling the interviewer about what's happening in China. Why China? Because it's the second largest economy in the world, and chances are good that you will be working with Chinese companies in your first job. China's version of Twitter is called Sina Weibo and is used by more than 260,000 companies, primarily for marketing and damage control, like making apologies to consumers for poor service or gaffes that customers found offensive. The term itself literally means "New-Wave Micro-Blog." The messages are called micro-blogs and can include videos, images, and hyperlinks. It has approximately 500 million users, about 30 percent of all Chinese Internet users. More than a hundred million messages are sent over Sina Weibo each day.

The Chinese version is at www.weibo.com, and the English version, partially launched in January 2013, is http://www.weiboenglish.com.

The problem with Twitter is that it can become addictive. You can receive and send tweets all day and come up with little helpful information for your job search. Twitter will suck up your time like nothing else. To use it effectively, first develop a plan similar to Kara's.

Kara from North Carolina. Kara graduated from a North Carolina college with a bachelor's degree in communications. Kara used Twitter in a very creative manner. First, she created a job-hunting plan for Twitter, and then she worked her plan. She targeted local corporate presidents and CEOs, and in doing so, found the president of a local company and learned that he made frequent visits to his company's district and regional offices. In addition, she learned that he attended trade shows across the US. He used Twitter to keep his constituents apprised of his whereabouts. Kara bought into his network and began responding to his tweets that highlighted his itinerary. She tweeted her interest in his travels, his company, and his mission, all of which caught his attention. Kara was, in effect, building a relationship. One of her tweets to the president focused on her college experience and her search for an internship. He responded by requesting that Kara call his administrative assistant to schedule a personal interview at the company home office. Kara's interview was a hit and she landed her internship.

The Internet is filled with advice for using Twitter. So are media pundits. And so is your next-door neighbor. You could spend the next ten years reading everyone's take on Twitter, but here are sources you will find useful:

Fastweb, www.fastweb.com/career-planning. This site provides useful information for job searching with Twitter. The advice is written in nontechnical terms, so everyone can understand and apply the basic and advanced rules.

Twitter, www.twitter.com. The company itself provides timely advice for using its product. The landscape is always changing, so check the Twitter website periodically.

There are many other tidbits of advice online for using Twitter for job hunting. Most of what you read has limited value, and some information is just plain misleading. For example, Twitter can send you a stream of jobs, but few may match your background and experience.

Also, create a separate Twitter account exclusively for job-hunting purposes. Do not load your new Twitter account with sophomoric images, and make sure it jibes with your resume and LinkedIn profile. Be consistent.

Going forward, keep on top of Twitter because its model will change. The company went public in November 2013, and it is now trading on the NYSE. Interestingly, when it went public, the company had yet to make a dime in profit. If it wants to serve as a public company, it will need to find a way to make money, and this means changing the model. Twitter is led by a bright group of people under the direction of its CEO, Dick Costolo.

YouTube

Can a video be a tool to reach the Promised Land—that is, a job that will pay your daily costs for food, shelter, clothing, insurance, transportation, recreation, and money to give back to the community? Yes, it can, but you must be judicious when using a video as a tool for finding your first job. First, remove anything from your archives that will make you look foolish and immature. If you have a video that presents you in a good light, submit it to a potential employer as an addendum to your digital resume. The video does not replace the resume, contrary to what you hear from video aficionados.

Employers like to see evidence that you were able to initiate a project and see it through to a successful conclusion. An example might be a video showing how you assembled a campaign to raise funds for fighting leukemia or heart disease. Another example might be an instructional video that you made for teaching early childhood yoga. Whatever you do, refrain from submitting a video with marginal value. There is nothing more harmful to your candidacy than a video that lacks mature subject matter and competent production.

Peggy McKee of Career Confidential specializes in job-hunting strategies, one of which is producing videos. I recommend that you access her website now for more information at www.careerconfidential.com.

Facebook

Some social media sites, like Facebook, include job postings by companies, both large and small, some of which include the names of their executives, hiring managers, and human resources directors.

Facebook has taken a beating for a number of reasons, one of which is its reputation for being a hangout for high school and college students to have fun, like posting pictures of themselves doing things that adults consider immature.

Once you have your Facebook images blasted all over the world, how do you regroup? We all know that once your images are out there it is difficult to get rid of them. The following sites are the best ones I've found for learning how to delete images and search history:

1. www.facebook.com/help/search/?q=how+do+i+delete+my +account
2. www.grovo.com/facebook-timeline/clear-search-history

Create a new Facebook account for job-hunting purposes only. Make sure it is in sync with your new Twitter account.

Indeed

Indeed goes back to 2004 and ranks high among social media job-hunting sites. Indeed is really a job aggregator that lists thousands of job postings from competitors' websites, job boards, company career pages, newspapers, and any other source that posts job opportunities. Enter a job title, a specific company, if you wish, and a location. Indeed provides all similar job listings in your location.

However, there is a yellow flag with Indeed job postings. Most do not provide the name of the hiring manager. Sending a resume off to a job number is a waste of time. To be productive, you must send your resume or career profile to a named person with a title. You can find those names on LinkedIn or by calling the company customer service department and asking for the name of a specific department hiring manager or human resources director.

Indeed works the other side of the job search business as well. You can upload your resume at no charge. The advanced search option permits you to dwell on a specific job you have in mind.

Simply Hired

Simply Hired is a job aggregator similar to Indeed. However, it not only posts jobs but also provides job trend information, including the latest on salaries. It has a convenient "Jobs by Category" list for quick access to specific jobs in a specific location. For example, I clicked on "Accounting" and up came a multitude of accounting-related jobs worldwide.

Regarding salaries, I clicked on "Teachers" and learned that the average salary for high school Spanish teachers was $37,000 per year. However, that is an average. In Chicago, that number will be much higher, and in Billings, Montana, it will be lower.

Under "Healthcare" there were many professional jobs posted. There were job listings for support personnel as well as healthcare administrators.

Employment trend information is a valuable feature. This feature compares specific job trends using metrics derived from Simply Hired's database of users. When I clicked "Accounting," I learned there has been virtually no increase in the number of accounting jobs available during the past two years.

Craigslist

I'm surprised at how many job seekers ignore Craigslist. It is probably the number one place to find local jobs. Small businesses employ more than 75 percent of American workers, and most look for local workers using local media to post these openings. The postings on Craigslist are interesting and cover the full gamut of industries and jobs. For example, I checked Craigslist recently and found a retail sales consultant position with AT&T in Flemington, New Jersey. What an interesting entry-level position with a great American name in the communications industry! Also, I viewed a sales position for a family-owned-and-operated fencing company in New Jersey, *and* the posting included a phone number. You know how convenient that is. All you need to do is call the number and ask for the name and contact information for the hiring manager to begin building a personal relationship.

I suggest that you set aside ten minutes each day to check Craigslist for job postings in your local area. Craigslist jobs have a tendency to come and go quickly because of the local listing feature. Act quickly when you see something interesting.

Pinterest

This site has been attracting millions of visitors, but it is not by any means your ticket to the Promised Land. Pinterest is a site where users share their special interests by posting or pinning their photos on a pinboard. It's clever, cute, and entertaining but has little value for job hunting. However, companies are now using Pinterest, and they may begin pinning job opportunities on their company pinboards. Check this site occasionally for changes that may target job hunters.

LinkedIn

The social medium that will be the most valuable in your search for employment is LinkedIn (www.linkedin.com). Click now for an overview and to sign on. LinkedIn is a site designed exclusively for the workplace, and if used properly, it can be one of your most important job-hunting tools.

After you sign on for free, you will be able to post your photo and your profile, which is tantamount to placing your resume where hundreds of thousands of workers and hiring managers can see it.

Both companies and individuals can post their profiles on LinkedIn. For example, I just entered the name of an American corporate icon, Harley-Davidson (www.harley-davidson.com). The motorcycle manufacturer has been in business for one hundred years. The company is based in Wisconsin and has regional offices and dealerships in every state in the US. Here's what else I did once I was on LinkedIn: I conducted a search for the name of the Harley-Davidson human resources director and got it immediately along with her photo and contact information. The entire process took less than a minute and gave me the name of a key player in one of the most respected companies in the US. By the way, check the Harley-Davidson website for career postings. It may have something just for you.

I find LinkedIn a valuable source for finding both job candidates and client companies. Each day, I receive several invitations from workers at every level to join their LinkedIn network. After viewing their online profiles, I either accept or decline, depending on several criteria I use to sort out workers who will be valuable members of my network.

LinkedIn has several levels of membership. The higher the level of membership, the higher the cost. As you go up the chain, you will have access to more information and more details about the individuals or companies you want to reach. I suggest that you take the lowest level of membership, which is free, a price that I like very much. Take time out now and sign on because LinkedIn is *the* one social media/networking site dedicated exclusively to the world of work.

LinkedIn members hold positions from entry-level support workers to managers, directors, vice presidents, presidents, and CEOs. Once you become familiar with LinkedIn, you can become a member of a subgroup dedicated to one specific area of employment, such as marketing, sales, or information technology. Once your name is identified with such a group, you will be notified of job openings across the entire spectrum of businesses. For example, recently I received notices from the International Society for Technology Education (ISTE) for the following job openings:

- Editorial Director, Victoria's Secret
- President, Connecticut Audubon Society
- President, Columbia Consulting Group
- Business Development Director, Simply Hired

Of course, these are jobs for experienced workers, but LinkedIn has not forgotten entry-level job candidates. It has created a special group tailor-made for you called "Recent College Grads."

This special group is a must for recent college graduates seeking entry-level positions or above. Once you are in, you will receive daily reports about the state of the job market generally, and job postings specifically. Every "Recent College Grads" posting includes job opportunities, so check this site every day. Here are just a few of the jobs I saw recently:

- Business Analyst
- Technical Customer Support Specialist
- Business Intelligence Trainee
- Sales Representative
- Java Developer Trainee

In addition, a number of recruiters belong to this group and post jobs frequently. You cannot go wrong accessing "Recent College Grads" every day.

IS USING SOCIAL MEDIA THE KEY TO FINDING A JOB?

The noise on the street considers social media the panacea for finding a job. What you frequently hear is that face-to-face communication, shaking hands, and having a cup of joe with a hiring manager are passé. In fact, in an article in the *Wall Street Journal* by Phyllis Korkki in her Workstation column, I read the following: "Old-fashioned personal networking can still be an effective way to land a job, but online networking now supplements it in many fields." I have to say that I don't agree with Phyllis because the evidence shows that using digital media exclusively is the least effective method of finding a job. Sorry, Phyllis.

WRITING A DIGITAL PROFILE TO USE WITH SOCIAL MEDIA

The digital profile is a document used with social media like LinkedIn. It is a condensed version of your resume with modifications required by the site posting it. The key point to remember is that your digital profile must be consistent with your resume. Most social media will define the format of your profile and even limit its length. When you are constructing your profile, have your written resume at your side and use it as a guide. For more information about creating a digital profile and to see a sample, refer to chapter 16.

GOING FORWARD

Remember the primary message of this book is that company hiring authorities don't hire resumes, tweets, YouTube videos, texts, or emails. They hire warm, living human beings, like you, who take the time to find their names and then see them personally.

Social media sites are not replacing personal communication. They are simply tools for job hunting and will reap benefits for you . . . if used creatively.

CHAPTER TAKEAWAYS

- *Use social media as a tool, not a panacea, for job hunting.*
- *LinkedIn is where the hiring managers hang out.*
- *Your resume and digital profiles must say the same thing.*
- *Clean up your social media profile.*

JOB HUNTER'S LIBRARY

Eric Schmidt and Jared Cohen, *The New Digital Age*, Knopf, 2013.

PART 3

FINDING EMPLOYERS
AND STARTING YOUR
OWN BUSINESS

Chapter 10

How to Find Employers

In this chapter, we will discover how to find employers. You may be shocked to learn that your future boss may be sitting next to you at Starbucks. The people you need to contact personally are hiring managers and human resources directors. These are the people in large companies or small businesses who decide who is hired and who is not.

If you are seeking a job in sales, the person you want to reach is the director of sales. If you are pursuing a marketing job, the person you should see is the director of marketing. If technology is your focus, the person you need to see is the chief technology officer (CTO) or chief information officer (CIO). If you are seeking a position in finance, the person you need to reach is the chief financial officer, the CFO. If you are not sure what role you would like and are seeking any entry-level position, the person you need to see is the human resources director.

Sometimes people at the highest departmental rank will refer you to a subordinate who handles entry-level positions. That happens frequently. See the person to whom you are referred and do not consider this a put-down. However, be assured that any person who is hired at any level is always approved by the department head. For entry-level positions, the first interview is usually with the human resources director. This person will send the best candidates to the hiring manager, who ultimately will make the final decision.

HOW DO YOU FIND THE DECISION MAKERS?

How do you go about finding these people? How do you learn their names and contact information? You may have had the experience of calling a company and asking for the director of sales to apply for a job only to have the receptionist tell you that all job applicants must go through the human resources department. That is not unusual for entry-level candidates, but you must take it to the next level by asking for the name and contact information of the human resources director.

You must contact the hiring authority by name to make real progress. You can learn who that person is by using several methods:

- Googling the company and position
- Reviewing a company website
- Calling the company customer services department and asking for the name of the person you want to see
- Using LinkedIn and entering the name of a company and a position
- Leaving the house and attending conferences and trade shows that take place almost every day in most large- and medium-sized cities across the country

The best way to find your first job is to leave the house and seek out hiring authorities personally. Jobs are not located in your home. When you leave home and go where the jobs are, you never know where the fun will end, or when someone will say, "Your hired!"

THE PROACTIVE JOB HUNTER

People who have the authority to hire you are lurking everywhere. You can find them in airports, on airplanes, in restaurants, and at bars, tapas joints, Starbucks, sports events—any location where people gather. However, just being in a crowd is not enough; you must be proactive.

When you are in Starbucks ordering a grande cappuccino, most likely the first thing you will do is look for a table that is unoccupied so you can whip out your smartphone or iPad and begin texting or tweeting with your friends. This is not the way you find your potential boss.

Select a table occupied by living, breathing human beings, particularly those dressed in business attire, because they are the people you want to know. Instead of tweeting your life away, begin a conversation with the woman who is dressed for success and pounding away on her laptop. How do you begin the conversation? Begin with that all-time favorite, the weather: "It's really hot out today. Good thing this place has air-conditioning. By the way, you look like the president of a company. What do you do?" You have just opened the door, and who knows what is inside.

Let me tell you how one CEO found many entry-level employees for his sixty-million-dollar company, which produced science supplies for schools and colleges.

Paul from Buffalo. Paul started his business by purchasing a failing mom-and-pop company that produced a hobby kit of science materials for kids at the elementary school level and sold them in small department stores. He transformed that kit into a major product in the school science supply business because he always found the right workers to get the job done.

When I visited the company's home office in Buffalo, New York, I noticed an unusually high number of young adults, probably in the twenty- to thirty-year-old age bracket. Paul told me that he made a practice of hiring young college graduates because they were smart, energetic, and passionate about finding their niche in the world of work. Paul even paid tuition for promising workers to continue their formal graduate level education.

I was surprised at his answer to my question, "Where do you find such good people?" He responded that he traveled frequently by air and made a practice of getting to the airport early for worker-hunting purposes. When he saw a person who was acceptably dressed and not jabbering away on a phone, he began a conversation, which was really the beginning of an interview. If he liked what he saw and heard, the next step was to request a resume and schedule a personal interview at his home office. His method of recruiting had a very high success rate because it began with a personal meeting, not a resume hurled through space. Many of his entry-level employees went on to become managers and directors.

HIRING MANAGERS ARE DRESSED FOR SUCCESS

One never knows the status of the person in business attire, but it's your job to find out. What's that you say? "Nobody really dresses up anymore. The world of work has gone casual." Don't drink the Kool-Aid. Business executives on the job always dress in business attire. The adult world of work really works that way. Don't let anyone kid you about that. Even in the technology world, executive-level people are dressed a cut above the people working in the trenches. Look for the people in business attire and you will find hiring managers, and even people like Paul, the CEO. Let me give you an example of how people of different rank dress in the business world.

Long Hair in Boston. I had an appointment with the CEO of a successful educational technology company in Boston about a director of marketing position. I entered the building wearing a suit, tie, and leather shoes . . . all traditional business attire. What I saw was close to mayhem. There were young workers everywhere in a large open space. Some were chatting animatedly with colleagues; others were sitting in a corner banging away on laptops; still others were drinking sodas and looking into space. All had one thing in common: *very casual dress* and waist-length hair for both the male and female employees. (Don't get me wrong. I have nothing against long hair, but I think there are some unwritten work rules that govern how we look and what we wear under certain circumstances.)

When I entered the executive offices, the scene changed dramatically. The CEO wore traditional business attire, and so did the human resources director, and so did the vice president for marketing.

There are two takeaways from this example:

1. When you see people dressed in business attire, they are usually managerial-level people who have hiring authority. You want to meet them personally.
2. Always dress in business attire when you go for a personal interview. After you are hired, you can dress as the culture dictates, which is mostly casual in today's world. The exceptions are outside salespeople, who always dress in traditional business attire because they are out meeting customers.

LOOKING FOR HIRING MANAGERS IN THE YELLOW PAGES

Another way to find employers may shock you. It is using the good, old Yellow Pages. Prior to 1990, people used print books to find just about everything, including employers. One of the most useful books was the Yellow Pages phone directory. It is still being published for every location in the US, and it is a fascinating book to review. As all of you know, the Yellow Pages are online, too. This directory for a large city like Chicago, Dallas, or New York City could run over a thousand pages. It lists all businesses alphabetically under industry headings.

I just clicked on www.yellowpages.com and then entered "cosmetic companies, New York" and got 799 hits, almost every single one a company dealing in cosmetics, from manufacturing to retail sales.

If you live in Chicago, one of the first major headings in the Chicago Yellow Pages is "Accounting," where you will find the names of hundreds of accounting firms, complete with addresses and phone numbers and possibly a website if the company listing is a display ad.

How to Use the Yellow Pages

Using the Yellow Pages, a mere phone directory, to look for a job in the digital age? What is this, some kind of joke? Before you write off the Yellow Pages, read this next story.

Alan from Chicago. Alan was a middle school teacher in Chicago when he decided to explore alternate career opportunities. A friend of his was a sales rep for a textbook publishing company and suggested that he explore this line of work. Bright guy that Alan was, he went to the Chicago Yellow Pages and found the major heading "Publishers." Under that heading were dozens of publishers listed by type, and he found twelve companies that published textbooks. He called each company and asked for the name of the sales manager for the Chicago Metro Area, and armed with these twelve names he began a search for his first job in the private sector. He called each manager and asked for a personal interview. The result? Five personal interviews and three job offers. He accepted an offer from a prominent publisher at a base salary that was twice what he was making as a teacher, plus

> a commission plan that yielded 50 percent of his base salary for meeting revenue targets, plus a company car, plus benefits.

Are the Yellow Pages for Real?

Could anything sounding so *yesterday* really help you find that first job in today's digital world? In the 2012 edition of the classic job-hunting book titled, *What Color is Your Parachute?*, Richard Bolles lists the five best ways to look for a job. Guess what is number three? Using the Yellow Pages. Bolles's research revealed a 69 percent success rate for candidates using this method.

Want to get that monkey called "student loan" off your back? Try the Yellow Pages. You can use either the print or the digital editions, but I believe you will find the print edition more helpful. If you know the industry you want to explore, just go to that major heading and find the firms listed under that heading. If you are not sure what you want to do, flip through the Yellow Pages and note the major industry headings. One of them might be your cup of coffee. Finance. Banking. Publishing. Retailing. Agriculture. Automobiles. Insurance. Healthcare. It's all there, in the Yellow Pages.

Caution: Do not let your friends know about this best-kept secret for job hunting. Keep this one all to yourself, and soon you may have a job while your friends are still whining, "There's nothing out there!" On second thought, let them in on the Yellow Pages secret. Heck, we're all in this together!

BACK TO THE FUTURE . . . AGAIN. FINDING EMPLOYERS USING THE NEWSPAPER

You can scan either the print or digital versions of local, regional, or national newspapers. One of the best if you want to get the broad picture is the *Wall Street Journal*. I call this daily newspaper

America's most honest publication because its agenda is helping people make money. I suggest that you subscribe to the *Journal* if you want an education about how the world of work *really* works.

I found the following quote in an op-ed written by Brad Smith, Executive Vice President and General Counsel of Microsoft, which appeared in an October 2012 issue of the *Journal*: "Many American companies are now creating more jobs for which they can't find qualified applicants . . . At Microsoft, we have more than 6,000 open jobs in the US, a 15% increase from a year ago. Some 3,400 of these positions are for engineers, software developers and researchers."

Smith goes on to say that colleges need to try new methods for educating students so they will be better qualified to meet the needs of companies in the digital age. What Smith says is what you will hear from executives in companies across the US. Unfortunately, some people who are new to the job market believe that sources like newspapers and phone directories are of little value when you are seeking your first job. Well, think again and start reading traditional media, because there you will find information that will help you find that first job.

The Microsoft URL is www.microsoft.com. What are you waiting for, humanities and STEM majors? A couple of clicks will tell you what's happening at MS. It's a great employer, and it might have a job for you. In addition, you do not have to be a whiz-bang techie to get a job there. Click, click, click.

What else can the newspapers do for you? The local newspaper is where local employers will advertise local jobs. You will find their job postings in the classified sections of print and digital newspapers. Usually, the weekend versions carry the most job postings.

FINDING EMPLOYERS THROUGH INTERNSHIPS

Some real-life examples will illustrate how to go about navigating the adult world of work for the first time through paid or unpaid internships, a good segue to that first job. They are available through many companies before or after you graduate. Here's a good example:

Kelsey from Washington, DC. In May of 2011, Kelsey graduated, *cum laude*, with a BA in political science and American studies from William Smith College in upstate New York, and by June she was employed with one of the icons in the public relations world in Washington, DC. How did she do this with the economy in turmoil and the unemployment rate hovering near 9.5 percent? What Kelsey did was a textbook example of how you find that first job. In the summers prior to her junior and senior years, she found two different internships in Washington, DC. Knowing she wanted to live in the area, she was excited to work hard and make contacts that would land her in the city full-time after graduation. The jobs were not glamorous, but she hung in there and in the process made numerous business acquaintances. During March of her senior year, she skipped the usual spring break junket to Cancún. Instead, she sat down at her kitchen table and reached out to anyone and everyone she knew in DC, and ended up applying to a company Google deemed to be one of the top ten public relations firms in DC. Because of her previous two internships and strong written and verbal skills, Kelsey landed a gig at her number one spot for an internship and hoped to turn it into a job by the end of the summer. She was hired less than a month after graduation.

Kelsey was not just lucky. She made a plan, worked her plan, and it paid off with a job. First, she had the foresight to find summer internships during her undergraduate years. Next, she did not sit at home firing off tweets and resumes to unknown entities like Job #126, or Employment Manager, or Second Ring of the Planet Saturn. She left the house and contacted potential employers in the flesh. Now that's the way a college graduate finds her first job!

Internships, paid and unpaid, are available, and you can find them on the websites of employers you are exploring. Also, Google "internships for college grads" and you will find much information about how to explore this route to permanent employment.

HOW TO USE NETWORKING SOURCES

The primary purpose of networking is to connect personally with someone who can help you secure a job. Who are these people? Everyone who is presently employed by a company or who owns a business is a networking source. Where do you find them? They are as close as your next-door neighbor. Here are sources for connecting with a person who can steer you in the right direction.

Your Former Boss

When you were employed part-time during college or after you received your diploma, you reported to someone who is familiar with your services. Contact that person and ask for the names of hiring managers. Also, you might ask that person for a letter of recommendation. Do not overlook this obvious source. Most people are willing to help an entry-level candidate find a job. Here's an example of what can happen when you solicit the help of a former boss or coworker.

Laura from New Jersey. When she graduated from Penn State with a BA in communications, Laura thought the world was waiting for her with great jobs paying big bucks. However, her first job was a part-time stint running a Christmas show for a local department store in Philadelphia. When that job ended, she solicited help from her original networking source who gave her the name of a hiring manager at a video production company in Philadelphia. She was hired as a temp worker for the receptionist who was just going on a three-month pregnancy leave. Laura worked the front desk and was noticed by the executive staff. Coincidentally, a position titled operations manager opened up, and Laura hit pay dirt. She was hired full-time with a successful video production company and a year later was promoted to production manager.

Laura says it is all about getting your foot in the door, even as a part-time worker, and that you can do that using referral sources. Her use of networking and planning was successful.

Does the networking thing really work? Here's another example of what a former boss can do for you:

Alice from Pennsylvania. When Alice graduated from James Madison University with a bachelor's degree in music education, she was not sure about pursuing a career in the classroom and looked at other opportunities in the business of music. While working as a volunteer host at JMU's public radio station, Alice took advantage of radio industry job opportunities posted by NPR and the Corporation for Public Broadcasting.

It so happened that the station chief engineer, to whom she reported, noticed an opening for which he thought Alice would be interested and qualified. He brought it to Alice's attention and the job was right up her alley. KCND, a start-up radio station in Bismarck, North Dakota, had a full-time opening for a classical music host/producer. Alice submitted her resume, audition tape, and photo immediately. After several phone interviews with the station's general manager and operations manager, she was offered an on-air, full-time afternoon hosting position, which she accepted.

Breaking into professional radio in a specialized area like classical music is no easy task, but Alice applied her intelligence, energy, and passion to her advantage. Luckily for Alice, KCND's general manager was intent on hiring a new staff to include veteran broadcasters and young, up-and-coming radio hosts, both from the local area and from out of town.

Though the pay was minimal, Alice received valuable working experience at her first job out of college, and since then has gone on to work successfully for other public radio stations. Now she is the program director for WWFM, The Classical Network, based in Trenton, NJ. Listen to Alice every morning by tuning in to WWFM, 89.1 on your radio dial.

This is another real-life example of how you get that first job, even without the experience that you have been led to believe you must have. Don't listen to the crowd. Follow your heart, hit the streets, and meet employers personally. Take the risk and you *will* find that first job.

Your Friends' Parents

This is a frequently overlooked networking resource. Assume that you have twenty-five good friends, all with parents who are working. That gives you fifty potential networking sources. Ask these parents where they work, and ask for the names of the human resources directors and other hiring managers. Ask if they would introduce you to these people and follow up by contacting them for an appointment. Do not wait two weeks to follow up. If the introduction is made on a Monday, follow up no later than Tuesday by phone or email to request an appointment for a personal interview.

Referrals

The entry-level candidate who has been referred by an employee of the company has the best chance of getting the job. In fact, many companies give monetary rewards to employees who refer a candidate who is hired. It's tough to beat an entry-level candidate who is referred to the human resources director and hiring manager by a valued employee.

Looking down the road a year or two after you are employed, you will see that an internal candidate has the best chance at winning a higher-level job, which usually includes a promotion. The networking continues even while you are employed. This does not ensure that the company always gets the best candidate, but that's the way it works. Fair or not, that is just the way it works.

LinkedIn Contacts

The best digital job-networking site is LinkedIn. That's the purpose of it: networking with hiring authorities. If you are interested in the broadly defined area of information technology, enter that in the LinkedIn search box and you will find the names and contact information for many people who are there to help you connect. I did that just now and came up with the names of 134 contacts, all of them networking sources who could lead to a job. Refer back to chapter 6 for more about using LinkedIn.

USING THE COLD-CALL METHOD TO FIND HIRING MANAGERS

Before we even begin our discussion, we need to be mindful of the importance of people called "gatekeepers," those who control access to the people you want to see. There are gatekeepers in every company, but at this point, the one you need to be concerned with is the receptionist at the front desk. This person can make or break you, and you must treat this person with respect and build a relationship quickly. Your appearance and introductory remarks are critical. The receptionist is trained to get rid of anyone demanding, disrespectful, or dressed like a slob.

The Cold-Call Process

The process begins by entering an office without an appointment and telling the receptionist that you are seeking a position and would like to meet with the human resources director or hiring manager for a specific department. If you are focusing on a specific position, maybe associate marketing manager, ask to see the hiring manager in charge of marketing. If you are seeking a position in sales, ask for the sales manager. Your introductory statement to the receptionist, accompanied with a smile, might go something like this: "Good morning, Ms. Jones. My name is William Foster. I'm a recent graduate of Wake Forest University, and I'm seeking a position in information technology. May I please speak with your technology director?"

The receptionist, whose name will be on the reception desk, will respond in one of several ways:

1. "Our technology director is Mrs. Deborah George and I'll see if she's available." Your response might be, "Thank you. I'd appreciate only a few minutes of her time. I know she's a busy person."
2. "Our technology director is Mr. Adams, but he's out of the office today." Your response might be, "Thank you. In that case, may I speak with his administrative assistant to make an appointment to see him?"
3. "We do not have a technology director." Your response might be, "Thank you. In that case, may I speak with the human resources director?"
4. "I'm sorry, you need an appointment to see any of our staff members." Your response might be, "Thank you. May

I please have the name of your human resources director and the email address and phone number? I'll call for an appointment as you suggested."

Note that your response should always begin with a thank you. Also, note that you never just say thank you and walk out. That is not the way it works in the business world. You are here because this is a business deal. You are selling yourself and the company is always looking for new talent, like you. Be professionally assertive, but courteous, until you get what you want and need.

Cold Calls Are Always in Style

Some consider making personal calls on potential employers without an appointment something out of yesterday's playbook. Wrong! The purpose of the cold call is to arrange a personal interview with a hiring manager. When you knock on doors, you never know who will answer and offer you a job. Cold-calling is not easy, but the more calls you make, the greater your chances of striking pay dirt. Also, you risk rejection, and that is not easy if you take it personally. However, the more times you do it, your technique will improve and you will learn that possible rejection is not a personal assault but part of the business process.

The odds of something happening are in your favor. Assume that you make fifteen cold calls per week to potential employers in an industrial or office park. At the end of one month, you will have made sixty calls where you spoke with a real person, a receptionist, hiring manager, or administrative assistant. Assuming a success rate of only 10 percent, at the end of one month, you will have met personally with six hiring managers. Compare that to the number of personal interviews you will have had if you stayed at home and fired off resumes to unknown entities.

HOW TO FIND EMPLOYERS AT CONFERENCES AND TRADE SHOWS

The best way to find potential employers in the flesh is to attend conferences, trade shows, job fairs, and conventions. This is where you will find a multitude of potential employers, all under one roof. I believe that attending conferences at major convention centers like McCormick Place in Chicago or the Javits Center in New York City is the best use of your job-hunting time. In fact, I so strongly believe in this method of finding a job that I've devoted an entire chapter to it. In chapter 13, I'll tell you where the convention halls are located and advise you what to do once you're there and faced with hundreds or thousands of booths occupied by potential employers. I know from first-hand experience that many candidates have met their potential employers on the floor of a convention center; in fact, candidates have even been hired on the floor. You will not find a better way to make productive use of your job-hunting time and effort. Here is an example of what to expect:

BookExpo America (BEA). This is the largest trade show in America for the book publishing industry. BEA held its 2013 annual convention at the Javits Center in New York City. More than 1,200 companies hosted exhibits on the conference center floor, all staffed by publishing company employees. Some held editorial positions, some were marketing managers, some came from sales, others from finance, and still others from information technology. Where in the world could you find so many potential employers under one roof, in the flesh?

By the way, BEA will be at the Javits Center in 2014 and 2015, too. I hope to see you there. Business, humanities, and STEM majors, check it out at www.bookexpoamerica.com.

USING SOCIAL MEDIA TO MAKE THE RIGHT CONNECTION

Using social media creatively can return positive benefits, but as I've said in chapter 6, it's necessary to proceed with caution. Studies show that using social media is the least effective way to find employment. But I have found one exception, LinkedIn, which you may consider a networking place as well.

USING JOB BOARDS

As with social media, the job boards have been disappointing with a success rate of less than 15 percent for both candidates and companies. My assessment of the boards is that they fail to connect you with a named person, a hiring authority, and, in many cases, even a named company. When you respond to a posting on a board, your resume goes to Job #234 or Position #456. You might as well send your resume to Jupiter or Mars.

REVIEWING CORPORATE WEBSITES

If you want to see what's happening at consumer goods companies, like Proctor & Gamble, it makes sense to review their websites and check out their career pages. However, do not assume that all available jobs are posted on company websites. Many jobs, entry-level as well as established jobs, are not posted. They are filled by workers being promoted from within the company, by referrals from employees, by recruiters, and through job boards. In many cases, companies use several different sources to find qualified candidates.

GOING FORWARD

This chapter reviewed some of the best tried-and-true methods of finding a job. In the next chapter, I'll tell you where to find those elusive first jobs. Don't go away!

CHAPTER TAKEAWAYS

- *Nothing happens until you leave the house to meet potential employers personally.*
- *Attending conferences is the best way to meet potential employers.*
- *Dress and appearance do matter, especially during the interview process.*
- *Treat the gatekeepers with respect.*

JOB HUNTER'S LIBRARY

Sheryl Sandberg, *Lean In,* Knopf, 2013.

Editors, *Standard & Poor's 500 Guide 2013*, McGraw-Hill, 2013.

Chapter 11

Where to Find Employers

The scope of the American job market is vast, so vast that it can be confusing to listen to the gurus on CNBC, Bloomberg, and Fox as they speak glibly about the world of work using a vocabulary that leaves one in the dark. Occasionally, you will hear them talk about the size of the American workforce and how that relates to being employed or unemployed. You will hear them talk about job sectors and economic cycles, too, but how does all of this relate to learning *where* one can find employers at any given time in the economic cycle?

In order to put the American economy into proper perspective, one must compare it to the rest of the world. The comparison is nothing less than startling. Just our American workforce of 155 million alone makes it equivalent to the seventh largest nation in the world.

THE SIZE OF THE AMERICAN WORKFORCE

The large size of our workforce makes it a difficult entity to move up or down, and explains why the employment rate is the most lagging indicator when the economy is coming out of a recession. You do not easily manipulate a demographic like 155 million people. Ask any worker who was laid off during the severe recession of 2007 to 2009 how challenging it was to find a new job during that period. However, there were jobs available, and you could find them if you knew where to look.

The size of our workforce explains why immigrants flock to the US both legally and illegally year after year. Only in America are so many jobs available. Immigrants continue to come here, even during a severe recession, for one reason: jobs! Immigrants know where to find the jobs, whether they're entry-level like basic landscaping, or skilled work like performing brain surgery. They do not sit there and whine, "There's nothing out there."

IS THERE ANYTHING OUT THERE FOR ME?

Armed with your college degree there is something out there for you. Living in a country that can generate 155 million jobs is about as good as it gets. It's just a matter of finding out where jobs are available and how to go about looking for them using your intelligence, your energy, and your work plan.

To begin learning where the jobs are, let's divide the workforce into bite-size chunks for easy understanding. Let's explore the broad divisions in our economy, which can be refined into numerous subsections, to learn where employers are.

AMERICAN JOB SECTORS: WHERE EMPLOYERS ARE LOCATED

How many times have you heard, "You have a degree and there are hundreds of companies just waiting for you"? It all sounds so easy. However, where and how do you tap into our vast job market? Does it make any difference where you work? Isn't working as associate director of marketing with a manufacturer like Ford Motors the same as working as associate director of marketing for Apple? Marketing is marketing. It makes no difference. Or does it? Are there significant differences between working for a *service producer* MassMutual Financial Group and working for a *goods producer* like PepsiCo?

The short answer is yes. There is a difference, but how do you know which sectors and which companies to explore for potential employment? Do you just throw darts at the stock listings in the *Wall Street Journal* and hope for the best?

The American economy is so large and varied that we need a road map to learn how it breaks down into its component parts. Knowing something about the components will provide direction for your search and save you time and energy. In addition, knowledge of the differences between a *service producer* and a *goods producer* will help you to understand what your interests are and what kind of work you might like to do.

THE TWO MAIN PARTS OF THE AMERICAN WORKPLACE

The Bureau of Labor Statistics divides the American economy into two main parts or job sectors, the *goods producing industries* and the *services producing industries*. What will it be for you? Assistant event planning manager for Hyatt, a services producing company, or associate customer service representative for California-based Callaway Golf Company, a goods producing company? (By the way, both have jobs available. Go to their websites and click on "Careers" at www.hyatt.com and www.callawaygolf.com.) For a detailed look at these sectors, consult the Bureau of Labor Statistics, www.bls.gov, and the latest edition of the *Occupational Outlook Handbook*. Before we get into the two main job sectors, let's take a quick look at some important numbers to set the stage.

The total of all goods and services, known as the Gross Domestic Product (GDP), produced by all businesses in 2012 was approximately $16 trillion. In anyone's book, that is a lot of money, and it makes the US the world's largest economy. Of the 500 largest companies in the world, 132 are American. Our workforce, as reported above, numbers 155 million workers.

Let's examine each sector, keeping in mind that you will probably be working in one of these two sectors. (Others might be working in government jobs, something entirely different.) Also, use this as an opportunity to learn more about your work aptitude and what you would like to do with your life in the world of work.

The Goods Producing Sector

Any industry that produces something tangible in a factory, plant, or mill falls into this category. These are industries like agriculture, food, shelter, clothing, technology, hardware, forestry, construction, manufacturing, chemicals, mining, oil, gas extraction, and the like. There are many subsets in each category, but we will examine just one of these industries, manufacturing, in more detail because this sector produces millions of jobs.

The Manufacturers

Contrary to what you might hear, the US is still the number one manufacturing country in the world. True, much US manufacturing has moved overseas in the past fifty years, mainly because of the demands for high wages and benefits by unions, but we have not abandoned manufacturing to become a services producing country only.

The world's largest manufacturer is the Texas-based gas and oil producer ExxonMobil. Exxon's 2012 revenues were *$452 billion*, and the company employs 77,000 workers. Other American manufacturers in the top twenty worldwide are Chevron and ConocoPhillips, both oil and gas manufacturers; Boeing; General Motors; and General Electric. So much for the "manufacturing is dead in America" theory.

A Note to Women about the Petroleum Industry

The stereotype of the worker in the oil and gas business is, "Big, burly, macho guy. Beard. Heavy drinking. Cursing. Dirty clothes." Think again. According to a 2013 BLS report, 46 percent of the new jobs in the petroleum business went to women. No, that is not a mistake. Check this out at www.bls.gov.

Once again, the numbers tell it all. Regardless of your gender, religion, race, or ethnicity, go for any job in an industry that interests you. Work stereotypes are falling fast, and the playing field is quite level. Don't fall for the hype. Just go for it!

Who Are the Manufacturers and Where Are Manufacturing Jobs Located?

In addition to those listed above, manufacturers are companies like Dow Chemical, Ford, Chrysler, Caterpillar, John Deere, Kellogg, Proctor & Gamble, US Steel, and Nike. Manufacturing in the US is not dead by any means. In fact, 12 percent of our GDP (Gross Domestic Product, the dollar total of all goods and services) comes from manufacturing. Large manufacturers employ hundreds of thousands of workers in a variety of jobs like sales, marketing, finance, human resources, information technology, and finance.

You do not have to live in the headquarters city of a large company to be employed by it. While a large company like Ford has home offices in Detroit, Michigan, it maintains manufacturing plants and regional offices scattered in dozens of locations across the US and abroad. There are job opportunities at every location.

In addition, working for a manufacturing company does not always mean working on an assembly line or loading boxcars with finished goods. In fact, most jobs in manufacturing are "clean-hands" jobs.

Is the manufacturing sector right for you? If you get a kick out of seeing a Boeing 747 defy gravity and lift off the runway to a cruising altitude of 38,000 feet, you might want to look at airline manufacturers like Boeing and Lockheed Martin for your first job. Click on their websites and view their career pages at www.boeing.com and www. lockheedmartin.com. In addition, there are many jobs available with passenger airlines like Delta and United. I like this entry-level job that a person I know just landed in Minneapolis. This is a reservationist job working at the Delta call center in Minneapolis, one of Delta's many reservation centers throughout the US. The position pays $11 per hour and carries a full benefits package. Annual salary at $11 per hour for a forty-hour workweek is $21,120 per year. Add 30 percent of your base salary for benefits (the value of vacation time, insurance, paid holidays, and sick days), and your true compensation is $27,456. But that's not all. This person and his wife and all family members can fly anywhere in the Delta network absolutely free! And after ten years of employment with Delta, the free airfare benefit becomes a *lifetime* benefit. Interested? Click here: www.deltajobs.net. Welcome aboard!

The chemical industry is another manufacturer providing jobs for thousands of workers. There is room for everyone in manufacturing, regardless of major, and there may be a spot for you at Dow Chemical (www.dow.com). This Fortune 500 company, which produces chemicals for the agriculture industry, is considered one of the best employers in America. A recent *Wall Street Journal* article profiled a twenty-two-year-old graduate of Iowa State who accepted a sales position with Dow at a base salary of $50,000 plus bonuses and benefits. What a great first job!

There are millions of jobs in the American manufacturing sector, and there could be one tailor-made for you. Check them out. If you would rather work in another part of the world, here are the five largest manufacturing countries including the US:

1. United States
2. China
3. Japan
4. Germany
5. Russia

Food, Shelter, Clothing: The Big Three of the Goods Producers

I've always considered the big three a cut above the other goods producers for an obvious reason. People need food, shelter, and clothing to survive. The big three will always provide an abundance of jobs.

Food and Agriculture Companies

A frequently overlooked industry is agriculture. It's a large industry employing millions of workers in jobs as diverse as driving a tractor on a soybean farm in Iowa, to operating a computer that controls machines pouring ketchup into bottles at H. J. Heinz, the food company headquartered in Pittsburgh, Pennsylvania. The last time I checked the Heinz website, I noted that there were many jobs available. Check it out at www.heinz.com. You do not have to be an agriculture major to participate in this booming industry. The US is home to over 315 million people, and all of them must eat every day to survive. You get the picture. America is a hungry country!

If you live in the Northeast and want to work for a first-class regional food company, check out Wakefern at www.wakefern.com. It's the nation's largest retailer-owned cooperative and wholesale distributor of food products to supermarkets. The last time I checked the job board, I saw more than a dozen Wakefern jobs ranging from entry-level to managerial positions.

Don't wait to check out the food-related companies because smart job seekers are all over their jobs like flies on honey. The food industry is almost recession-proof, because people will always need to eat, hard times or not.

The job outlook in the food and agriculture industry is very promising. The Bureau of Labor Statistics forecasts robust growth and many new jobs over the next ten years, as you can see from this BLS chart.

Position	Projected Job Growth to 2020
Farm equipment mechanics and service technicians	13.4%
Animal, plant, and food scientists	10.4%
Agricultural engineers	9.1%
Agriculture and food-science technicians	7.0%
Farm products buyers and purchasing agents	5.5%

The total number of new agriculture-related jobs through 2020 is projected to be in excess of one million workers. With this kind of job outlook in one of our largest industries, food production, it is no wonder why America is called the breadbasket of the world.

Clothing Companies

Like people, clothing companies come in different sizes and shapes. They offer millions of jobs across the country, most of them behind the scenes. Mistakenly, most people view jobs in the clothing industry as behind-the-counter salespeople and checkout clerks. The reality is that the overwhelming numbers of jobs in the clothing business are those you will never see on the store floor. These are jobs in marketing, finance, fashion design, purchasing, human resources, legal, information technology, and web merchandising. Included in this category are basic clothing retailers like Macy's, JCPenney, Target, Walmart, Kohl's, and Sears, where you can buy reasonably priced basics like shoes, underwear, jeans, and shirts. Another category of companies in the clothing business consists of fashion producers and retailers like Talbots, Nordstrom, Bloomingdale's, and Brooks Brothers.

Some clothing companies specialize in shoes and sporting gear and include Nike, Adidas, New Balance, Aéropostale, and Lululemon Athletica. These companies provide many interesting jobs all across the US for college graduates like you.

 By the way, a ***Real World Fave*** in this category is Lululemon, a Vancouver, British Columbia-based company that manufactures and sells high-quality and fashionable yoga apparel and running gear, mainly for women. One of its brilliant marketing initiatives is conducting yoga classes in public parks and in-store locations several times each week with qualified instructors.

This company is a Wall Street favorite, too, because it makes money for shareholders in a very competitive market. The former CEO, Christine Day, has built a great international company, and if you are smart, you will review the website now at www.lululemon.

com. The last time I checked its career page, I saw assistant store manager positions open in Chicago and Palo Alto, California; human resources jobs at the home office; and support jobs at many locations across the US, Asia, and Europe. People who work with Lululemon consider it a fun place to be. Check it out!

To put the clothing industry in perspective, let's look at the numbers. According to research released by the NPD Group, sales of men's clothing in 2013 reached $59 billion. Sales of apparel for women in 2013 reached $112 billion as reported by Bain & Company. The grand total: $171 billion!

Shelter Companies

Shelter includes houses and commercial buildings, and everything therein required to protect you from the elements and to make your life more comfortable. It is a vast industry and includes companies such as Toll Brothers, a high-end residential homebuilder, and commercial builders like The Trump Organization, headed by Donald Trump. Included in this industry are furniture producers like Ikea and Ethan Allen, and home improvement producers like Home Depot and Lowe's. Here are examples of two shelter companies:

Ryan Homes. Ryan builds residential housing developments in the Northeastern United States. Prices for individual houses are in the $450,000 to $800,000 price range. Ryan hires and trains recent college graduates for a variety of jobs in marketing, sales, information technology, finance, land purchasing, construction supervision, and customer service. Check out the website for current job opportunities at www.nvrinc.com.

Weyerhaeuser. This company claims to be inspired by trees, which is understandable. It produces wood products for residential and commercial buildings and its annual revenue is approximately $20 billion. The company has been in business for more than 100 years, is based near Tacoma, Washington, and has offices and job opportunities across the country and abroad. This company will be around longer than you and I will be—not a bad place to land when you are seeking long-term employment. Check it out at www.weyerhaeuser.com.

The Services Providing Sector

The Bureau of Labor Statistics defines this sector as that which has to do with producing an intangible product. Included in this group are educational services, health care and social assistance, government, finance, insurance, computer and information technology, entertainment, transportation, recreation, professional and business services, and many other services. This sector is expected to grow at double-digit rates in the near future fueled by technology.

Service providers are companies like Microsoft, Adobe, Bank of America, Google, Wells Fargo, Travelers, Pearson, McGraw-Hill, and Salesforce.com.

Like manufacturers, large service producers have offices in locations all across the US. For example, Travelers employs thousands of workers in locations away from its home office in Hartford, Connecticut.

Technology companies are always inventing new products and services and are likely places to find technical and nontechnical work. Check out Microsoft and Salesforce.com, two interesting technology companies in the services sector. Both have jobs available. Click on www.microsoft.com and www.salesforce.com.

The services sector is sometimes described as the "people sector." If meeting and greeting the public is something that appeals to you, explore the services companies. There are thousands of them across the country, both large and small, and one of them has a job just for you. It's a matter of finding them, and you will, if you follow the instructions in this book.

Public Sector Work

The public sector consists of all elected and appointed government jobs on the federal, state, and local levels. The public sector employs more than twenty million workers in jobs as diverse as the president of the United States, US senators and ambassadors, and administrative assistants working for local government, like for the mayor of a small town in Wisconsin.

In addition, there are thousands of workers employed by the political parties. Both the Republican National Committee (RNC) and the Democratic National Committee (DNC) have national headquarters in Washington, DC, and regional offices in every state. If you like the idea of working in a government job, go for it! Start exploring this sector by checking out these websites for job openings at www.rnc.org and www.dnc.org. You may be pleasantly surprised.

Local Government

Jobs in towns, cities, or counties are just around the corner but are often overlooked as places for employment. For those who are seeking a career in government or politics, this is a good place to start.

Do you envision yourself as "Congresswoman from Florida"? A good place to start is at the local, grassroots level. Here you will learn how government works and the role you can play in it. Former congressman from Massachusetts, Tip O'Neill, said, "All politics is local." Successful politicians are successful because they know what works on their own turf.

How do you get started? Easy. Just go to your state website. For example, assuming that you live in Stockton, California, enter this URL: www.stocktongov.com. You will find a list of both full-time salaried jobs and part-time hourly jobs. There are specific instructions for applying for all government jobs, one of which is applying online. If you see something you like, complete the application and go to the next step, which is making a personal visit to the Stockton city offices. Do not sit at home and wait for an answer.

Put on your business clothes, and with your career profile or resume in hand, make a personal visit to the government office and tell the receptionist you are there to see the mayor (or the highest-ranking official for that government entity) about job opportunities. Should you really ask to see the highest-level official? The short answer is yes, unequivocally. Tell the gatekeeper that you would like to be mayor some day and would like her help. Injecting a sense of humor into a conversation with a gatekeeper is a good way to find what you want. These are key players in the employment process, so you need to build that personal relationship. If you cannot arrange a personal visit with the mayor or other high-level official, ask the receptionist to give your credentials to the mayor or the mayor's administrative assistant. Several days later, follow up by calling the mayor's office to make sure it received your resume. Remember to request a personal interview.

Many times, government jobs at any level are awarded to those who know a prominent government official or businessperson. If you have family members or friends who work in government (or business), use their names as the referral agents.

State Government

Follow the same process to explore jobs at the state level. For example, assuming that you live in Nebraska, enter www.nebraska.gov and see what happens. You will find many different departments and a listing of jobs at different locations throughout the state. Follow the instructions for applying online, and then visit the office personally, repeating the procedure you used at the local level.

You cannot circumvent the rules and regulations for government jobs because there is legislation governing the employment process. Always try to use a referral source for government jobs.

Federal Government

This is the largest employer in the country. The employment process here becomes a bit more complicated because the federal government employs more than four million workers in a variety of interesting jobs spanning every possible occupation, according to statistics released by the US Office of Personnel Management.

A common misconception is that federal government jobs are located primarily in Washington, DC. Once again, the BLS stats set us straight: 87 percent of federal government jobs are located outside of Washington, DC.

Go to the BLS website and read the article titled, "How to Get a Job in the Federal Government" by Olivia Crosby. The information and instructions in this article will demystify the federal government employment process, save you time, and possibly lead to employment.

Nonprofit Companies

Our economy can be divided further into nonprofit and for-profit companies. The Bureau of Labor Statistics defines the nonprofit category as "organizations that are neither for-profit businesses nor government agencies. Nonprofits are a subset of private industry. Nonprofit organizations may generate revenue, but this revenue cannot be distributed to owners or employees as they might be in a for-profit business. Nonprofits include, but are not limited to, hospitals, churches, educational institutions, social welfare organizations, and charitable organizations. More than one million charitable organizations work to benefit a variety of different causes, such as disaster relief, civil rights, community development, environmental advocacy, and the arts. Charitable organizations also include hospitals and private schools. More than half of all hospitals and almost a third of postsecondary educational institutions are nonprofit."

Nonprofit companies are frequently involved in charitable works, like providing medical care for the disadvantaged in the US and abroad, educational services for certain socioeconomic groups, and work training for the unemployed.

Some nonprofits operate in much the same manner as for-profit companies because they must make money to pay their employees and support the corporate infrastructure. Two such companies are the College Board and Educational Testing Services (ETS). Both produce and sell products for the K–12 and higher education markets. Check out their websites for job opportunities at www.ets.org and www.collegeboard.org. Both of these companies offer pay scales and benefits packages that are on par, or above, what you'd find in the private sector. The College Board is based in New York City and ETS is based in Princeton, New Jersey, but both have regional offices across the US where jobs are available. Did you click?

Foundations

Some nonprofits are called "foundations," like the Ford Foundation, the Bill & Melinda Gates Foundation, and the Robert Wood Johnson Foundation. They employ thousands of workers in a variety of jobs ranging from sales representatives to marketing directors to chief technology officers. Compensation at these organizations is about 10 percent lower than comparable jobs in the for-profit world. However, the benefits are usually much better, the culture more stimulating, and the opportunity for long-term employment much greater. These organizations seek out workers who are passionate about doing good things for others and who care about a rewarding, satisfying, and fulfilling career.

For-Profit Companies

These organizations make a profit after accounting for expenses and distribute that profit to owners, employees, and shareholders. This group consists of all publicly owned companies like McDonald's, Ford, and Target. The goods producers and services providers, discussed above, are included in this category. Others in this group are single proprietorships, partnerships, and small businesses that you will find on the main street of Anywhere, USA.

The Best Industries in the For-Profit Sector

The workplace is vast and it takes time to determine where to start looking for that first job. Here are some of my favorites based on personal experience, research, work experience, and anecdotal information from a variety of sources. These are industries that employ millions of workers and provide an opportunity to take home more than just a paycheck. Workers in these industries find that the monetary rewards are attractive as well. Three of my faves are in education, insurance, and security.

The Education Industry

The broadly defined education industry consists of for-profit schools like University of Phoenix online, DeVry Institute of Technology, McGraw-Hill Education, Scholastic, and Highlights for Children. There are nonprofits, too, like Educational Testing Service (ETS), the College Board, Measured Progress (www.measuredprogress.org), and MIND Research Institute (www.mindresearch.net).

These companies are scattered throughout the US and offer jobs spanning the entire range of specialties, like sales, marketing, finance, editorial, product development, information technology, and human resources. Workers in the education industry find much job satisfaction because their products, instructional materials, and services benefit individuals and the country as a whole. Here is an example of the influence a worker in this industry can have:

Margaret from New Jersey. Margaret was an editor with a large K–12 publishing company that specialized in producing social studies texts and materials. Some of the products she edited included American history, world cultures, and government texts. Thousands, perhaps millions, of students using these core products acquired the concepts and skills necessary for an understanding of the heritage of the United States because of Margaret's work. If you are seeking work satisfaction, it does not get better than working in the education industry.

The Insurance Industry

This industry is frequently characterized as boring and concerned only with making money at the expense of policyholders. Who wants to do something as unexciting as selling policies for life, auto, homeowners, short- and long-term disability, or flood insurance, or retirement instruments like annuities? All of this is just an invention to make money, right?

Well, think again. Interestingly, the insurance industry in the United States was founded by none other than Benjamin Franklin, who recognized insurance as something to minimize risk and deal with unforeseen occurrences like a fire that consumes your home and all of its contents. In so doing, Franklin gave birth to an industry where it is almost impossible to fail, and which employs some of the most brilliant mathematical minds on earth, who often serve as the industry's actuaries and underwriters.

In addition, insurance products have become a necessity to living as a responsible, self-sufficient human being. Insurance policies provide monetary benefits to policyholders who suffer misfortunes, whether it be an illness that costs thousands of dollars to treat, or an accident that causes temporary or permanent disability resulting in loss of wages, which in turn can cause inestimable hardship. Here is an example:

Chicken Man. I was riding my bike through a rural part of Pennsylvania one morning when a bantam chicken ran into the front wheel of my bike. I was partially disabled for eight months following fourteen days in the hospital for a fractured pelvis, a torn rotator cuff, a concussion, and multiple lacerations, contusions, and abrasions. During that time, I had no income or disability payments from my employer. My expenses (mortgage, car payments, etc.), however, continued as usual.

Here's how the insurance industry rescued "Chicken Man," as I was called by a TV reporter on the late evening news. I would have defaulted on the mortgage and car loan but for a long-term disability insurance policy that I had purchased, and which had become effective only five days before the accident. That policy covered almost 100 percent of my expenses during my disability. Without it, I could not have survived financially.

Joanne, the insurance agent who sold me life insurance and homeowners insurance, had been after me for months to buy a long-term disability policy because my employer did not provide that in my benefits package. I finally said, "Okay, Joanne. Get off my case! Write up the damn policy and don't bug me anymore." She did just that, and five days later, I was hit by the chicken. To this day, I thank Joanne for taking time to educate me about the unknown risks that we face every time we get out of bed in the morning.

What did Joanne get out of this? First, she received commission on the policy, and she got great satisfaction performing a good deed for another person. Thanks, Joanne. Without you, I would have been in dire financial straits.

Who said insurance is boring and only for aggressive insurance agents who are interested only in bringing home the bacon? This is a good industry, one that can provide not only a handsome income, but also much job satisfaction educating dummies like me about risk.

Later in this chapter, I will give you the names of some of my favorite insurance companies.

The Security Industry

The security industry has been growing exponentially, primarily because of cybercrime against both governments and companies.

It includes a wide variety of initiatives, from preventing cheating on exams, to securing private property, financial information, and confidential data, to reducing the threat of terrorist attacks. There are many companies in the security industry, and each limits its activities to one or two specialties. Here are two examples:

Caveon. This company specializes in preventing cheating on academic exams, like the SAT, and on various certification exams. Check it out at www.caveon.com. Its list of clients includes the College Board, IBM, Microsoft, Atlanta Public Schools, American Board of Internal Medicine, Hewlett-Packard, and the Association of Government Accountants. Caveon is an interesting place to work and provides an increasing number of jobs. Give it a click to learn if there is anything at Caveon for you.

Raytheon. This company is frequently called a defense contractor because it builds weapons systems that are used for our national protection. However, Raytheon also builds cybersecurity systems to get rid of hackers, worms, trojan horses, and other forms of cyberwarfare. Check out its website and review the career pages for exciting job opportunities at www.raytheon.com.

Real World Faves

Best Companies to Work For

My advice is to concentrate on companies that have been in business for many years and that have been profitable. Target companies whose products and services are in constant demand throughout the business cycle and that have a good reputation for fair play with their workers. Why spend your time throwing darts at the entire board of American goods and services producers? To get you headed in the right direction, here is a list of my favorite goods and services producers:

Salesforce.com, www.salesforce.com. This is the preeminent cloud-computing company headed by the highly respected CEO, Marc Benioff. Recently, the company created a new division dedicated to the institutional school market because colleges and universities are moving to the cloud. The stock price has been moving up steadily over the past three years because company revenues have been increasing, and because investors consider Salesforce.com to be the best of breed.

Texas Instruments, www.ti.com. TI, as it is now called, has been around for the past eighty years. It's not a Johnny-come-lately to the technology world and produces more than upscale calculators. TI produces technology products like RFID barcodes and sophisticated semiconductors, those little beasts that make your digital toys run. TI has a presence in thirty-five countries and employs 35,000 workers. Its revenues topped $12 billion in 2012. The company is based in Dallas, Texas, and has offices scattered throughout the US and abroad.

TI has a reputation for treating its workers like family despite its size, which explains why people work there for many years. TI has one of the best mentoring programs in the business, and one of its most attractive benefits is a profit-sharing program that has made many workers very wealthy.

Please note that TI is very meticulous when it comes to hiring workers at any level for any position, probably one of the reasons why this is such a successful company. The hiring process could span several months, but it is worth the time and effort.

ETS, www.ets.org. These folks construct a variety of exams used in schools and colleges. The ETS family includes five subsidiary companies. This nonprofit company is located in Lawrence, New Jersey, and has annual revenues exceeding $1 billion. There is money in the testing business! Most jobs are located on its beautiful corporate campus near Princeton, New Jersey, where you will be happy when the human resources manager says, "You're hired!" Jobs are available in other locations as well.

Southwest Airlines, www.southwest.com. If you like profitability in a company profile, then Southwest Airlines is for you. The company was founded in 1967 and is headquartered in Dallas, Texas. Southwest has been profitable almost every quarter for the past twenty years and has provided thousands of jobs for workers across the country. While other airlines have been going broke, Southwest has been making money. Under the leadership of its likeable CEO, Gary Kelly, it is doing something right. People like to work at Southwest.

Tiffany & Company, www.tiffany.com. This American icon of upscale jewelry and fine home furnishings has been in business since 1837. Do you want to work in a pleasant environment surrounded by beautiful objects for the home and personal adornment? Do you get high looking into a flawless two-carat diamond that could one day be yours? If the answer is yes, go to its website. By the way, if you are bilingual in French and English, you will want to check out Tiffany job opportunities in Paris, France.

Starbucks, www.starbucks.com. Decades ago, when Starbucks came on the scene, people asked, "What can a coffeehouse do for America? What's all the fuss about another coffee joint?" Well, for starters, a good cup of joe in the morning is the traditional way most Americans begin their day. A cup of morning coffee is just as much a part of our culture as the demitasse-size cup of super-strong espresso that the Italians drink before going to work. However, there's more to this story than drinking coffee.

Starbucks provides both part-time and full-time jobs for millions of Americans from coast to coast and treats them fairly. Many workers who start as baristas (don't you love the job title?) move up to management and executive-level positions. In addition, the CEO, Howard Schultz, has made a concerted effort to bring jobs back to America by using only American manufacturers to provide essential items like paper coffee cups.

With the recent acquisition of Teavana Holdings, Starbucks is not only America's coffeehouse but also America's teahouse as well. Starbucks has a bright future, and I recommend that you check out the website for job opportunities. You will see jobs in supply chain operations, finance, global development, information technology, retail sales, coffee-roasting house operations, and many others.

For the seventh year in a row, the Ethisphere Institute has named Starbucks on its list of the world's most ethical companies. *Fortune* magazine has named Starbucks on its list of the one hundred best American companies for employment. The company has been around since 1971, and I predict it will still be here when you are looking for an encore career. Did you check the career page on the website? And don't forget to ask for the name of the hiring manager the next time you drop in for a Caramel Mocha Frappuccino.

Costco, www.costco.com. The company makes money two ways: by selling its products to customers and from collecting membership fees. Hoover's, a company that provides information about almost every company in the US (www.hoovers.com), describes Costco as follows: "Walmart isn't a behemoth in *every* business. Costco is the nation's largest wholesale club operator (ahead of Walmart's Sam's Club). The firm operates more than 640 membership warehouse stores. Primarily under the Costco Wholesale banner, it serves some 71 million members in 40-plus US states, as well as in Australia, Canada, Japan, Mexico, Puerto Rico, South Korea, Taiwan, and the UK. Stores offer discount prices on an average of about 4,000 products (many in bulk packaging), ranging from alcoholic beverages and appliances to fresh food, pharmaceuticals, and tires. Certain club memberships also offer products and services, such as car and home insurance, mortgage and real estate services, and travel packages."

Costco's 2012 revenues totaled $24 billion. That's a lot of money spent on groceries and household goods. Costco has nowhere to go but up, and that means job opportunities for workers across America. By the way, Costco sells more wine than any other company in the world. And in 2012, Costco sold 137 million rotisserie chickens and 130 million hotdogs.

Hungry for a good job and a rotisserie chicken? Work at Costco.

The Coca-Cola Company, www.coca-cola.com. This hundred-year-old company has provided jobs for millions of people not only in the US, but also throughout the world. Coca-Cola treats its workers well and is in an expanding mode. Many of Coca-Cola's workers are nearing retirement age, and younger workers are taking over. They have new ideas, use technology effectively, and are positioning Coca-Cola to reach new levels of performance and revenue.

Dow Chemical Company, www.dow.com. Dow can be considered part of the food industry because of the many products it produces for agriculture. It is considered by many to be one of America's best employers.

Whole Foods Market, www.wholefoodsmarket.com. This company deserves an A+ for leading America toward better eating habits by selling foods that are free from chemicals and pollutants that are harmful to our health. In addition, the CEO has made a commitment to collaborating with the community to provide assistance to those in need.

The company is based in Austin, Texas, and is considered one of the most socially responsible companies in the world. The company employs approximately 60,000 workers, and its 2012 revenues were $12 billion. *Fortune* magazine ranks Whole Foods in the top one hundred best companies to work for. Whole Foods has an excellent benefits program for its employees and has a career path for workers seeking long-term employment.

Medtronic, www.medtronic.com. This is a medical devices manufacturer based in Minneapolis. It produces state-of-the-art cardiac devices like defibrillators.

McDonald's, www.mcdonalds.com. This company is expanding its fast-food menu constantly and is adding more healthy items to its menu. There is a McDonald's in every country on the planet. It has been in business for over sixty years. Over the years, it has been a leader in community outreach.

General Electric, www.ge.com. GE has its fingers in many manufacturing pots and is a very profitable company. It employs tens of thousands of workers around the world.

Home Depot, www.homedepot.com. Where else can you find houseplants, lightbulbs, kitchen appliances, and sheets of plywood for home construction all under one roof? This is a very profitable company with locations across the US and abroad. It is active in community outreach.

Walmart, www.walmart.com. This is the world's largest retailer because it offers the number one staple—food—at reasonable prices. This is a nonunion employer and has incurred the wrath of union bosses who want to crack the code. Don't fall for their negative attacks against Walmart. This is a good company with many job opportunities for entry-level and experienced workers.

Raytheon, www.raytheon.com. See my description earlier in this chapter for more information on this Boston-based company.

Explore the career pages of these companies and apply for a position that matches your profile. Many offer entry-level positions, so you will need to find the names of the human resources directors and send your complete career profile packages to these individuals. (See chapter 16 for a description of the career profile and instructions for preparing one.) You can find the name and contact information for the human resources directors by calling the customer service department.

 The Best Conservative Growth Companies
Here are my favorite companies in the conservative growth industries of education, insurance, and pharmaceuticals. Check them out by reviewing their websites and checking online sources like Hoover's (www.hoovers.com) for company information. Be sure to learn the length of time they have been in business, their growth in revenue and profitability, their community outreach initiatives, their numbers of employees, their key executives, their benefits plans, and their job openings.

Highlights for Children, www.highlights.com. This Columbus, Ohio, education company produces print and technology instructional materials for the K–12 market.

MIND Research Institute, www.mindresearch.net. Based in Irvine, California, MIND publishes K–12 technology products for mathematics instruction.

Measured Progress, www.measuredprogress.org. This New Hampshire-based company has been in business for close to thirty years and produces both formative and summative testing and assessment products for K–12 school districts and state departments of education.

MassMutual Financial Group, www.massmutual.com. You cannot argue with more than one hundred years of continuous profitable operations. Want long-term employment? Try MassMutual.

State Farm, www.statefarm.com. This is the best of the automobile insurers. Many of its agents have made State Farm a family business, and it is not unusual to see several generations of State Farm agents in one location.

Pfizer, www.pfizer.com. Pfizer is an icon in the pharmaceutical business and employs thousands of workers in a diverse array of jobs. It's one of the best in the business.

Johnson and Johnson, www.jnj.com. J&J, as it is called, produces not only lifesaving medicines, but also everyday health and grooming products.

SMALL BUSINESSES CREATE THE MOST JOBS

In this chapter, we have concentrated on large companies to illustrate the American job sectors and to learn what kinds of companies fall into the various industries. A common misperception about the market is that most jobs are created by the types of large businesses cited above, like Costco, Coca-Cola, Starbucks, and Dow Chemical.

While it is true that large companies employ tens of thousands of workers, small businesses create most of the jobs in America. These are no-name companies that you might find in shopping malls, on Main Street, USA, or in industrial parks. Their names might be Faulkner Toyota, Lincoln Tech Consulting, Kim's Hairstyling, or Maplewood Physical Therapy.

How do you find employment with a small business? Take a stroll through your local mall or industrial park, and you will find them. Look through your Yellow Pages directory and check your local newspapers, and you will find them. Look on Craigslist, and you will find them.

In a 2012 study of the job market, *Inc.* magazine learned that small businesses employ sixty to ninety-five million workers at any given time. However, *Inc.* also noted that small businesses account for job losses in greater numbers than do large companies.

This is such an important segment of our workforce that the federal government created a special department devoted to small business operations. It is called the Small Business Administration. Review the website for additional information at www.sba.gov.

FASTEST-GROWING PRIVATE COMPANIES

The *Portland Business Journal* recently cited the fastest-growing private companies in the Pacific Northwest. If you live in Washington or Oregon, go to www.bizjournals.com/portland/event/77621 for a listing of these companies. One of them may be just right for you.

Other regional business journals will provide a similar list of companies in your local area. Google the business journal in your location.

THE *REAL WORLD* WAY TO LEARN WHERE THE EMPLOYERS ARE

The best way to find employment opportunities regardless of your major is to contact hiring authorities in the flesh to say hello. That is the first step in establishing a relationship, which is what you need to do to secure employment. Contrary to what you might have learned on the street, sitting at your computer and firing off resumes day after day is the least productive way to find employers. The reason is that *companies do not hire resumes; rather, they hire warm, living, human beings* who have used their creativity to seek them out personally.

Before sending a resume or making a cold call, learn the name and title of the person associated with the employment process. Sending a resume to Sally Singleton or asking to speak with Robert Jones is much different than sending it to Job Box 29 or "Hiring Authority." In addition, if your friends tell you the best way to find a job is to use Twitter, Facebook, career centers, job boards, and postings on corporate websites, they are sadly mistaken. The proven way to find a job is by doing a lot of hard work, by knocking on doors of companies in your area, and by being alert to opportunities with low visibility. They can be with large companies, like Johnson & Johnson, or small companies, like your neighborhood branch bank or your local car dealer. Can you really find a job that way? Well, take a look at this next real-life example.

Valet Jobs Available at Toyota

Recently, I took my car to the local Toyota dealer for service. While waiting for the service tech to complete the oil change and lube, I noticed a sign at the service manager's counter. It read: "Valet needed. Full-Time. Salary and Benefits." I didn't know what a valet at a car dealership did, so I asked the service manager and learned that this person drove cars from the service area to the waiting area, took cars to the car wash, and accompanied owners to their cars' locations when service was complete. The job paid $11 per hour plus benefits and possible overtime. That's $440 per week, $1,760 per month, and $21,120 per year. Add another 30 percent for benefits like insurance and vacation time, and the job is worth $27,456 a year. Not much, you say? And why would anyone with a college degree want to drive cars around the service area of a car dealership? Well, here's the rest of the story.

The service manager told me that the valet position was her entry-level job, and after twelve months, she was promoted to assistant manager and then service manager at more than double her salary. In addition, she said that the valet position could be a stepping-stone to a sales position with Toyota, a reputable manufacturer with the bestselling car in the US, the Toyota Camry.

Selling quality cars is often an overlooked opportunity, and some consider it a "no-brainer" job. Think again. A good car sales

representative can make a very good income, work flexible hours, and provide a necessary service to the public. If you really want an interesting sales job with very high income potential, sell cars like Mercedes, Lexus, BMW, or Volvo. You need high-level communication skills to sell high-end products, skills like those acquired in college. Consider what happened to Tom.

Tom from Boston. When I was sales manager for a school publishing company, one of my sales reps, Tom, told me he was leaving the company to sell Volvos in a wealthy Boston suburb. In so many words, I told Tom he had lost his mind. "When you sell instructional materials to schools, you are doing good things for teachers and kids," I told him. However, when school budgets are cut, purchases of instructional materials are put on hold, and you do not make your sales quota. You risk being fired. Tom was intent on working for Volvo and left the publisher.

Six months later, I was passing the Volvo dealership where Tom worked and stopped in to say hello. I had to wait for an hour, as he was closing a deal and another customer was waiting for him. He told me that he was making twice as

much as he did with the publisher, and he had free time to pursue community activities as well. I thought about what skills Tom possessed to be successful as a high-end car sales rep. It all comes down to this: having passion for your job, demonstrating superb communication skills, and using your intelligence and energy to be the best you can possibly be.

I'M READY TO MOVE. WHERE ARE THE BEST LOCATIONS FOR JOB HUNTING?

Certain metropolitan areas across the country offer more job opportunities than others. For example, at the beginning of July 2013, the following states and cities had high rates of employment opportunities, according to the Brookings Institution:

1. *Texas.* Throughout the state, employment opportunities are plentiful, especially in the oil and gas industry. Six major cities showing the most robust job growth were Austin, San Antonio, El Paso, McAllen, Dallas, and Houston. Austin

leads the pack with many job openings in state government and at the University of Texas. Also, Austin has become one of the fastest-growing high-tech areas in the country and provides many jobs in that industry.

Texas is the leading state in the country for job growth because of a favorable business climate. For this reason, many companies are locating their headquarters or regional offices in Texas. Arguably, Texas is the best-run state in the entire country. Taxes in Texas are low, there are reasonable rules and regulations for businesses, and the climate is favorable.

If you are seeking a new location to begin your work cycle, think about relocating to Texas. Two of the best places are Austin and San Antonio, both having an ideal semitropical climate and very favorable cultural and educational opportunities.

2. *Oklahoma City, Oklahoma.* You will find many job opportunities here in the petroleum industry.

3. *Omaha, Nebraska.* For careers in agribusiness, this is one of the best places to be.

4. *Salt Lake City, Utah.* This area offers many job opportunities in the booming mining industry and the recreation industry.

5. *Pittsburgh, Pennsylvania.* Pittsburgh has a robust education environment. Noted universities like Carnegie Mellon and Duquesne are located here, and they provide many job opportunities. The area supports many manufacturers, and as we know, they produce jobs by the bucketful.

6. *San Jose, California.* Did you ever hear of Silicon Valley? This is the heart of the technology industry. If you like bits and bytes, this is the place for you.

7. *Knoxville, Tennessee.* This city is noted for providing job opportunities in health care and in education at the University of Tennessee. In addition, factories in Knoxville manufacture parts for Volkswagen, whose major US plant

is in Chattanooga. Drive west ninety minutes to Nashville, and you will find Vanderbilt University, known not only for academic excellence, but also for its world-class medical center, which provides countless jobs for those interested in careers in medicine.

8. ***Charleston, South Carolina.*** This pleasant city is home to many manufacturers. One of the largest is airplane manufacturer Boeing.

9. ***Upper Midwest.*** The upper Midwest (South Dakota and North Dakota specifically) is one of the hottest spots in America for job opportunities. The reason? This area has huge deposits of natural gas and oil, which are being extracted using new technology. If you like to work outside doing some heavy lifting in the gas and oil patch, you could make $90,000 per year. The unemployment rate in this area as of January 2013 was only 3 percent, the lowest in the nation.

WHAT DO HIRING AUTHORITIES SAY?

Recently, I attended an education industry conference in Baltimore and talked with several vice presidents in charge of sales, marketing, and product development. (By the way, the education industry consists of those companies that produce and provide instructional materials, supplies, and services to K–12 schools and postsecondary institutions. It has nothing to do with teaching. Some companies in the education industry are McGraw-Hill, the College Board, ETS, Pearson, Scholastic, and a host of other companies both large and small.) Their takes on entry-level candidates with either a bachelor's or master's were almost identical.

All said they would run to see a candidate who knocked on their doors without an appointment. They considered resumes that come in through human resources or addressed to Job Box 29 just that: resumes unattached to a live human. Even if the cold-call candidate did not connect on that first call, the vice presidents said they would put him or her on a "must see" list when they had the time. All said that cold calls really work. Are you ready to hit the street?

GOING FORWARD

If you spent four to six years getting a bachelor's or master's degree, then you must know how to communicate. It is time to put those skills to work by leaving your house. Should you start knocking on the doors of every car dealership in your area? Why not? Alternatively, there are branch banks, homebuilders, or large retailers like Home Depot, Lowe's, Costco, Walmart, or even your local fine dining restaurant. Add the business parks where you will find the headquarter offices and regional offices of larger companies like Texas Instruments.

The personal contact strategy works for everyone, even if it might be your second, third, or fourth job with a track record of successful experience to back up your candidacy. Remember this, because at some time while you are navigating the world of work, you will be fired or laid off for some reason, and you will be looking again. Welcome to the real world!

In this chapter, you learned *where* to find jobs. In the next chapter, I'll tell you *how* to find jobs at conferences and trade shows. Stick around.

CHAPTER TAKEAWAYS

- *Nothing happens until you leave the house.*
- *Landing your first job is not the end of your search. It is the beginning of a lifelong search for meaning and understanding.*
- *Work for companies whose products and services interest you.*
- *Evaluate the ethical conduct of every potential employer on your target list.*

JOB HUNTER'S LIBRARY

Rory Freedman and Kim Barnouin, *Skinny Bitch*, Running Press, 2005. The authors advocate a straight vegan diet, but what interested me most about it was its analysis of the food industry, one of my faves. This book has been on the bestseller lists in the US and UK for five years and has become a classic.

Robert Kaplan, *What You're Really Meant to Do*, Harvard Business Review Press, 2013.

Enrico Noretti, *The New Geography of Jobs*, First Mariner Books, 2013.

Chapter 12

Finding Employers at Trade Shows, Conferences, and Business Parks

A trade show is a gathering of workers from companies in a specific industry. The purpose of a trade show is to give companies an opportunity to display their products and advertise their services in exhibit booths located on convention center floors.

Trade shows go by different names, but all mean the same thing. They might be called trade fairs, trade exhibitions, exhibits, expos, or trade conferences. They are held at convention centers, which are located in cities or state capitals. Sometimes they are held in hotels or resorts that have large rooms for hosting exhibits and smaller rooms to host "breakout sessions" where industry experts present new products or discuss research and industry trends.

Industry professional organizations host these shows, which are extremely costly to sponsor. Some of those costs are defrayed by member dues and by conference attendance fees.

An example of a trade show is the world's largest technology show called the Consumer Electronics Show (CES), which is held in January each year in Las Vegas. In 2013, attendance at this show exceeded 150,000, including 35,000 people from foreign countries. More than 3,250 companies attended and hosted exhibits.

Can you imagine 3,250 potential employers under one roof? If you are interested in technology, you cannot afford to miss CES. For more information and to register for the next show, click here at www.consumerelectronicsshow.com.

Attending trade shows, or industry conferences, is the most productive method for job hunting right in your own hometown. But how do you know where to go, and what do you do once you find yourself in a convention hall? In this chapter, I will give you instructions for attending trade shows, as well as the names and locations of the major convention centers across the country.

PREPARATION FOR ATTENDING A TRADE SHOW

One does not just show up at a trade show and expect miracles to happen. In order to reap maximum benefits from attending a trade show, serious planning must be done. Here's a checklist and suggestions for planning purposes:

- Your primary purpose for attending these events is to visit the many exhibit booths where you will find hiring managers. Many shows hold exhibits only on specific days and at specific hours. For example, the dates listed for CES, the technology conference in Las Vegas, may be January 10–16, but the exhibits may be open only on January 11–15, from 10 a.m. to 6 p.m. You can find this information online or by calling the conference center or the organization hosting the show. This is important because you are attending the conference primarily to visit the exhibit booths where you will find the hiring managers. There is no need to attend the conference on days when the exhibits are not open.

- The conference organization usually publishes a list of companies attending (online and in the printed conference program) and the names of the representatives who will be attending, along with their contact information. Obtain this list either online or at the conference center because it will provide the names and contact information for key executives and hiring managers.

- Bring at least a hundred business cards and two dozen resumes to the conference each day. The exchange of business cards is the accepted way to build your list of networking contacts.

- When you enter the conference center to attend the show, first go to the registration desk to pay the exhibit fee, obtain your name tag, and pick up the conference program, which is usually tucked in a tote bag. Make sure you get the conference program because it will provide the names of the companies attending, the names of company representatives, and their exhibit booth numbers. Always wear your name tag.

- Almost all shows charge a fee for attendance. Usually, fees vary with the number of days you will attend, your affiliation, and your work status. Usually, there is a steep discount or no charge at all for students. Even if you have already graduated, tell the registration person that you are a recent college graduate and you are attending only to visit the exhibits to find employment opportunities. You may be able to enter paying the student rate, which many times is the best price . . . *free.*

- As an example of fees to attend specialized conferences, a technology education industry trade show called EdNET could charge up to $900 for admission, but the fee is worth it. The reason is that 600 hiring authorities attend this annual show, including CEOs; presidents; vice presidents for sales, marketing, and product development; chief technology and information officers; and human resources directors. During this three-day conference, you will hear noted keynote speakers, participate in breakout sessions, and have an opportunity to present yourself for two minutes in front of 600 hiring authorities. It is an excellent opportunity to present your candidacy to 600 hiring authorities and to advertise that you are a job candidate seeking your first job. It does not get better than that. Negotiate the lowest entrance fee for this and every conference. Many large trade shows, which are open to the general public, charge very low fees for attendance, in the range of $50 to $100. Always try to negotiate the lowest possible fee.

- If you are coming from a distance and plan to stay overnight near the conference enter, make hotel reservations in advance. If the conference center is in a large city like Los Angeles, local hotel rates will be quite steep. Find a hotel or motel just out of town at a more reasonable room rate, and then drive to the conference center each day. Also, some conference organizations negotiate lower room rates with hotels and motels in the area, so always check this out online six months in advance.

- Dress at trade shows is usually casual, but you as a job candidate should always be dressed as though you were going for an interview. You are there on business, not to work in an exhibit booth. You are there to sell your candidacy, and you should be dressed with that in mind.

WHAT EXACTLY DO YOU DO AT A TRADE SHOW OR CONFERENCE?

Are you ready for a bit of fun? This is where you will have a good time in a very relaxed environment and meet hundreds of full-time company workers, many of whom will be hiring managers.

Exhibit halls are usually crowded with customers who are there to get product information and to visit company representatives. This is a place where business is done in a pleasant way.

Usually, people working in the various exhibit booths will be dressed informally, many times wearing a casual shirt or top bearing the name of the company and the company logo. Remember, however, that you are not a worker here and you should be in business attire.

After you register and get your name tag, enter the exhibit hall and begin visiting each booth. You may want to begin in the first aisle and proceed around the hall until you have stopped at each exhibit booth. If there are hundreds of exhibits, this may take two or even three days.

When you enter an exhibit booth, view the products on display and ask one of the representatives to explain what the company does. Establish a personal relationship by learning what the person's job is, how he or she likes working for the company, and if he or she would recommend working there. After you establish the relationship, tell the person you are job hunting and ask to speak with any hiring manager who may be there. If you are interested in marketing and the director of marketing is not there for some reason, get that person's name and contact information, and follow up with a phone call or email when you return to your home office.

WHAT DO YOU SAY AFTER "HELLO"?

If all of this is new to you, here's a script you might use to break the ice and get in the game, remembering that veteran workers are always eager to help an entry-level person. Establish the relationship by addressing the workers by name, which is always on the name tag.

"Hello, Justin. My name is Julia, and I'm here for two reasons and would appreciate your help. First, I would like to know more about your company and what you do. Second, I'm seeking employment and would like to see the hiring manager for marketing if this person is attending the conference. If not, would you please write his or her name and contact information on the back of your business card for me? Also, could you give me the name and contact information for the company human resources director?"

Before you leave the exhibit booth, give your business card to your new contact and write on the back, "Seeking employment and would appreciate your help. Thanks! Julia."

If a hiring manager you want to see is in the booth, request a few minutes for an informal interview and give that person your resume. The way to get this moving without feeling awkward is to say something like this:

"Bill, here's my resume and if you have the time now, maybe you could take a minute to review it. I have a bachelor's in business administration from Penn State. Note my experience in volunteer marketing work for nonprofit companies. If you don't have time now, could we make an appointment to sit down later and chat for a few minutes, maybe over a cup of coffee or lunch? My treat, of course."

HOW TO RECOGNIZE A HIRING MANAGER AND EXECUTIVE

In the exhibit booths and on the floor, you will see people dressed in formal business attire. Most often, these are the company executives. These are people you need to meet. Lacking an introduction, you just have to wing it. Walk up to that person and say something like this:

"I can tell by the way you're dressed that you must be running the show here. My name is Julia, and I'm here job hunting. I graduated recently from the University of Wisconsin with a major in communications, and I'm looking for a position in sales. Could you steer me in the right direction? I would really appreciate your help."

This person will probably smile and appreciate your sense of humor and your subtle note of respect and recognition. The odds of getting a positive response are in your favor because veteran business execs remember when they were starting out like you, and they are willing to lend a hand to a newcomer.

LUNCHTIME

On the convention center floor there will be restaurants, kiosks selling hotdogs and soft drinks, and sometimes bars selling alcoholic drinks. This is another place to meet people. After you buy a burger and a Coke, find a table that is partially occupied. Take a seat, introduce yourself to the person next to you, and go into your sales pitch. Lunch is not just lunch; it's a networking opportunity. You never select an empty table, whip out your smartphone, and begin texting. Never. You paid good money to work this conference. Why waste your time and money tweeting when you should be meeting potential employers?

Thirsty for a Cold Beer? If there are alcoholic drinks being sold, *never* buy them. Do not even think of it. A cardinal rule is never to drink anything alcoholic, even if others around you are. You are here on business, not to throw down a beer or a Chardonnay. Many of the people here are hiring managers, and they could be sizing up your personal habits. Company managers do not hire entry-level candidates, or veteran candidates, who drink while job hunting.

FINDING JOB OPPORTUNITIES WITH CONVENTION CENTERS

When you review the conference center website, always check out the career postings. Convention centers, such as McCormick Place in Chicago, are profit-making organizations and employ many workers across all specialties. These are good full-time jobs in sales, marketing, technology, finance, and human resources. In addition, go to the conference center offices and inquire about job opportunities when you attend the conference.

WHERE ARE CONFERENCE CENTERS LOCATED?

Every city and state has convention centers where trade shows and job fairs are held. Contact the convention centers on my list, and you will learn the dates and names of the trade shows for the entire year, and these sites will provide links to the names of the companies attending. In addition, you will be able to learn the price of admission and be able to access other pertinent information that will make your visit there more profitable. As an example of what I'm talking about, go to the huge convention center in Chicago. It's called McCormick Place and the URL is www.mccormickplace.com.

Managers and directors from sales, marketing, product development, technology, advertising, human resources, event planning, and finance work in the exhibit booths. Stop at a booth, introduce yourself, and ask for help securing employment. Does it get any easier than that? Potential employers are not hiding under rocks; rather, you will find them at convention centers, the names and locations of which are just a couple of clicks away.

CONFERENCE AND CONVENTION CENTERS: WHERE THE BIG GUYS HANG OUT

My state-by-state list of convention and conference sites is your key to learning where you will find hiring authorities, upcoming conferences, and exhibits. Use this information to plan your job search. The big guys, the hiring authorities, always attend trade shows and conventions in order to meet their key customers, keep up with industry trends, *and* to recruit workers for all levels of employment. Recruiters often attend these shows to prospect for new clients, to seek workers for positions they have available, or to look for qualified candidates to place in their databases for future reference. In fact, I have attended hundreds of conferences to recruit job candidates and seek new clients. In the job-hunting world, trade shows and conferences *are* the Promised Land. Visiting these shows is the best way to begin your job search. Find the location closest to you and click away. You will not be sorry.

Convention Centers by State

Here is the list of convention centers in your state. Locate the one closest to you and access the convention website. A few clicks could lead to your first job.

Alabama

Birmingham-Jefferson   Convention Complex
www.bjcc.org
2100 Richard Arrington Jr. Boulevard North
Birmingham, AL 35203
(205) 458-8400

Alaska

Anchorage Convention Centers
www.anchorageconventioncenters.com
555 West Fifth Avenue
Anchorage, AK 99501
(907) 263-2800

Juneau Centennial Hall Convention Center
www.juneau.org/centennial
101 Egan Drive
Juneau, AK 99801
(907) 586-5283

Arizona

Phoenix Convention Center
www.phoenixconventioncenter.com
100 N 3rd Street
Phoenix, AZ 85004
(602) 262-6225

Arkansas

Statehouse Convention Center
www.littlerockmeetings.com
#1 Statehouse Plaza
Little Rock, AR 72201
(501) 376-4781
(800) 844-4781

California

Long Beach Convention and Entertainment Center
www.longbeachcc.com
300 E Ocean Boulevard
Long Beach, CA 90802
(562) 436-3636

Los Angeles Convention Center
www.lacclink.com
1201 South Figueroa Street
(between Wilshire Blvd and 7th St)
Los Angeles, CA 90015
(213) 741-1151

San Diego Convention Center
www.visitsandiego.com
111 West Harbor Drive
San Diego, CA 92101
(619) 525-5000

Moscone Center
www.moscone.com
747 Howard Street, 5th Flr.
San Francisco, CA 94103
(415) 974-4000

Colorado

Colorado Convention Center
www.denverconvention.com
700 14th Street
Denver, CO 80202
(303) 228-8000

Connecticut

XL Center (formerly the Hartford Civic Center)
www.xlcenter.com
One Civic Center Plaza
Hartford, CT 06103
(860) 249-6333

Delaware

Delaware does not have a major convention center. Check the convention center in the closest neighboring city and state, which is Philadelphia, PA.

District of Columbia

Walter E. Washington Convention Center
www.dcconvention.com
801 Mount Vernon Place NW
Washington, DC 20001
(202) 249-3000

Florida

Fort Lauderdale/Broward County Convention Center
www.ftlauderdalecc.com
1950 Eisenhower Blvd.
Fort Lauderdale, FL 33316
(954) 765-5900

Miami Beach Convention Center
www.miamibeachconvention.com

1901 Convention Center Dr.
Miami Beach, FL 33139
(305) 673-7311

Orange County Convention Center
www.occc.net
9800 International Dr.
Orlando, FL 32819
(407) 685-9800

Tampa Convention Center
www.tampaconventioncenter.com
333 S Franklin St.
Tampa, FL 33602
(813) 274-8511

Georgia

Georgia World Congress Center
www.gwcc.com
285 Andrew Young International Blvd. NW
Atlanta, GA 30313
(404) 223-4000

Hawaii

Hawaii Convention Center
www.hawaiiconvention.com
1801 Kalakaua Avenue
Honolulu, HI 96815
(808) 943-3500

Idaho

Boise Center
www.boisecentre.com
850 West Front St.
Boise, ID 83702
(208) 336-8900

Illinois

McCormick Place
www.mccormickplace.com

2301 S Lake Shore Drive
Chicago, IL 60616
(312) 791-7000

Navy Pier
www.navypier.com
600 East Grand Avenue
Chicago, IL 60611
(312) 595-7437

Indiana

Indiana Convention Center
www.icclos.com
100 South Capital Avenue
Indianapolis, IN 46225
(317) 262-3400

Iowa

Iowa Events Center
www.iowaeventscenter.com
730 Third St.
Des Moines, IA 50309
(515) 564-8000

Kentucky

Kentucky International Convention Center
www.kyconvention.org
221 Fourth Street
Louisville, KY 40202
(502) 595-4381

Louisiana

Ernest N. Morial Convention Center
www.mccno.com
900 Convention Center Blvd.
New Orleans, LA 70130

(504) 582-3000

Maine

Cumberland County Civic Center
www.theciviccenter.com
One Civic Center Sq.
Portland, ME 04101
(207) 775-3481

Maryland

Baltimore Convention Center
www.bccenter.org
1 West Pratt Street
Baltimore, MD 21201
(410) 649-7000

Massachusetts

Boston Convention and Exhibition Center
www.bostonconventioncenter.com
415 Summer Street
Boston, MA 02210
(617) 954-2000

John B. Hynes Veterans Memorial Convention Center
www.massconvention.com
900 Boylston Street
Boston, MA 02115
(617) 954-2000

Michigan

Cobo Conference/Exhibition Center
www.cobocenter.com
One Washington Blvd.
Detroit, MI 48226
(313) 877-8777

Minnesota

Mayo Civic Center
www.mayociviccenter.com
30 Civic Center Dr. SE
Rochester, MN 55904
(507) 328-2220

Duluth Entertainment Convention
Center
www.decc.org
350 Harbor Dr.
Duluth, MN 55802
(218) 722-5573

Minneapolis Convention Center
www.minneapolisconventioncenter.
com
1301 Second Avenue S.
Minneapolis, MN 55403
(612) 335-6000

Mississippi

Mississippi Coast Convention Center
www.mscoastconventioncenter.com
2350 Beach Boulevard
Biloxi, MI 39531
(228) 594-3700

Missouri

Kansas City Convention & Entertainment Centers
www.kcconvention.com
301 West 13th Street
Suite 100
Kansas City, MO 64105
(816) 513-5000

America's Center Convention Complex

www.explorestlouis.com
701 Convention Plaza, Suite 300
St. Louis, MO 63101
(800) 916-0092

Montana

Butte Silver Bow Civic Center
www.butteciviccenter.com
1340 Harrison Avenue
Butte, MT 59701
(406) 497-6400

Mansfield Convention Center
www.greatfallsmt.net/mansfieldcenter/mansfield-convention-center
2 Park Drive S
Great Falls, MT 59401
(406) 455-8510

Helena Civic Center
www.helenaciviccenter.com
340 Neill Avenue
Helena, MT 59601
(406) 447-8481

Nebraska

CenturyLink Center
www.centurylinkcenteromaha.com
455 N 10th Street
Omaha, NE 68102
(402) 341-1500

Nevada

Las Vegas Convention and Visitors
Authority
www.lvcva.com
3150 Paradise Rd.
Las Vegas, NV 89109
(702) 892-0711

New Hampshire

Check the convention center in your closest neighboring state.

New Jersey

Atlantic City Convention Center
www.accenter.com
1 Convention Blvd.
Atlantic City, NJ 08401
(609) 449-2000

Meadowlands Exposition Center
www.mecexpo.com
355 Plaza Dr.
Secaucus, NJ 07094
(201) 330-7773

Edison Conference Center
www.njexpocenter.com
97 Sunfield Avenue
Edison, NJ 08837
(732) 417-1400

Garden State Convention and Exhibit Center
www.gsec.com
50 Atrium Dr.
Somerset, NJ 08873
(732) 469-4000

Wildwoods Convention Center
www.wildwoodsnj.com/cc/
4501 Boardwalk
Wildwood, NJ 08260
(609) 729-9000

New Mexico

Albuquerque Convention Center
www.albuquerquecc.com

402 2nd Street NW
Albuquerque, NM 87102
(505) 768-4575

New York

Buffalo Niagra Convention Center
www.buffaloconvention.com
Convention Center Plaza
Buffalo, NY 14202
(716) 855-5555

Jacob K. Javits Convention Center
www.javitscenter.com
655 West 34th Street
New York, NY 10001
(212) 216-2000

North Carolina

Charlotte Convention Center
www.charlotteconventionctr.com
100 Paul Buck Blvd.
Charlotte, NC 28217
(704) 339-6000

Metrolina Expo Center
www.metrolinatradeshowexpo.com
7100 Statesville Road
Charlotte, NC 28221
(704) 596-4650

North Dakota

Check the convention center in your closest neighboring state.

Ohio

Duke Energy Convention Center
www.duke-energycenter.com
525 Elm Street
Cincinnati, OH 45202
(513) 419-7300

Cleveland Convention Center
www.clevcc.com
500 Lakeside Avenue
Cleveland, OH 44114
(216) 928-1600

I X Center
www.ixcenter.com
6200 Riverside Drive
Cleveland, OH 44135
(216) 676-6000

Dayton Convention Center
www.daytonconventioncenter.com
22 E Fifth St.
Dayton, OH 45402
(937) 333-4700

Seagate Convention Centre
www.toledo-seagate.com
401 Jefferson Avenue
Toledo, OH 43604
(419) 321-5007

Oklahoma

Cox Convention Center
www.coxconventioncenter.com
1 Myriad Gardens
Oklahoma City, OK 73102
(405) 602-8500

Cox Business Center
www.coxcentertulsa.com
100 Civic Center
Tulsa, OK 74103
(918) 894-4350

Oregon

Oregon Convention Center

www.oregoncc.com
777 N Martin Luther King Blvd.
Portland, OR 97232
(503) 235-7575

Pennsylvania

Pennsylvania Convention Center
www.paconvention.com
1101 Arch Street
Philadelphia, PA 19107
(215) 418-4700

Lawrence Convention Center
www.pittsburghcc.com
1000 Ft. Duquense Blvd.
Pittsburgh, PA 15222
(412) 565-6000

Rhode Island

Rhode Island Convention Center
www.riconvention.com
One Sabin Street
Providence, RI 02903
(401) 458-6000

South Carolina

Charleston Convention Center
www.charlestonconventioncenter.
com
5001 Coliseum Drive North
Charleston, SC 29418
(843) 529-5050

Palmetto International Exposition
Center
www.palmettoexpo.com
One Exposition Avenue
Greenville, SC 29607
(864) 233-2562

South Dakota

Sioux Empire Fairgrounds
www.siouxempirefair.org
Sioux Empire Fair Office
4000 W 12th Street
Sioux Falls, SD 57107
(605) 367-7178

Tennessee

Nashville Convention Center
www.nashvilleconventionctr.com
601 Commerce St.
Nashville, TN 37203
(615) 742-2002

Texas

Austin Convention Center
www.austinconventioncenter.com
500 E First St.
Austin, TX 78701
(512) 404-4000

Kay Baily Hutchinson Convention
Center
www.dallasconventioncenter.com
650 S Griffin St.
Dallas, TX 75202
(214) 939-2750

George R. Brown Convention Center
www.houstonconventioncenter.com
1001 Avenida de las Americas
Houston, TX 77010
(713) 853-8090

Henry B. Gonzalez Convention
Center
www.sahbgcc.com
200 E Market Streets
San Antonio, TX 78205
(877) 504-8895

Waco Convention Center
www.wacocc.com
100 Washington Ave.
Waco, TX 76702
(254) 750-5810

Utah

Salt Palace Convention Center
www.saltpalace.com
100 SW Temple
Salt Lake City, UT 84101
(801) 534-4777

Dixie Convention Center
www.dixiecenter.com
1835 Convention Center Drive
St. George, UT 84790
(435) 628-7003

Vermont

Check the convention center in your
closest neighboring state.

Virginia

The Virginia Beach Convention
Center
www.vbcvb.com
1000 19th Street
Virginia Beach, VA 23451
(757) 385-2000

Washington

Meydenbauer Center
www.meydenbauer.com
11100 NE Sixth St.
Bellevue, WA 98004
(425) 637-1020

Washington State Convention and
Trade Center
www.wscc.com
800 Convention Place
Seattle, WA 98101
(206) 694-5000

Spokane Center
www.spokanecenter.com
334 W Spokane Falls Boulevard
Spokane, WA 99201
(509) 353-6500

West Virginia

Charleston Civic Center
www.charlestonciviccenter.com
200 Civic Center Dr.
Charleston, WV 25301
(304) 345-1500

Wisconsin

Wisconsin Center
www.wisconsincenter.org
400 W Wisconsin Ave.
Milwaukee, WI 53203
(414) 908-6000

Wyoming

Casper Events Center
www.caspereventscenter.com
One Events Drive
Caspar, WY 82601
(307) 235-8441

Convention Center Spotlight

Several convention centers deserve special attention because of their strategic locations and the kinds of trade shows and conferences they attract. Here are eight that I like:

Washington, DC

Our nation's capital has one of the most frequently used convention centers for regional and national trade shows and conferences. Check the website (www.dcconvention.com) frequently because conventions in Washington draw a large number of both vendors and attendees. Hiring managers and top-level executives of major companies attend DC conventions.

Also, many large DC hotels, such as Marriott, Holiday Inn, and Hilton, host trade shows, and I suggest checking their websites for conference information. If you can't find it online, call the hotel and ask to speak with the conference manager.

Florida

The Orange County Convention Center, www.occc.net. Located in Orlando, this is one of the busiest convention centers in the world, hosting national and international conferences. There are two separate facilities a block apart, and each can accommodate tens of thousands of visitors at one time. The convention halls are massive, so be prepared to do a lot of walking. Some conventions to attend here are the Orlando Home Show, the Florida Educational Technology Conference, and the Golf Industry Show. The Golf Show attracts 500 companies, which exhibit here. That means there are 500 potential employers all gathered under one roof. Attendance usually runs over 50,000. Do you like the sporting industry? Attend the Golf Show.

The Tampa Convention Center, www.tampaconventioncenter.com. This is one of the premier conference centers in the Southeast. It accommodates medium-sized conferences that attract hundreds of companies exhibiting their products and services. Its location is on the waterfront in downtown Tampa.

Miami Beach Convention Center, www.miamibeachconvention.com. The Americas' largest jewelry show is held here each year. It is sponsored by the Jewelers International Showcase (JIS) and features three shows annually that attract hundreds of exhibitors and thousands of attendees. The October show has about 1,200 exhibit booths, and the April show, 300 booths. The JIS trade shows attract companies and attendees from 50 countries in the Caribbean, Latin America, and North America. If you like gold, silver, diamonds, rubies, and pearls, this is the place to go to find a job in the jewelry industry. And, if you speak Spanish, you never know where the fun will end!

Georgia

The Atlanta Convention Center, www.atlconventioncenter.com. This large conference facility (more than 800,000 square feet) attracts many national and international trade shows each year. For example, the International Society for Technology in Education (ISTE) will hold its 2014 convention here the last week in June, and the anticipated attendance is more than 15,000 attendees. This conference will host more than 500 exhibiting companies that produce educational technology products for K–12 and higher education. More than 4,500 company representatives will work the booths. One of them could be the hiring manager of your future employer. As instructional materials are transitioning from textbooks to digital products, the education industry will need more workers, like you. If you live in the South or Southeast, you cannot afford to miss this show.

Hawaii

The Hawaii Convention Center, www.meethawaii.com. This one-million-square-foot convention center is just down the street from famed Waikiki beach and is ranked one of the best of its kind in the world. It holds many large and small conferences around the calendar, many of them with exhibitors staffed by key employees, like hiring managers.

The Society for Industrial and Organizational Psychology (SIOP) will hold its twenty-ninth annual convention here May 15, 2014 to May 17, 2014. Those of you interested in careers relating to psychology should attend this conference, which attracts about 4,000 attendees from across the globe.

By the way, the convention center itself is a prospect for your first job. The convention center has a number of full-time sales reps and a complete staff of IT workers and an active marketing department. Check out the careers listed under "Jobs" on its website.

Ready for some sun, some surf, and a luau on weekends after convention hours? That's working in Hawaii. Does it get any better than that? Did you check out the job pages?

Illinois

McCormick Place, www.mccormickplace.com. This facility is located along the lakefront in Chicago and is Illinois's largest convention facility. Go there now on your smartphone, iPad, tablet, or laptop. Click on "Full Calendar" and then go to the "Monthly Calendar." As an example of what you might find, when I did this, I saw that the first show of the 2013 calendar year was the Chicago Boat, Sports, and RV Show scheduled for January 8–13. Click on the show title and it will take you to the website for the Chicago Boat Show, which will provide you with all the information you need to know, including the names and addresses of hundreds of companies that will be exhibiting there.

Indiana

The Indianapolis Convention Center, www.icclos.com.   This popular conference center hosts many national and regional conferences representing all industries. Its central location and reasonable attendance fees make it a popular location.

One of the most important annual conferences held here is the Indiana Bankers Association. I checked out a recent conference and it listed all of the attending banks, including many national financial institutions, *and it listed the names of the attendees from each bank.* Pay dirt!

One of the main premises of this book is to show you that the most important step in the job-hunting process is to learn the names of hiring managers. I found that Joe Hanson was listed as an attendee for Bank of Indiana. I Googled his name and affiliation, and here's what I found on LinkedIn: "Joe Hanson, EVP Capital Development and Strategic Initiatives at Indianapolis Neighborhood Housing Partnership (INHP)." Joe has moved on from Bank of Indiana, where he was employed in 2012 and had attended the annual Indiana Bankers Association conference at the convention center. Now he has an executive vice president position with an important nonprofit in Indianapolis. How easy does it get? You now have the name of a high-level hiring manager because you had the smarts to look at the website for the Indiana Convention Center, the place where the hiring managers hang out.

Iowa

Iowa Events Center, www.iowaeventscenter.com. The Iowa Power Farming trade show is held here each January and is organized by the Iowa-Nebraska Equipment Dealers Association. The convention brings together under one roof manufacturers and dealers of farming equipment, all of which are potential job targets. If you are interested in agribusiness, where better to find a job than in Iowa, at the Iowa Events Center in Des Moines?

By the way, when I reviewed the Iowa Events Center website, I found an interesting array of job opportunities, and a listing of internships for marketing, sales, events management, and food and beverage operations.

Kansas

The Kansas City Convention Center, www.kcconvention.com. The conferences you will find here are varied and interesting. For example, there were two conferences that caught my attention. One was ETS (Educational Testing Service), which focuses on K–12 and higher education testing and assessment. The program included seminars on career opportunities with ETS, one of the *Real World Faves* (see page 160).

Another trade show appealing to those interested in college coaching careers was the 2013 Collegiate Strength and Conditioning Coaches Association Annual Conference. The conference website itself had interesting positions and internships posted at various colleges and universities throughout the country. It never ceases to amaze me how much information can be found at conferences and trade shows.

Best Trade Shows by Industry

The following list of annual trade shows by industry could be your ticket to that first job. Click on the show nearest to your location or the show focusing on an area of interest, like photography, housing, travel, or educational technology and publishing. These organizations hold annual conferences in different locations each year.

American Booksellers Association (ABA), www.bookweb.com. The ABA holds an annual conference and several regional conferences where you can see many companies in the print and digital publishing industry. The 2014 and 2015 annual conventions will be held at the Javits Center in New York City.

American Association of School Administrators (AASA), www. aasa.org. Hundreds of companies exhibit here to display their products to school superintendents and other high-level school administrators. The companies attending this convention are publishers and producers of instructional materials, school supply companies, bus companies, insurance companies, security companies, and more.

Association of Educational Publishers (AEP), www.aepweb.org. This organization sponsors an annual conference in June each year in Washington, DC. Attendees include high-level educational technology and publishing company executives, all of whom are hiring authorities. In 2013, this organization merged with the Association of American Publishers (AAP).

American Library Association (ALA), www.ala.org. This conference is devoted to books and digital products related to public and school libraries and online education. It's a fascinating show with hundreds of exhibitors from the education, publishing, and online learning industries. Once you are on this website, click on "Education and Careers." You will not be sorry because you may find your first job right here.

Association for Supervision and Curriculum Development (ASCD), www.ascd.org. Members of ASCD are involved with curriculum at K–12 schools. Thousands of these administrators, called curriculum coordinators or assistant superintendents for curriculum, attend this show. The conference is held in a different location each year.

American Society for Training and Development (ASTD), www. astd.org. This nonprofit organization is devoted to training and professional development for educators and government workers. It holds an annual plenary conference in a major city plus four regional conferences. The 2013 annual conference was held in Dallas, May 19-22, and attracted approximately 9,000 attendees from eighty different countries. More than 300 companies exhibited their products and services. The fee for entrance to view the exhibits? Free! Track the annual and regional conferences because this is where you will meet many employers in the flesh, each one being the source for a possible first job. Think of it. Three hundred potential employers gathered under one roof. Does job hunting get any easier than that?

BookExpo America (BEA), www.bookexpoamerica.com. BookExpo America is the largest trade show in America for the book publishing industry. BEA held its 2013 annual convention at the Javits Center in New York City. More than 1,200 companies hosted exhibits on the conference center floor, all staffed by full-time employees. Some held editorial positions, some were marketing managers, some came from sales, others from finance, and still others from information technology. Where in the world could you find so many potential employers under one roof?

Who attends BEA? Here is an example of the caliber of attendees at this convention. A New York City-based trade publisher, Skyhorse Publishing Inc. (www.skyhorsepublishing.com), the publisher of this book, attends BEA and displays its publications in an exhibit staffed by some of its key employees, like Jay Cassell, who is the editorial director. He is in charge of the entire editorial staff at Skyhorse and is the person you need to see for potential job opportunities, entry-level or above. If you had attended BEA in May 2013, you would have had the opportunity to connect personally with Jay Cassell, the hiring manager for a major publisher.

By the way, BEA will be at the Javits Center in 2014 and 2015, too. I hope to see you there.

Consortium for School Networking (CoSN), www.cosn.org. This organization conducts an annual conference attended by hundreds of executive-level hiring managers from the educational technology industry. The location changes each year. CoSN is based in Washington, DC, and posts job openings on its website. Check it out.

The EdNET Conference, www.ednetinsight.com. The conference is held in a different city each year in September. In 2012, it was held in Baltimore, Maryland. In 2013, it was held in Denver, Colorado, at the Sheraton Hotel and Conference Center. In 2014, the conference will be held in Baltimore, September 28–30. If you are interested in the education business, which consists of companies that produce instructional materials and services for K–12 and higher education, how better could you spend $500 or less if you negotiate a lower fee? Check out the website now to learn more.

Florida Educational Technology Conference (FETC), www.fetc. org. The organization hosts an annual convention in Orlando, Florida. Its focus is educational technology. Hundreds of educational technology companies exhibit at this conference, and if you like technology and its application in the education process, you cannot afford to miss this one. By the way, bring a few dozen resumes because you will find a hiring manager in almost every exhibit booth.

International Reading Association (IRA), www.reading.org. This organization is for teachers and administrators who teach reading and literacy classes to K–12 students. When you access this site, click on "Career Center," where you will find ten or more pages of open positions for educators, both beginning and experienced. If you are an educator interested in literacy education, you have hit the jackpot.

International Society for Technology in Education (ISTE), www. iste.org. This show focuses on products and services related to education and is held each year in June at a different big city location. If you are interested in an industry that makes a difference for kids, this one is for you. Do not miss it because here you will find hundreds of exhibitors under one roof. Each is a potential employer, so bring along a bundle of resumes.

Additional Education Conferences

National Association of Biology Teachers (NABT), www.nabt.org
National Council for the Social Studies (NCSS), www.ncss.org
National Council for Teachers of English (NCTE), www.ncte.org
National Council of Teachers of Mathematics (NCTM), www.nctm.org
National Science Teachers Association (NSTA), www.nsta.org
Software and Information Industry Association (SIIA), www.siia.org
Texas Computer Education Association (TCEA), www.tcea.org

International Book Fairs for Education

Several international publishing conventions are held each year, so if you are in the area, plan to attend. You will find thousands of companies from America and around the world that will host exhibits staffed by workers who will tell you about job opportunities and provide the names and contact information for hiring managers. Foreign companies may be looking for workers to represent their interests in America, and you might be the one. Here are some of the best international trade fairs in the education and communication industries.

Frankfurt Book Fair, www.buchmesse.de/en/company. This convention attracts 7,000 exhibitors from around the world and is considered the mother of all international book fairs. It is held in Frankfurt, Germany, every October. Can you imagine 7,000 potential employers under one roof?

The London Book Fair (LBF), www.londonbookfair.co.uk. This is a major bookseller event and is held in London each spring. It attracts close to 1,000 exhibitors ranging from retail booksellers to educational publishers, and communications companies in general.

Bologna Children's Book Fair, www.bolognachildrensbookfair. com. This interesting book fair has been displaying products related to children's education since 1964. Hundreds of companies publishing books and digital products for children exhibit here. It's located in an attractive place, Bologna, Italy, and is held each March. Check it out if you happen to be in Italy in spring.

Beijing International Book Fair (BIBF), www.combinedbook. com. If you find yourself in China during the month of August, visit this fascinating conference to meet more than 500 exhibitors from around the world, with an emphasis on Asian companies. This is a long way to go to meet American companies, but you will find many here exhibiting alongside their foreign counterparts. This annual book fair takes place in Beijing.

The Homebuilding and Improvement Industry

If you recall the three necessities for survival—food, shelter, and clothing—you will not be surprised to learn there are many home shows throughout the US that attract thousands of companies exhibiting their products. Each one is a potential employer. Where do you find them? At conference centers throughout the US.

For example, do you live in or near the Chicago area? There are several home shows in different area locations hosting many hundreds of exhibitors. Who knows, one of them may provide your first job. Click here: www.chicagohomeshow.net.

There are so many home shows that it would take many pages to list all of them here. An easy route to find these conferences is to Google "home shows" in your local area. Sometimes these shows combine homebuilding and improvement companies with garden and horticulture organizations. As an example of what you will find, I'll highlight just two:

National Association of Home Builders (NAHB), www.hahb.com. The annual convention is called the NAHB International Builders Show. The 2015 conference is in Las Vegas in January. At this show, you will find approximately 1,000 exhibiting companies, all potential employers. If the shelter part of survival intrigues you, attend this show and other home shows that take place in major cities. In addition to providing an opportunity to meet hiring managers, or workers who can lead you to them, this show will provide an education about how the shelter industry works in the US. Attend this show or other regional home shows, and your knowledge of the housing industry will increase exponentially. When you visit the website, click on "Careers and Industry Jobs." When I visited the career pages, I found an entry-level job titled "computer support specialist," a position requiring a college degree and knowledge of several common applications.

To find other home shows in your area, do a Google search. For example, if you enter "Philadelphia Home Show," here is what you will get:

Philadelphia Home Show, www.phillyhomeshow.com. This conference takes place in Philly each February and hosts hundreds of exhibitors, some national and most local. While you're there, remember to have one of those famous Philadelphia cheesesteak sandwiches. Also visit the Philadelphia Art Museum, where you can have your picture taken beside the famous bronze of Rocky.

The Transportation Industry

In addition to food, shelter, and clothing, transportation has become one of the basics for living. The transportation industry conducts hundreds of conventions each year in locations throughout the country, and it would be impossible to list all of them. As you did for the housing industry, Google "Auto Shows" in the largest city close to home, and you will find all the information you need. Here is an example of a major transportation show to get you started:

New York International Auto Show, www.autoshowny.com. This conference is one of the largest auto shows in the country and hosts hundreds of companies, which exhibit on the floor of the Javits Center. By attending this conference you will find potential job opportunities in the automobile industry. Guaranteed.

The Insurance Industry

In this century, insurance of every type has become a necessity to live as a self-sufficient human being. Like it or not, you need insurance. Many insurance companies have been in business continuously for more than a hundred years and are attractive places for long-term employment. The industry hosts many conventions throughout the calendar year in many different cities. Here is an example:

The National Association of Mutual Insurance Companies (NAMIC), www.namic.org. This is one of the largest insurance organizations in the business and hosts an annual convention at a different location each year. The 2014 national convention will be held in September at the Gaylord National Resort and Conference Center in National Harbor, Maryland. More than 300 companies will exhibit, and there will be more than 1,000 senior executives from the insurance industry in attendance.

The Insurance Journal. Like other essential industries, the insurance industry holds hundreds of national and regional conferences, and the best place for information about where they are and when they are held is to visit the *Insurance Journal* online at www.insurancejournal.com.

If you like the idea of long-term employment, make it a point to attend an insurance industry conference. Attending conferences not only opens the door for job opportunities, but also provides an education about that industry and how it works.

FINDING EMPLOYERS AT OFFICE, BUSINESS, AND INDUSTRIAL PARKS

In every metropolitan area of the country, you will find office, business, and industrial parks—places where hundreds of different companies locate their home offices or regional offices. Some parks specialize in one particular industry, while others are diversified. For example, an industrial park in Langhorne, Pennsylvania, specializes in medical offices for both physicians and dentists. An industrial park in Portland, Maine, hosts a diversified group of companies, including J.Weston Walch Publishing, a ninety-year-old educational publisher.

How do you contact companies in a business or industrial park? Easy. You leave the house at 8 a.m. in your business attire and armed with business cards and two dozen career profiles or resumes to distribute to hiring managers and human resources directors. You go from door to door and request a personal meeting with the hiring manager in charge of your field of interest. This process is referred to as a cold call—that is, one made without an appointment. Instructions for the cold-call process are in chapter 10.

One might ask, "Do I make a cold call on every business in the business park?" If you are job hunting for any kind of job, regardless of industry or position, the answer is *yes*. If you are interested only in positions with insurance companies as an underwriter, sales representative, or claims adjuster, you narrow the cold calls to insurance companies. You determine who these companies are by checking out the names of the companies in the business or office park on the website beforehand.

Use the Internet to Find Business Parks

There are many business, office, and industrial parks in major cities, and the best way to find out where they are is to Google an entry like, "business parks in Denver, Colorado." I did just that and found the Denver Tech Center, an area along the I-25 corridor southeast of Denver. This area is home to more than sixty companies spanning a number of industries. The list of companies on the website includes Agilent Technologies, Boeing, Cargill, Centex Homes, JPMorgan, Kodiak Petroleum, Morgan Stanley, Nissan Motor, Time Warner Cable, and Western Union. These are either home offices or regional offices and are potential employers. If you live in the Denver Metro Area, start cold-calling the companies located here to find your first job.

For industrial parks in Houston, Texas, for example, Google "Houston industrial parks." When I did that, I found the Beltway Industrial Park, where light manufacturing companies are located. Industrial parks in other locations host large manufacturers as well as warehouses and regional offices.

Do you live in Seattle? Enter "Seattle business parks." I did that and found enough potential employers, and their locations, to keep me busy job hunting for the next six months.

No matter where you live in the US, you will find office parks, business parks, and industrial parks. Google using all three names, and you will find companies galore to explore for your first job.

GOING FORWARD

Attending trades shows and conferences is the best method for finding hiring managers who are there in the flesh, ready and waiting for both customers and candidates for open positions. There are conferences every month in every large metropolitan area, and all you need to do to learn the who/when/where is to search the convention center websites listed above.

Cold-calling companies at business, office, and industrial parks is another ideal way to find that first job. Many open positions are not advertised in print or online, but you can find them by calling the many companies located in these business parks.

But wait! If working for someone else is not your idea of a good time, and you want to start your own business, read chapter 13. It's coming up next.

CHAPTER TAKEAWAYS

- *The best place to meet hiring managers and key executives is at conferences and trade shows.*
- *Office, business, and industrial parks are where you will meet potential employers personally.*
- *Never drink alcoholic beverages while job hunting. Never!*

JOB HUNTER'S LIBRARY

Michael Farr, *100 Fastest-Growing Careers*, JIST, 2010.

Chapter 13

Starting Your Own Business

Join the thousands who have decided to start their own businesses instead of working for someone else. Just because you have a college degree does not mean that you must work for a big corporation or even a small business, which is defined as having 500 employees or less. Working for a company, particularly a large one, where the ground rules can be oppressive, may not be your idea of a good time. Thousands of recent college graduates feel the same way. In fact, in a recent op-ed in the September 12, 2013, issue of the *Wall Street Journal*, Bill Aulet, head of the Martin Trust Center for MIT Entrepreneurship, claims that 20 percent of college undergrads are interested in pursuing their own businesses rather than casting their lot with a corporation.

But how do you start your own business? What must you do before hanging out a sign with your name on it? Only people who do not have college degrees start their own businesses, right? Isn't it true that most business owners have money in the family, and are mostly upper class? To clear up those misconceptions, here is the profile of people who start their own businesses, according to an article that appeared in the November 12, 2012, issue of the *Wall Street Journal*: "95.1 percent of people who start their own businesses have a college undergraduate degree or higher. Forty-seven percent have advanced degrees. Less than 1 percent come from extremely rich or extremely poor backgrounds. 71.5 percent come from a middle-class background. Seventy percent used their own savings as the source to fund their own businesses."

I like numbers. They always set the record straight.

HOW DO YOU GET STARTED?

Let's consider what Richard Branson, founder and CEO of Virgin Airlines, said in his first blog for LinkedIn, posted in 2012: "As LinkedIn is a business that started in a living room, much like Virgin began in a basement, I thought my first blog on the site should be about how to simply start a successful business." Here are Branson's five top tips:

1. Listen more than you talk.
2. Keep it simple.
3. Take pride in your work.
4. Have fun; success will follow.
5. Rip it up and start again.

These are the first steps that Richard Branson took when founding Virgin Airlines, arguably one of the most successful airlines on the planet. Branson always has good ideas for entrepreneurs and has authored twelve books about starting businesses and how to run them. I've suggested two of them at the end of this chapter for your "Job Hunter's Library."

By the way, Branson did not have a college degree when he founded Virgin Airlines. His age? Twenty-four. Go to LinkedIn and read the rest of Branson's first blog. You can learn much from him. He's been there, done that.

MORE FAMOUS ENTREPRENEURS

If you explore how other entrepreneurs founded their businesses, the story will be similar to Branson's. Take Bill Gates and Microsoft.

He dropped out of Harvard after his sophomore year and founded Microsoft. His age? Twenty-one.

I'm sure you've heard by now that Steve Jobs and Steve Wozniak both dropped out of college after their first year and founded Apple Computer working out of a garage. Both were in their early twenties. And then we have Larry Ellison, founder and CEO of Oracle, who bypassed college altogether and founded one of the world's largest software companies. (By the way, Ellison just purchased the entire island of Kauai in the Hawaiian Islands. Yes, the entire thing, not just a couple of acres.)

Facebook? Mark Zuckerberg, another person with big dreams and little appetite for the pace of a college education, founded it. He's another Harvard dropout who had a better idea and followed his dreams. Mark is in his late twenties now, and after his company went public in June 2012, Mark's net worth was close to $14 *billion.*

Welcome to the Real World is not saying that only college dropouts launch successful businesses. Most businesses are founded by college graduates, like you, as the numbers above indicate. Let's also be realistic about the money. Not every entrepreneur will be worth $10 billion, but what's wrong with a cool million? That sounds like a big number, but after you get into your own business, a million may sound like chump change.

I WANT TO DO IT MY WAY

These behemoths in the technology world all started as someone's dream, and many times most started in a garage. (We're not sure why garages are so attractive for entrepreneurs. That's just the way it is.) If Gates and Zuckerberg could do it, so can you. The business you start does not have to be another Microsoft in order to be successful. There are thousands of small businesses founded, owned, and operated successfully by someone who had the courage to say, "I want to do it my way."

If the thought of working for a company that has your name on it really turns you on, go for it! There are many books and websites that will provide ideas about how to get started, and remember to check my website for information, inspiration, encouragement, and ideas at www.firstjobsforcollegegrads.com.

STARTING YOUR OWN BUSINESS AS A SOLE PROPRIETOR

Can you really start your own business and make a living at it? How long does it take before you can make serious money to become self-sufficient? The world is filled with good examples of small businesses that are successful. Take a walk down Main Street, USA, and talk to the owner of a storefront business, and you will get the answer. Here's an example of a business started by a college grad who found the corporate world not to his liking.

You do not have to work for a large company to become a self-sufficient worker. If the entrepreneurial life is appealing, select something that you really like and pursue it. It does not have to be glamorous, but it does have to fulfill a need that people will always have for goods or services. Here's an example of an entrepreneur who found a need nobody had addressed and turned in into a profitable business:

Gary Schultz from Philadelphia. Several years ago, I tired of the annual window-washing chore, so I went to the Yellow Pages and found Gary's Window Washing. Gary did an excellent job washing our windows both inside and out while paying attention to details like washing the screens, cleaning the windowsills, and wiping down the hardware and window frames. The job took Gary about six hours, and we paid him $400, which translates into $66 per hour. That's the going rate in our area. We have employed Gary for the past five years. He begins work at the appointed hour, supplies all window-cleaning products, and maintains a high quality of work. He runs a very good business.

Recently, Gary added another service to his business—residential exterior power-washing—which is a perfect complement to the window-washing business.

Gary graduated from Temple University in Philadelphia with a bachelor's in business administration and began working in the corporate world with several large companies, one of which was General Electric. He was not happy and decided to make it on his own. He researched several opportunities and found there was no competition in the residential window-washing business. He started out with a modest investment and a few years later had two people working for him.

I can hear the snickering now. Window washing with a college degree? You have to be kidding! Well, what if I told you that Gary's business generates a revenue stream approaching six figures and he works only ten months of the year? (Gary works only ten months because inclement weather in January and February prevents him from working outside.) Now what do you think about the residential window-washing business?

Compare that to a corporate job. An average entry-level corporate job will bring in about $35,000 per year. Assume that you are promoted after three years, and then you will be making about $55,000 per year. You will get two weeks' vacation, report to work each day at a specific time, and will be confined to working in a corporate kennel.

However, this is not the end of Gary's story. He has created the Window Business Start-Up Kit, which you will find on his website at www.windowcleaningcash.com. This kit consists of a sixty-page manual, a thirty-five-minute video, and one year of phone and email support. The price? $68. Buy Gary's package and study what he has to say. It cuts through the hype written by MBAs selling you textbook promises. Gary explains the reality of starting your own business.

Thanks, Gary. See you next year when you come to wash our windows, and by the way, please power-wash our house, too. I'll write you a check for $850. Thanks!

Gary's story is about how to make a living on your own terms. You, like Gary, have a college degree, which is one of the factors that makes for a successful entrepreneur. Owning and operating your own business is one of the most satisfying things you can do. Your business will provide a good income, the option to work on your own terms, and provide time to give back to the community by participating in your choice of outreach programs. The term "work" does not always mean putting in time with a Fortune 500 company.

WHAT KIND OF BUSINESS CAN I START?

The list of business ventures is endless, but a good place to start is to envision a business in which you have an interest or a passion. Food. Shelter. Clothing. Transportation. Technology. Insurance. Education. These are necessities that all people need, regardless of age, gender, geography, race, or religion.

Businesses on Main Street, USA

The next time you are out of the house, look at the businesses on either side of Main Street. More than half will be selling food, shelter, clothing, and related products. The point is this: if you want to strike out on your own as an entrepreneur rather than work for someone else, just do it. Play to your passion. Do something that turns you on every day, as Branson said.

Ideas for Your Own Business

Here are three entry-level start-up ideas to get you thinking about your own business:

1. Produce and sell a much-needed product like bread and related baked goods.
2. Provide services for homes and businesses as Gary does.
3. Sell products of any kind as an independent sales representative.

Number three is the least expensive way to start working on your own. Independent sales reps carry products related to one specific industry, like cutlery. Sales reps working in this narrow market niche might carry products for three or more different manufacturers, both domestic and foreign, and sell them to restaurants, both large and small, or to wholesalers—that is, companies that distribute and sell not only knives but also related products such as metal cooking pots and pans. I know a sales rep who sells only knives in the Mid-Atlantic region, and he makes a small fortune. His slogan? "My products are a cut above the rest."

Starting a Business with a Partner

Another way to start your own business is with a partner who has similar interests and values. Selecting the right partner is an important first step and requires a complete examination of that person's skills, energy, intelligence, passion for self-employment, ethics, values, and interest in the ideas you have for starting a business. Researching your potential partner is critical. If you select just a good friend instead of a good friend who is compatible with you in every way, your business could turn into a nightmare. Many entrepreneurs have failed because they selected the wrong partner. Selecting the right partner will result in a successful business that brings satisfaction and money to both partners. Here's a good example of a successful partnership.

Chris from Silver Spring, Maryland. Chris said "good-bye" to the corporate world and turned his interest in cinematography into a thriving video production company. This is not a business for the faint of heart. It requires exceptional written and verbal communication skills, bottom-line business skills, creativity, imagination, and technical expertise. While Chris possessed all of those qualities, the time requirements for operating a successful media business are significant. Chris came across a partner with similar skills, and together they founded Rafferty-Weiss Media (www.raffertyweiss.com). Check out their website for a peek at a successful and creative partnership with a nationwide reputation for producing products of excellent quality.

Starting Your Own Business with a Franchise

A popular way to start your own business is to purchase a franchise, but how this operates is frequently misunderstood. It's a common business model. The franchise industry focuses on products and services related to food, shelter, and clothing. Some of these industries are restaurants, cleaning services, hotels, and a variety of retail stores.

How a Franchise Works

There are two entities involved in the franchise operation. First is the *franchisor*, which is the company that owns the brand name, like McDonald's. The other part is the *franchisee,* the person who sells the goods or products at an individual store. The franchisor, or parent company, if you will, provides the location, training, marketing and sales support, advertising, and other requirements needed to run a business. The company charges the individual store operator a franchise fee to begin the business, and takes a percentage of the business revenues.

Of course, the first names that come to mind are McDonald's, Burger King, Starbucks, Dairy Queen, Chipotle, KFC, and the like. Almost all of the individual stores in the fast-food market are franchises. Purchasing one costs serious money. For example, McDonald's requires a minimum of $250,000 in cash. You cannot borrow this amount; it must be $250,000 that is unencumbered, and that is just the beginning. Before you are finished, it will cost anywhere from $600,000 to $1.5 million to purchase a McDonald's franchise.

However, other franchise opportunities are interesting and available for as little as $10,000. There are hundreds of websites that provide information, not only about cost, but also about the process. One that I like is Top 100 Franchises at www.top100franchises.net.

When I last checked this website, I found franchises in the $10,000 to $200,000 range. One that I like is ServPro, a house-cleaning and restoration business that has an excellent nationwide reputation for good service. The franchise cost is $25,000. At the high end was a Checkers Drive-In restaurant, where a franchise will cost approximately $200,000. I like their burgers, medium-well with an order of fries and a large diet Coke.

Franchise Resources

Here are several online sources to learn more about franchise operations and opportunities:

Top 100 Franchises, www.top100franchises.net

Franchise Opportunities, www.franchiseopportunities.com

Franchise Direct, www.franchisedirect.com

RESOURCES FOR ENTREPRENEURS

Recently, *Forbes* ran an article titled, "The Best Organizations for Entrepreneurs" (www.forbes.com). You can access this article online for interesting and valuable sources of support for getting started in your own business. Navigate this list for information on how to start a business and how to connect with others doing the same thing.

Entrepreneurs Organization, www.eonetowork.org. This organization provides general information about starting businesses across the country.

Young Entrepreneur Council, www.theyec.org

Young Presidents' Organization, www.ypo.org

FoundersCard, www.founderscard.com

Vistage, www.vistage.com

Small Giants, www.smallgiants.org. This is a close-knit organization for entrepreneurs of all sizes and provides training.

The Technology Council of Greater Kansas City, www.kcnext.com. Specializing in Kansas City-area tech jobs, the organization offers support and advice for entrepreneurs, regardless of location.

Built in Chicago, www.builtinchicago.org. BIC concentrates on technology opportunities in the Chicago area.

Corporate Alliance, www.corporatealliance.net. This organization has offices in California and Utah and provides support, training, and networking services.

OKAY, WHERE'S THE MONEY?

A good question all entrepreneurs ask is, "Where do I get the money to start a business?" It's a valid question and one that cannot be answered easily. Some businesses can be started with absolutely nothing in your bank account; others can take substantial amounts of money. How much you will need depends on what you intend to do. Let's get practical and explore how you can find a few bucks to start your business:

1. **Your own personal savings.** This may not be much, because you've just recently graduated college, but even if you have only $1,000 saved, this could be enough to get you started. Remember Gary from Philadelphia? How much could it have cost to buy supplies to start a window-washing business?

2. **Family money.** Most entrepreneurs find start-up money from parents and other family members. This can be dicey. Mom and Dad are not going to be happy about lending you more money if you already have a loan to repay, and if you have been sitting around the house whining, "There's nothing out there." However, it's worth a try. The way to approach this is to prepare a detailed business plan and present it to your parents just as you would to a loan officer at a bank. If they say no, move on to other family members, like a favorite aunt or uncle, or better yet, your grandparents. Grandparents love their grandchildren and will do most anything to make them happy and successful. There is one caveat about asking family members for money: promise to repay it, every last cent. You are not a charity case, and your parents and other family members have their own lives to support financially. Present a written statement for family members stating when you will begin repaying the loan.

3. **Banks.** Local banks make money by lending money to entrepreneurs like you. You must have a detailed business plan to get anywhere, but you can do that. There are online sources that give advice about preparing a credible business plan. Approach the most local of banks in your area, an independent bank, not a branch of Wells Fargo. The process is to learn the name of the bank loan officer and make an appointment for a personal interview to present your business plan, your resume and your career profile. This is a no-nonsense deal, so dress accordingly. Bankers are not impressed with sneakers, backpacks, T-shirts, and waist-length hair.

4. **Angel funding sources.** These are individuals or small organizations that provide seed money to entrepreneurs. Finding these sources takes time and research. You can find these money sources online, by networking through social media like LinkedIn, or through loan officers at a local bank.

What can be more exciting than saying good-bye to the corporate world and doing it your way? Chris from Silver Spring did it. So did Gary from Philadelphia. So did Bill Gates. So did Mark Zuckerberg. So can you!

GOING FORWARD

The business of starting your own business does not have to be complicated. The beginning of any entrepreneurial adventure is planning and research, so I'll repeat a **Real World** rule: *Plan your work. Work your plan.*

Owning a business requires your undivided attention and much time. However, if you like what you are doing, who cares how many hours you put into it?

CHAPTER TAKEAWAYS

- *Plan your work. Work your plan.*
- *Follow your passion.*
- *Select a business that provides basic goods and services for customers.*
- *You alone can make a difference by applying your intelligence and energy to an idea about which you are passionate.*

JOB HUNTER'S LIBRARY

Richard Branson, *Losing My Virginity*, Virgin Books, 2013.

Richard Branson, *Like a Virgin*, Virgin Books, 2012.

Martha Shirk and Anna Wadia, *Kitchen Table Entrepreneurs*, Basic Books, 2009.

Lewis Schiff, *Business Brilliant*, Harper Business, 2013.

Stephen Fishman, *Working for Yourself*, NOLO, 2011.

Brian Tracy, *GOALS!* Berrett-Koehler, 2010.

Bill Aulet, *Disciplined Entrepreneurship*, Wiley, 2013.

Chapter 14

Jobs for Returning Military Personnel

First off, I want to extend my thanks to all military personnel who have sacrificed to make our country safe and secure for our 315 million American citizens. Placing yourself in harm's way for the security of our country is admirable indeed, and I am grateful.

Every year, approximately 160,000 men and women are discharged from active military service. Returning veterans have a number of challenges facing them when they reenter civilian life, one of which is finding that important first job after leaving active duty. Some already have a bachelor's or master's degree, and others may have completed only a few years of undergraduate work and intend to return to college. Still others may be returning with no college experience whatsoever. I urge those of you to continue your education as soon as possible.

EDUCATION! EDUCATION! EDUCATION!

Education is necessary to remain competitive in today's changing job market, but obtaining a college degree costs money. At one time, the GI Bill paid for a college degree, but now full tuition reimbursement is no longer a government benefit. However, there are low-interest government loans available for veterans, and you should take advantage of these loans as soon as possible. Outright assistance for army veterans was curtailed in May 2013 because of cuts to our federal budget, but check frequently to see if the education assistance program has been reinstated. It's sad to say that veterans benefits are now subject to political agendas.

Tuition Assistance Programs. Military personnel still in service and who are reading this book may want to tap into the Tuition Assistance program. For example, those serving in the navy could earn their college degree for free under the navy tuition assistance program. The navy offers active-duty sailors several programs to support their education goals, including tuition assistance reimbursement for college courses taken during off-duty hours. In addition, the navy TA program extends to active-duty reservists. Check it out by clicking here: www.military.com/education/money-for-school/navy-tuition-assistance.html. Other branches of the military have similar TA programs for active military personnel, but there are strict rules and regulations attached.

The GI Bill Education Benefits program does provide some tuition assistance for discharged military personnel, but there are many rules attached, so you must constantly check to see how the program is administered.

DELAYS IN RECEIVING GOVERNMENT BENEFITS

Unfortunately, there has been a delay in getting the paperwork processed for veterans benefits after discharge. The snag in Washington is the result of a digital system that does not work well and has forced the veterans administration to process claims using paper and pen. There have been promises from government officials to rectify the problems, but nothing has been done. It is a broken system, causing a delay of almost one year after discharge for vets to receive benefits that are due.

I urge both veterans and non-veterans to lobby congressional representatives to fix the problem. In addition, you can send your message directly to the president's office. I have taken up your cause by sending stern email messages to my New Jersey senator, Robert Menendez, demanding that he and other members of Congress take up your cause and get this problem fixed. There is no reason why you should wait a year or more to receive what is owed to you for your service to our country and for your sacrifice.

While waiting for your benefits to be processed, I urge veterans to pursue jobs in the civilian workforce. The advice that follows applies to both civilians and military personnel. The rules are the same, but you do hold an advantage because of the skills you acquired in the military.

WORKING IN CIVILIAN JOBS

As you begin your life after military service, you will find that potential employers cutting across all industries are eager to assist military veterans returning to the workforce. Most companies will consider your military experience a big plus. Company hiring managers and human resources directors know that the military honed your leadership skills and sense of mission in a unique way. They will welcome your candidacy, even if you do not have a college degree. They know that you bring much to the table because of your real-life experience and your maturity.

Your military experience will work in your favor while competing in the job market. There are many nonprofit organizations and government agencies ready to help you. However, you must be proactive and position your candidacy for jobs as a returning military person. Companies large and small have already made public through a variety of media sources that they are seeking your candidacy, and I urge you to reach out to these companies. Here's an example:

Early in 2013, Walmart (www.walmart.com) said that it is reserving 100,000 jobs just for returning military personnel. The company has been ranked as one of the Top 100 Military-Friendly Employers by both *Forbes* (www.forbes.com) and Military Friendly (www.militaryfriendly.com). The Walmart website will take you to the right place, but it is somewhat cumbersome, so here are rudimentary directions. On the home page, click on "See All Departments." At the bottom of this page, you will find a menu that includes "Careers." Click on it and then click on "People," and you will see a special section titled, "Military." You can take it from there and find advice and a listing of job opportunities under twenty-two separate categories. The company says, "Walmart offers something for every military skill set and background." This site has much to offer, so plan to spend ample time here to see what is available.

Later in this chapter, I will give you the names and websites of companies that have advertised similar initiatives for veterans. Stay current on the many career-counseling opportunities provided by the government and nonprofit agencies by frequently conducting online searches.

EMPLOYMENT ADVANTAGES FOR MILITARY PERSONNEL

Military veterans returning to the civilian workforce hold a deck of aces. Employers consider candidates with military experience as having a good sense of mission, leadership skills, and a desire to excel. Some companies will consider your military experience more valuable than comparable experience in the civilian workforce.

An alternative to seeking a corporate job is to consider starting your own business. The discipline you learned in the military is a requirement for owning any business. There are many examples to follow, like that of West Point graduate Captain Kiel King. Here is what he did after discharge, in his own words:

Captain Kiel King from New York. "First, I medically retired as a captain. Upon returning to the United States from Germany, I spoke with the Lucas Group, an executive recruiting firm that specializes in placing military personnel. My bachelor's degree is in chemistry and life sciences, but it did not come into play while taking my interview with the Coca-Cola Bottling Company. I was hired after the first interview. I started with Coca-Cola a month after leaving the military as a production manager. But, after one year, I was not truly working in a field that I enjoyed. I believe I was hired due to my leadership experience in the army and my education at West Point. After a bit of soul searching, I decided it was important to continue my education in an area that I truly loved and went back to school to complete a graduate degree in physical rehabilitation sciences.

I have since started my own company called Kings of Fitness where we operate under the mission to educate, motivate, and inspire individuals to live a healthy and physically active lifestyle. While I was in the army, helping people was extremely important to me, and now that I am medically retired, helping people is still the most important thing that gives me true job satisfaction. I did not feel I had that with Coca-Cola as great as they were with bringing me in.

I also had the fortunate opportunity to work with the Wounded Warrior Project on maintaining an updated resume. They are absolutely an amazing organization that cares. I still hear from them once a month when they check in to see how I am doing."

Captain King's story is interesting and all of us can learn from it. After his medical discharge, he immediately made a move to enter the civilian workforce. He did not just hang out for six months thinking about it. He interviewed with Coca-Cola and was hired after the first interview, which indicates how impressed the company must have been with the communication and leadership skills he learned in the army. After a year, he did some soul searching and found that working for someone else was not his thing. He returned to school for a master's in a field he liked, physical rehabilitation, and then started his own business in Wappingers Falls, New York, and named it Kings of Fitness, www.kingsoffitnesshv.com. Check it out.

It's a marvelous story and here is what we can learn from Captain King:

- Education must continue after discharge.
- Determine what you really like to do, and then do it.
- Take advantage of the many sources of help for veterans like the Wounded Warrior Project.

STARTING YOUR OWN BUSINESS

When you're thinking about starting your own business, look not only at local businesses you can start from your own home, but also at franchise opportunities that are military-friendly. Here's one franchise opportunity you may want to explore.

The Grilled Cheese Truck Inc., www.thegrilledcheesetruck.com. This Los Angeles-based company has plans to open franchised locations throughout the country. The company's franchise program is focused on the sale of franchises to US veterans, who will be among the first one hundred franchise owners of The Grilled Cheese Truck. As part of this strategy, the company recently announced an agreement with General Wesley Clark, a retired four-star general, to become the company's vice chairman and supervise the implementation of this national veteran franchise program.

Before moving on, read chapter 13. Here you will find guidelines and more information about starting your own business from scratch or by purchasing a franchise.

RESUME WRITING FOR VETERANS ENTERING THE CIVILIAN WORKFORCE

All workers seeking jobs have similar challenges. The same rules apply, even for writing a resume. Finding that first job is a daunting task for everyone, and you should follow the advice in this book and on my supporting website, www.firstjobsforcollegegrads.com.

Writing a resume for entry into the civilian workforce presents several challenges whether you hold a college degree or not. Construct a resume that makes sense to civilian hiring managers and human resources directors, most of whom have no military experience. Having little or no military experience means they will not be familiar with military jargon and acronyms that you considered second nature in the military. For example, the acronyms PFC (Private First Class), PO3 (Petty Officer 3rd Class), and SPECWARCOM (Special Warfare Command) will mean nothing to the civilian reader. In fact, the use of acronyms could be confusing and diminish your candidacy.

In the military, you used these acronyms on a daily basis and everyone knew what you were saying. In the civilian world, however, the acronyms mean little or nothing to many hiring managers.

Avoid Using Acronyms

When you write your resume, you can use acronyms, but only in parentheses following the actual word or phrase. For example, even what you assume everyone will know, like "USN (Ret)," could be meaningless to a civilian who never went past the Boy Scouts. The better way to state this would be "United States Navy, Retired (USN Ret)." Now everyone knows the meaning of the acronym. While many civilians would make a correct guess at the meaning of "USN (Ret)," there are other acronyms that would be very confusing. Here's an example:

On your resume, you will be listing the branch of service you were in and what your various assignments were. Let's assume that you were on special classified assignment with the United States Naval Special Warfare Command and you would like to include that on your resume. In military jargon, one would refer to your role in this elite branch of the navy as NAVSPECWARCOM. Everyone in the military knows the meaning of that acronym, but how about the human resources directors with Walmart? They would not have the slightest idea what that means. The proper way to present that on your resume in bullet format would be like this:

- Special classified assignment with the **United States Naval Special Warfare Command (NAVSPECWARCOM)**

The most junior human resources director will know what that means. Be sure to state your military training in detail on your resume. Do that by adding an addendum to your resume titled, "Military Training and Education." Highlight all of your field training and experience, all of your leadership roles, and all of the classes and academic courses you completed.

Do not get hung up on writing a resume. Hundreds of resume writing sources are on the Internet, and much of what you see is repetitious and confusing. Some professional resume writing services charge for advice and for constructing a resume. Just follow the rules for resume writing in chapter 15. Do not even think of paying someone to write a resume for you.

HELP FROM VETERANS ORGANIZATIONS

The list of nonprofit organizations offering assistance to returning military personnel is almost endless. Check the Internet frequently to learn who they are and what they can do for you. The following list will lead you in the right direction:

USO, www.uso.org. This organization was established in 1941 to assist military personnel on active duty and after discharge. There are USO facilities in twenty-six states plus Washington, DC, and overseas locations. All are dedicated to helping military personnel and their families with a variety of challenges and problems. In addition, the USO posts job openings on its website under "Career Opportunities." The last time I checked, there were thirteen posted jobs at different locations in the United States and abroad. Here is a list of the most frequently advertised jobs on the USO website:

- Regional Vice President
- Director of Operations
- Area Director
- Area Operations Manager
- Center Director
- Center Manager
- Duty Manager
- Information Specialist
- Programs Manager
- Programs Coordinator
- Administrative Assistant
- Mobile Program Manager
- Mobile Unit Manager
- Mobile Unit Coordinator
- Volunteer Coordinator
- Tours Manager
- Assistant Tours Manager

Check out these positions and the job descriptions. There may be something tailor-made for you.

Help for Wounded Veterans, www.oso.org. To help our wounded warriors and their families, the USO has launched Operation Enduring Care, a fund-raising campaign to bring aid to veterans wounded in action. This is a serious and unseen problem, as 40,000 men and women have been wounded physically in Iraq and Afghanistan, and more than 400,000 suffer from emotional wounds such as post-traumatic stress disorder. Unfortunately, the media has not done its fair share publicizing this problem. Do all you can to make this known by sending emails and tweets to your friends, congressional representatives, and the president. The USO website provides a link to all senators and representatives on the USO leadership team. All you need to do is click on their names to get into their websites. Voice your concerns and seek their aid.

To contribute to this worthy cause, click on www.uso.org, and then click on "Donations."

VFW, www.vfw.org. The VFW is one of the oldest veterans organizations, tracing its origins back to 1899. It has 1.9 million members who not only receive benefits and support, but also contribute their time on a voluntary basis to accomplish the objectives of the organization. The VFW has a powerful lobby group to keep members of Congress aware of the problems our military personnel face as the result of putting themselves in harm's way.

The VFW hosts an annual convention and participates in numerous patriotic functions throughout the nation. In addition, it is actively involved with many employment organizations to advertise the benefits of hiring vets. One such initiative involves the manufacturing sector of our economy that provides hands-on and managerial jobs to veterans.

GI Jobs, www.gijobs.com. For your general education about how to use your military experience in job hunting, this is a very helpful site. Included is a list of military-friendly colleges for those seeking a college degree. For example, click on "Military-Friendly Schools" and then click on "Arizona State University." Here you will find a special section titled, "Military Support."

US Department of Defense, www.defense.gov. This is a comprehensive site, so plan to spend quite a bit of time here. There are many jobs available with the Department of Defense and many opportunities are listed on this website.

Wounded Warrior Project (WWP), www.woundedwarriorproject. org. The Wounded Warrior Project works to raise awareness and enlist the public's aid for the needs of severely injured servicemen and servicewomen, help severely injured service members aid and assist each other, and provide unique, direct programs and services to meet their needs. Importantly, WWP also provides support for returning military personnel seeking civilian employment.

Yellow Ribbon Programs, www.yellowribbon.org. Yellow Ribbon programs counsel veterans and assist them in gaining funding and access to education programs ranging from associate's degrees to professional degrees. This is a far-ranging federal government program offering multiple options, and the place to begin exploring the program is on the following website: www.yellowribboneducationdecisions.com.

Military College Benefits, www.militaryeducationbdecisions.com. This website will help you navigate the education benefits you are entitled to receive for education. Check it out.

THE TOP ONE HUNDRED MILITARY-FRIENDLY EMPLOYERS

An important site to explore is Military Friendly, www.military-friendly.com, a department of Victory Media, a company dedicated to helping veterans find civilian employment. Review this website for a ranking of the best one hundred military-friendly employers in the US. Here you will find a description of these companies, along with their websites and a comprehensive description of their services for veterans. This is a great place to begin your job search.

So who are these military-friendly employers? They include a diverse group of companies, some of which are household names like McDonald's, General Electric, Lowe's, Verizon, and Hewlett-Packard. All of them are noted for valuing the skills and training that military personnel acquired while in service. Many have special training programs for veterans, and some even provide preferential treatment for military spouses. Two sectors I like are the manufacturers and the railroads.

Manufacturers

The National Association of Manufacturers is reaching out to help veterans as much as possible through a number of programs. The need for workers in the manufacturing sector is acute. According to the Institute for Veterans and Military Families (IVMF) at Syracuse University, there are an estimated 600,000 advanced manufacturing jobs unfilled in the US. More than 82 percent of manufacturers report they cannot find people to fill their skilled production jobs. Furthermore, up to 2.5 million manufacturing jobs will open up within five years as older workers retire.

Companies such as Alcoa, Boeing, Lockheed Martin, and General Electric are making a concerted effort to recruit veterans, and I urge you to contact these companies. Manufacturing companies are dead serious about hiring vets. Just these four companies alone have hired close to 65,000 veterans in the past ten years.

Railroad Companies

This booming industry is often overlooked by job seekers. According to the Association of American Railroads (AAR), some 500 companies and organizations in the railroad industry sought to hire about 5,000 veterans in 2012. These companies include freight carriers, intercity passenger and commuter railroads, and rail supply companies. As a growing number of current railroad employees look toward retirement, the number of job openings will begin to rise in future years. Ed Hamberger, president of the AAR, said, "Today, roughly 23 percent of the railroad workforce is eligible to retire by 2015."

Ray LaHood, former US Department of Transportation secretary, said that 25 percent of the industry's current employees are veterans. "Our veterans have the skills and real-life experiences that we need to help rebuild America," he said in a CNN interview.

HIGHLY RANKED MILITARY-FRIENDLY COMPANIES

Curious about other companies that value the skills and leadership traits of veterans? To get you started, here are the top ten ranked by AOL Jobs in cooperation with Career Builder:

1. United Services Automobile Association
2. United States Steel Corporation
3. Deloitte
4. Booz Allen Hamilton
5. Burlington Northern Sante Fe
6. ManTech International Corporation
7. Southern Company
8. Combined Insurance Company of America
9. General Electric
10. J. B. Hunt

Review the company websites and zero in on their career pages for job listings and advice for veterans.

Top-Rated Employers for Veterans to Explore
Here are ten employers you should definitely explore. My analysis of these companies has revealed that they have much to offer returning military personnel. Here you will find a variety of jobs spanning a variety of industries and companies.

Cleveland Clinic, www.my.clevelandclinic.org. Located in Cleveland, Ohio, this medical treatment center encourages returning military personnel to contact human resources for employment opportunities. It has a special category on its website for military, so check it out.

Lowe's, www.lowes.com. A WWII veteran, Carl Buchan, founded this major home supply company. Over the years, the company has taken good care of military personnel. Click on "Careers" and then on "Military" for more information and a listing of job opportunities. Lowe's is ranked #38 in GI Jobs' listing of the Top 100

Military-Friendly Employers. Lowe's boasts of having hired more than 14,000 veterans recently. In addition, Lowe's participates in the Military Spouse Employment Partnership, an initiative devoted to finding job opportunities for spouses of military personnel employed at Lowe's. Read more about it on the website.

United Rentals, www.unitedrentals.com. This is one of the largest tool and equipment rental companies in the world and offers many interesting opportunities for returning veterans. Under the "Careers" menu, click on "Military Recruiting." This company has great respect for the values and skills you learned in the military and is rated one of the best one hundred military-friendly employers. One of the testimonials is from Marc Elig, US Army, CW-4, who advises vets not to discount the skills learned in the military because companies like United Rentals will translate those skills into positions within the company.

USAA, www.ussa.com. United Services Automobile Association is a multiline insurer offering a variety of insurance products. Insurance is a booming business, and this nationwide insurer has reserved jobs in all departments of the company for returning vets. In addition, there are special programs for veterans and their spouses, such as those sponsored by the Junior Military Officer (JMO) program. The JMO program is designed to effectively transition JMOs into the company and provide the knowledge, skills, and awareness needed for a potential USAA leadership career. You will find sixteen program opportunities, each relating to a specific functional area within USAA.

Verizon, www.verizon.net. The country's largest wireless carrier offers employment opportunities in all states and is at the forefront of all forms of digital communication.

IHG, www.ihg.com. The Intercontinental Hotels Group includes famous names like Holiday Inn, Holiday Inn Express,

Intercontinental Hotels, Crown Plaza, and others. When you find the careers page, click on "Job Search," and then click on "Create a Profile." From the menu, click on "View Veterans Jobs." Here you will find more than 1,000 jobs listed by job title and location, both domestic and international.

Disney, www.disney.com. Go to the website, click on the "Careers" button, and then on "Working Here." Then click on "Heroes Work Here," and you will find a wealth of information about initiatives Disney offers to help returning military personnel get started on a meaningful career. You will see quotes from veterans about their work experience at Disney in a variety of positions involving finance, sales, security, and technology.

General Mills, www.generalmills.com. This is one of the leading food companies in the world and is based in Minneapolis. The company has offices in most major US locations. Click on the General Mills website for details about its help for veterans and for job listings.

Qualcomm, www.qualcomm.com. This company is a global semiconductor designer and a manufacturer and marketer of digital wireless telecommunications products. It is one of the best in the business and has been around since 1985, which is a long time in the digital technology business. Qualcomm is based in San Diego and employs 30,000 workers. Qualcomm has collaborated with Manpower San Diego to provide a number of information technology scholarships, exclusively for returning military personnel who served in Iraq and Afghanistan. Check with Manpower San Diego and Qualcomm human resources for more information about this and other programs for veterans.

Boeing, www.boeing.com. Rick Stephens, a Boeing senior vice president and marine corps veteran, said that Boeing has hired 3,000 veterans in the past two years. Boeing will need thousands of additional workers as orders for the new 757 Dreamliner keep pouring in. By the way, tune out the media noise on the lithium ion battery problems. Boeing solved this problem, and the Dreamliners are safe and back in the air. Land a job with this company and you will be a happy person.

General Electric, www.generalelectric.com. GE has announced that it plans to hire at least 1,000 returning military personnel this year. It is one of the world's largest manufacturers of products as diverse as jet engines and batteries.

Lockheed Martin, www.lockheedmartin.com. When you open this website, the first thing to hit you will be a close-up of the new F-35 jet fighter. It's worth the trip to the website just to see this new fighting machine. Click on "Careers," and the first heading is "Separating Military Personnel." What a great place to begin exploring Lockheed for exciting job opportunities. Click on "Transitioning Military" for an exciting ride to what may be your next job. As one of our largest defense contractors, Lockheed is one of the friendliest of employers for military personnel.

Walmart, www.walmart.com. Walmart has pledged to hire 100,000 veterans during the next five years. William Simon, president and CEO, recently said, "Let's be clear: hiring a veteran can be one of the best decisions any of us can make. These are leaders with discipline, training, and a passion for service."

The Blackstone Group, www.blackstone.com. This company is one of the world's leading investment and financial advisory firms and is headquartered in New York City. It has eight regional offices spread throughout the country and has offices abroad as well. Blackstone describes itself as "an alternative asset manager company" and its business includes "the management of corporate private equity funds, real estate opportunity funds, hedge funds, mezzanine funds, senior debt vehicles, proprietary hedge funds, and closed-end mutual funds." Blackstone recently announced its intention to focus on the aerospace and defense industries and has already appointed a senior executive, Jim Albaugh, to manage this operation. He had been CEO and president of Boeing Commercial Airplanes. CEO Stephen Schwarzman announced in April 2013 that Blackstone plans to hire 50,000 military veterans during the next five years. It has established a management training program, which is already up and running, and has partnered with President Obama, First Lady Michelle Obama, and Vice President Biden to implement a nationwide initiative called "Joining Forces" to encourage private companies to hire and train military personnel. The New York City phone number is (212) 583-5000. Call and ask for instructions on how to contact the hiring managers for their various departments. This may take some time, but stick with it until you find the right person.

Costco, www.costco.com. One of the largest companies in the world has made a commitment to hiring returning military personnel. We are not talking about cashier jobs or shelf-stocking jobs. Costco employs 174,000 workers, most working behind the scene in real estate, finance, marketing, technology, supply chain management, purchasing, construction, and human resources.

Evaluating an employer is an important task, and it takes time. It is worth the effort because you do not want to work with a company whose products and culture are not compatible with your agenda. For more help on evaluating a company, see chapter 23.

MILITARY-FRIENDLY COLLEGES AND LAW SCHOOLS

Many colleges and universities across the US are mindful of the challenges faced by veterans and have stepped up with substantial financial aid and counseling programs. When you contact the admissions departments at the colleges you are exploring, always discuss the programs offered for military personnel. You will be pleasantly surprised to learn about the substantial financial aid programs for veterans.

Help for veterans has come at a professional level, too. The following law schools have made special provisions to help vets with tuition, room, and board. Do not overlook these opportunities.

Law Schools Offering Special Help for Vets

1. Stanford Law School, www.law.stanford.edu
2. New York University School of Law, www.law.nyu.edu
3. Columbia Law School, www.law.columbia.edu.
4. Duke University School of Law, www.law.duke.edu
5. Northwestern University Law School, www.law.northwestern.edu
6. UC Berkeley School of Law, www.law.berkeley.edu
7. Harvard Law School, www.law.harvard.edu
8. Fordham Law School, www.law.fordham.edu

Many law schools work with the government-sponsored Yellow Ribbon programs that provide qualifying veterans with additional money to supplement GI Bill funding. Veterans, I urge you to explore these opportunities even though you might not have the educational prerequisites for law school admission. Contact all or some of these schools to learn what it takes to gain admission and if the legal field sparks your interest. Act on the advice you get from counselors. One day you may be arguing cases before the Supreme Court.

GOING FORWARD

Job hunting is a job in itself for candidates with or without a military background. The processes are the same, but military experience can be a big plus for your candidacy. There are several important rules to follow as you begin a search for civilian employment:

- A job is not going to fall out of the sky for anyone who sends a resume to a potential employer. The key point to remember is that hiring authorities do not hire military resumes, tweets, text messages or YouTube videos. They hire living human beings who had the smarts to meet with them personally to build a relationship. The main objective of submitting a resume is to get to the next step, a personal interview.

- Your successful military experience was the result of applying your intelligence, energy, and passion to complete a particular project. Do the same in your search for employment.
- Nothing just happens. Success is the result of planning and follow-through. Plan your work. Work your plan.
- Do not rely completely on technology to find your civilian job. Use it creatively but not exclusively. The best digital tool for job-hunting is LinkedIn.

CHAPTER TAKEAWAYS

- *Your military experience and training are of value to employers in all industries.*
- *Write your resume using civilian terminology, not military acronyms.*
- *Plan your work. Work your plan.*
- *Continue your education.*

JOB HUNTER'S LIBRARY

Thomas Ricks, *The Generals*, Penguin Press, 2012. This book reviews the reorganization of high-level military staff begun by General George Marshall before WWII. Leadership skills articulated in this book apply to the military and the civilian business world.

Colin Powell, *It Worked for Me*, Harper, 2013.

Chesley "Sully" Sullenberger, *Making a Difference*, William Morrow, 2012.

PART 4

WRITTEN COMMUNICATION: WRITE IT RIGHT!

Chapter 15

Writing a Resume and a Career Profile

The common wisdom is that your resume is the most important document for finding that first job. This is an outdated assumption. Submit only a resume to a prospective employer and you are just another look-alike candidate. Companies receive large quantities of resumes for each job posted. Remember, the US has a workforce of 155 million people, which generates a lot of action on the hiring front.

Workers in our economy move from job to job, and companies are always adjusting the size of their workforces. Workers are always on the move, too, for a variety of reasons. In fact, I take notice when I see a candidate who has more than five continuous years of employment with the same company on his or her resume. This is a positive checkpoint for your candidacy.

Candidates come to companies through job boards and social networks like Monster and LinkedIn, from recruiters, and from referrals. Large companies like Google, Caterpillar, and Microsoft receive upwards of 75,000 resumes per week in response to their job postings. Other large companies like Southwest Airlines have similar statistics.

In 2011, Southwest received 193,000 new resumes but hired only 4,300 new employees. Walmart hires 600,000 new employees each year and has a turnover rate of 44 percent, similar to that of other large retail companies. When Google posts a job on its website for a web designer, the company receives thousands of resumes in response from candidates in the US and foreign countries.

Keeping these numbers in mind, assume that you submit a run-of-the-mill resume in response to a Google posting and anxiously wait for a response. A week goes by and you get nothing in return, or maybe just a perfunctory, "We received your resume. Thanks." Six weeks transpire, and nothing. Three months? Nothing. Six months? Nothing. I know it's discouraging, but let's consider the odds. If 5,000 candidates submit similar resumes for the Google position, your chances of connecting are slim. What will make your candidacy different from the other 4,999 candidates? Is there anything you can do short of camping out at the doorstep of the company hiring manager? Yes, there is. It is a package of documents about you and your candidacy that I call the *career profile*.

THE CAREER PROFILE

The career profile replaces the stand-alone resume. It is the written version of who you are. In an ideal world, all candidates would be interviewed personally. There would be no phone screenings and no Skype interviews. It would be a face-to-face meeting where the hiring manager and candidate chat for an hour or two and get to know each other on a personal level. But that doesn't happen in today's world.

Time is of the essence in the business world, and hiring managers do all they can to shorten the hiring process, even hiring temp workers to screen resumes using the key word "technique." If your resume does not contain a sufficient number of company-defined "key words," your resume is discarded. Also, some large companies use digital screening software to evaluate your resume. You have no idea what key words and phrases the company has written into the screening program. That's why I advocate submitting more than a resume and why I advocate sending your credentials only to a named person with a job title and never to a box number or "staffing assistant."

How to Use the Career Profile

I designed the career profile to make your candidacy a compelling alternative to candidates who persist in the old way, which is sending only a resume to an unknown entity. How do you use it? When you submit your candidacy, you send a package of documents instead of just your resume. It will communicate the full range of your experience, expertise, education, and general background. It will distinguish your candidacy from the rest of the pack. Here are the six documents in your career profile:

1. Resume
2. Cover Letter
3. College transcript
4. Letters of reference or commendation for outstanding performance
5. Business and technology certifications
6. Your articles and blogs that have been published or posted to highlight your written skills

Don't you think the career profile will be more impressive to prospective employers than just another look-alike resume? Let's examine each part of the career profile, beginning with the resume.

THE RESUME AND HOW TO WRITE IT

Job candidates spend hundreds of hours writing the *perfect* resume based upon advice from peers, parents, college professors, and a variety of online resources. When you say "resume" everyone provides liberal suggestions and advice, believing their way is the best way. While some of this input may have value, most of it is redundant or based on personal experience, which may be outdated.

Even college professors get into the act and give advice to college students that has no relevance in the business world. For example, they call the resume a curriculum vitae, a term used only by the academic establishment. Do not refer to your resume as a CV. In the business world, it is still called a resume.

My advice for resume writing is based on my experience as an executive recruiter working in the employment industry every day. If you follow my instructions, you will construct a first-class resume that reflects what is current and acceptable in the business world. If you want confirmation, review a few online resume websites. One that I like best is Career Confidential at www.careerconfidential. com. The CEO, Peggy McKee, is one of the best in the business, and I suggest that you attend one of her many webinars, the cost of which is very attractive: *free.*

Professional Resume Writers

What about those professional resume writing services that charge $25 to $200 for designing your resume? If these resume-writing gurus sell their services, they must be good, right? Save your money. What you'll find here is all you need to write a first-class resume. Spend that money to attend a trade show or conference where you will find hundreds of hiring managers in person. You and I know this is money well spent because landing a job is a matter of building a personal relationship with hiring managers and other influential company workers like the director of human resources. The resume is only one of the tools at your disposal to reach the next step, the personal interview.

General Rules for Writing Your Resume

I have reviewed thousands of resumes. Few are outstanding. Many are just okay. And some are too cute. Cute resumes contain too many unnecessary stylistic mistakes like a nonstandard typeface, multiple colors, clip art, pictures, borders, and other design features. The basic rule is this: *Keep it simple. Keep it clean.* Remember, this is business communication, not a promotion piece for homecoming, and certainly not a menu for a French restaurant.

Recruiters working in the staffing business every day know how a resume should look, and they can tell you what mistakes to avoid. Here are the five most common mistakes candidates make on resumes:

Five Common Resume Mistakes

1. *Typos.* Correct spelling is your responsibility, not the spell-checker's responsibility. Later in this chapter, I will tell you about poor Patti from St. Louis to illustrate the importance of correct spelling.
2. *Grammar Mistakes.* Hiring managers expect grammatically correct resumes from college graduates. Make a mistake and you are finished. There is no second chance.
3. *Inconsistent Formatting and Style.* Use only one typeface and type size.
4. *Missing Metrics.* Quantify as much as possible. Generalities say nothing about your expertise or accomplishments.
5. *Gaps in Employment History.* You do have a work history, even though it may consist of part-time jobs during your college years. Make sure these are in chronological order.

The Purpose of a Resume

The resume has only one purpose: to take you to the next step, the personal interview. Everything else is secondary. In other words, the resume is a marketing and sales tool. You are selling yourself, your value to the employer, your background and experience, your academic record, your professional work experience, your intelligence, your energy, your passion, and your aspirations. It is not rocket science, and you need not spend $200 to get it done.

Resume Features That You Must Get Right

Resume File Name. This is one of the most important parts of your resume and one that is frequently overlooked. The file name must be brief and to the point so the reader will understand without hesitation who you are and what the file is all about. This is how your file name should be stated: Jerome Michaels. Ford Motors: Marketing Associate Candidate

Resume Length. The resume for an entry-level candidate and a resume for a candidate with twenty years of experience are obviously going to differ in length. Appearance, style, and format, however, are the same for all candidates. Length of resume for all entry-level candidates should be no more than two pages. However, for workers with, say, ten to twenty years of experience that includes executive-level positions and possibly publications, the resume could be three or four pages, or more.

Resume Appearance. Your resume is your personal appearance, in written form. Think of it as the way you would dress for a live interview: uncluttered and neat. Hiring managers are not interested in your picture, graphs, boxed items, borders, charts, shading, and clip art. Resist the temptation to include your picture on the resume even though you think you look like Miss or Mister America. You will see what we mean about the clean look in the next chapter.

Resume Formatting. Consistency is key from beginning to end. Use bullet points consisting of only one line instead of paragraphs in the body of the resume. Use only one typeface and size. The usual business font, the one that I see most frequently in business communication, is 12-point. Times New Roman. Use uppercase bold for major headings and lowercase regular type for text. Do not use a script typeface, like *Segoe Script*, under any circumstances. The typeface is not the tool to differentiate your candidacy from the rest of the pack.

Resume Style. Resume styles change over time. Today, readers are conditioned to view content in small bits and pieces. They lose interest when confronted with long paragraphs. Save that for your first novel. The way we convey information in the digital world is to construct the resume using bullet points instead of paragraphs, with one exception. The first major heading of your resume, "Objective" or "Summary," should be in paragraph form but not to exceed about six lines. Everything else should be listed in bullet points. See the sample resume in chapter 16.

Sometimes you will see "Summary" used instead of "Objective." "Objective" should be used when you are applying for a specific job, and "Summary" should be used if you are submitting your resume to a human resources director to make this key person aware of your search for an unspecified position in the company.

Resume Spelling. This may seem like a no-brainer, but I'm including it because I have seen too many spelling errors on resumes. A spelling error is nothing short of a job-killer. Make a spelling error and your candidacy is finished before you are even considered. You get no second chances. There is more on this topic later in the chapter under the major heading Spell Checkers. Do not miss it.

Resume Metrics. One of the most common mistakes candidates make is to list their bullet point achievements using broad generalities like, "Responded to a large number of customer service calls." The statement means much more to the hiring manager if it reads, "Responded to forty customer service calls per day over a three-month period."

The Major Headings of Your Resume

All resumes are constructed using the same general format: major headings under which follow bullet points listing the particulars. Here are the major parts of your resume:

1. Personal Identification
2. Objective or Summary
3. Work Experience
4. Awards, Recognition, Community Service
5. Technology Skills
6. Education

That is it. No "References on Request." No "Hobbies and Special Interests." Here's a review of each major heading with an explanatory note. You will find a sample resume in the following chapter, and I suggest referring to it as you read the following material.

IDENTIFICATION. The first item on your resume, at the top of the page and centered, is your name, address, phone number, and email address. Use only one phone number, the one that you use most frequently for both inbound and outbound calls. Remember that calls regarding employment matters come at all hours. The 9 a.m. to 5 p.m. window is no longer valid. Your address must include your street number, town, and zip code. Your name should be first, in uppercase bold. Beneath your name is the address, phone number, and email address in lowercase, regular type.

Recently, I have received resumes without an address, only a name, a phone number, a Twitter hash tag, and an email address. This is the result of a mistaken idea by tech gurus who believe that in a digital world, where you live is not important. Tell that to a human resources director and you are history. Do not buy into the hype. Use common sense. Always include your address.

OBJECTIVE or SUMMARY. This is nothing more than a marketing piece about the product you are selling: yourself. Write this in paragraph format and limit your self-advertisement to about six lines. In the next chapter, I will give you a sample summary.

A different objective should be written for each application to reflect the qualifications and requirements in the job description. Specifically, state your work expertise in terms that coincide with the job in question. Use key words from the job description and remember that the reader is thinking, "What can this person do for the hiring manager and the company going forward?" If there is just a general statement on a company website under careers that reads, "Customer Service Representative," think about what this position requires: excellent verbal and written skills. Build your statement around that premise.

There is no need to state your age or number of years in college, or to say something like, "seeking entry-level position." Rather, state specifically the position for which you are applying. "I am applying for the Associate Finance Manager position." If appropriate, quantify your experience. Once more, metrics are important. For example, if you are applying for an editorial position, state, "My written communication experience includes three years of writing full-page reviews of sporting events for the bimonthly college newspaper." In your cover letter you can elaborate on that experience.

WORK EXPERIENCE. Many of you will be seeking your first "real world" job, and as such have no full-time work experience. It is a frustrating problem, so what do you include under this heading? First, you probably have had a number of part-time positions that include the usual suspects, like retail work, landscaping, child care, and possibly an internship with a for-profit or nonprofit company. What should be included? Anything that relates most closely to the position for which you are applying. List all for-profit companies and nonprofit companies for which you worked during the school year, or summer months, or holiday breaks. Make this a chronological listing beginning with your most recent experience. Here's an example:

Educational Testing Service (ETS). Summer internship program working as Social Media Coordinator Assistant. June–September, 2015.

Run for the Cure. A nonprofit organization raising money for breast cancer research. Candidate Organizer. June–September, 2013, 2014.

To explain what you did at these companies, state three or four of your accomplishments and/or responsibilities. Below is an example. Note that each bullet point contains a specific metric, not a broad generality.

> *Educational Testing Service (ETS).* Summer internship program working as Social Media Coordinator Assistant. June–September, 2015.
>
> - Wrote Twitter feeds for dissemination to 500 school district superintendents.
> - Conducted LinkedIn searches for 15 job openings and supplied 75 qualified candidates.
> - Based on performance, offered three-month summer internship with ETS in 2016.

AWARDS, RECOGNITION, COMMUNITY SERVICE. This is a section not often found on resumes, but I encourage its inclusion based on my experience with hiring managers. I have noted that one of the first things that a hiring manger will see when scanning a resume is a major heading listing awards and recognition for outstanding achievement.

What do you include? Go back to your high school years and write a list of any citations you received for superlative performance. It could have been a certificate stating, "The Most Promising Politician in the Class of 2005." In college, it could have been making the Dean's List or graduating *cum laude.* You may have been given a bonus by the manager of the local Dairy Queen for selling a high quantity of ice cream over an eight-week period.

As for community service, many hiring managers and human resources directors will give you a big plus mark for your give-back to those in need. Many companies, like Starbucks, Microsoft, and

Bank of America, are community conscious and have their employees participate in outreach efforts. This section of your resume might look like this:

> ## AWARDS, RECOGNITION, COMMUNITY SERVICE
>
> - *Washington High School.* Written certificate from the principal: "Superlative Community Services Award, 2005."
> - *University of Wisconsin.* Received a written citation for achievement as, "Outstanding Sports Photography Award, 2012."
> - *Miami Herald Newspaper.* Published my article on the Opinion Page titled, "The Use of Twitter in the 2012 Presidential Campaign."
> - *University of Massachusetts, Amherst.* Dean's List, 2011, 2012, 2013.
> - *Montgomery County MD School District.* Spanish Literacy Program Volunteer, 2014.

Do you see how much this adds to your resume? In very specific terms, it tells the hiring manager who you are and what you have accomplished. With little full-time work experience, you need to flesh out your persona using every means possible.

TECHNOLOGY SKILLS. In today's world, we assume that college graduates have the technology skills required to be productive workers. However, hiring managers have been burned many times because of this false assumption. In other chapters of this book, I have highly recommended that you take an online course from HigherNext to obtain your Technology Certification Degree as verifiable proof to a hiring manager that you are up to speed. This is the place on your resume to include that achievement. It adds a reassuring amount of certainty about your technology skills. Absent a HigherNext certification (or other online certification), make a comprehensive list of your technology skills. Here is an example:

TECHNOLOGY SKILLS

- Social Media: Twitter, Facebook, LinkedIn, Indeed
- Personal Productivity: Word, Sage/Act, MS Excel, PowerPoint
- Programming: BASIC, Java, HTML

No matter what the job or industry, you will be required to use technology to meet your job requirements. If, for some reason, your technology skills are lacking, take online technology courses or courses at your local community college to enhance your candidacy.

EDUCATION. This is the last major heading on your resume and it is very straightforward. Chronologically list your college education and other professional development courses or courses of interest. Here is how this section should look:

EDUCATION

- Elon University, Elon, NC. Major: Events Management. Minor: Communications, 2013.
- Elon University Study Abroad in Art History Program, Florence, Italy, 2011.
- The International Culinary Center, New York City. Graduate level courses in Pastry Arts and Cake Design, 2010, 2011.
- HigherNext, Philadelphia, PA. Online Certified Business Laureate Degree, 2013.

The major heading, "Education," is the final part of your resume. Add nothing else here such as hobbies, references, favorite sports, ethnicity, gender, religion, or age.

THE COVER LETTER AND HOW TO WRITE IT

The purpose of a cover letter is frequently misunderstood. Google the words "cover letter" and you will get thousands of hits relating to every conceivable nuance of the term. However, the most important thing to remember about the cover letter is this: it is just one of the items in your career profile. Along with the other documents, it has a primary purpose: to take you to the next step, the personal interview with the hiring manager.

In chapter 17, I will go into detail on the cover letter and provide a sample. Do not lose sleep over this document. It is straightforward and easy to write with a little forethought and planning . . . and with a little help from this book.

YOUR COLLEGE TRANSCRIPT

Obtaining your college transcript is a task easily completed online. I conducted an online survey of five colleges and universities, and all but one offered transcripts bearing the institution's official seal, free of charge. Only one of my five survey targets, the University of Arizona, charged a $10 fee for obtaining the transcript online. If you order online, the processing time usually takes about two weeks. Plan ahead.

Why do I think the transcript should be a part of the career profile? In my recruiting business I have observed a growing trend toward college verification, mainly because of several high-profile cases where candidates outright lied about their academic credentials.

In one instance, the multinational recruiting firm, Heidrick & Struggles, a company with impeccable credentials, submitted a candidate for the presidency of a major company. The candidate was hired, but after several months a member of its board of directors began to question the new president's credentials relating to technology expertise. A subsequent investigation revealed that the candidate had intentionally misrepresented his master's degree credential. He stated under the education section of his resume that he had been awarded a master's degree in information technology in a particular year from a well-known university. The company and the Heidrick recruiter conducted an investigation and learned that in the year stated on the resume, the university did not even offer a master's degree in information technology. Ultimately, the president was fired, and Heidrick was embarrassed and returned its recruiting fee.

Transcripts and GPA. Adding an official transcript to your career profile not only adds to your personal credibility, but also provides you with a segue to highlight certain parts of your academic achievements related to the position in question. For example, if your overall GPA was 3.0 but 3.9 in your major, business administration, you could point out your business aptitude in your cover letter. This could be a deal-maker if you are applying for a position in finance and the hiring manager notes your sterling performance in business courses. The manager might not care if you had only a C+ average in your required social science courses.

LETTERS OF REFERENCE OR COMMENDATION FOR OUTSTANDING PERFORMANCE

This part of your career profile adds to your credibility as an entry-level job candidate. When a job candidate submits a reference letter, I always read it and sometimes follow up with a phone call or email to the individual who wrote it if I have any questions or if I need additional information. Once again, this document builds credibility, something that you need as an inexperienced worker.

The question you might have is, "Who do I ask to write this letter for me?" It is a valid question because you may not have a former boss to vouch for your good qualities. My suggestion is to begin with a professor in your major subject who thought highly of your work and commended you for excellent academic performance. Next in line would be your college advisor, if you did indeed have one.

Other references could be the person to whom you reported in one of your part-time jobs or in your community outreach ventures. If you played on any college sports teams, you could ask your coach for a letter of recommendation attesting to your strong team-building skills. Request your reference to comment on your strongest suit, your verbal and written communication skills, for example, and to highlight a project that you initiated and completed satisfactorily.

How many letters of reference do you include in the career profile? One or two at this stage of your job search. A potential employer who has made you an offer might request additional references, and at that time, you can solicit more from similar sources. I advise that you have more references lined up to meet that eventuality.

BUSINESS AND TECHNOLOGY CERTIFICATIONS

One of the most impressive documents in the career profile is a written business or technology certification from an online provider like HigherNext (www.highernext.com). This is particularly important for arts, humanities, and education majors. You will be competing with business and STEM majors, and you need these certifications to enhance your credibility. Usually these online certifications are inexpensive and can be completed in a relatively brief period of time. I suggest that you get busy with this now. You are going to need business and technology skill certification because you are now in business for yourself. Your work life is your own personal business. You are the CEO. (Review chapter 5 about certification.)

ARTICLES OR BLOGS YOU'VE PUBLISHED OR POSTED

Written communication is one of the key check marks on every candidate's profile, and how better to show these skills to a hiring manager than to include something that you have created and have had published either online or in print. I cannot emphasize enough the importance of correct written communication in the business world, and I will tell you a true story to emphasize the point.

Melody from Chicago. When I was editor in chief with a major publishing company, I frequently reviewed documents written by our consultants or sales reps. Most of these documents were well written, but what happened one day almost knocked me off my chair. Melody, one of our consultants who held a PhD in science education from the University of Chicago, asked me to review a post-sale instructional document for our K–6 science program, which had been adopted by a large school district. I had heard Melody make product presentations and her verbal skills were phenomenal. When she gave me her document for review, I was ready for a good read. What I found was shocking and left me wondering how the University of Chicago could have awarded a PhD to someone so lacking in written skills. Her document had errors in grammar and spelling, and just made no sense whatsoever. It was truly a word-salad. I did a total rewrite, motivated by the fact that the content was related to a curriculum area for which I was responsible. Her written document was going to be disseminated to hundreds of teachers and had to be perfect.

If you have any published blogs or articles, be sure to include them in your career profile. Of course, be sure that what you submit is perfect in every respect. Written communication is very exacting. Unlike verbal communication, where you can make midstream corrections, a written document is out there for everyone to see. Your article or blog does not have to be great-American-novel quality. It can be plain vanilla, interesting, or entertaining but serve as an example to the hiring manager that you are a literate person who can deliver written communications that will be a benefit to the company going forward.

WRITING A DIGITAL PROFILE

The digital profile for media such as LinkedIn or Twitter is similar in many respects to the resume. Its main characteristics are brevity and clarity. For example, with Twitter you have only 140 characters to tell who you are and what you want, so you must be creative. In today's digital world, it is important to get this right. Right now, you have much to do in preparation for your job search, like finding out where and when the next trade show is coming to the convention center near your home. I will guide you through the digital profile in chapter 16. Stick around.

SPELL-CHECKERS

I'm including this section on spell-checkers because I have seen many spelling errors on all types of written documents. This is often due to the assumption that the spell-checker will make everything right. Nothing could be further from the truth. Here's a real-life example:

Poor Patti from St. Louis. Patti was a worker with considerable communication skills. She worked in product development for a company producing testing and assessment products for the K–12 market. She had risen from an entry-level position to supervising manager and was ready for the next step ahead, a director-level position.

A Boston-based company was conducting a search for a director of professional services, and Patti was perfect for the job. The base salary was $135,000 plus a bonus of

$65,000, making the total annual compensation $200,000. In addition, the job carried an attractive benefits package. Patti revised her resume several times until she felt it was right for the position and I agreed. I told her to do a minor tweak on one section of her resume, run it through the spelling-and-grammar checker, proofread the document, and then submit it to the human resources director and the hiring manager.

The response from the company was devastating for Patti. The human resources director and the hiring manager told Patti they were rejecting her candidacy because of a spelling error on the resume. Patti lost the $200,000 job, not because she lacked written communication skills. She lost it because the spell-checker did not do its job. Apparently, Patti had failed to proofread her resume aloud before submitting it.

All of us have come to trust the spelling-and-grammar checker without question because it saves time. After all, this is a product made by Microsoft, so you should be able to trust its worthiness implicitly. Wrong! Not all spell-checkers are created equal. For example, I have found that the 2010 Word spell-checker is close to a disaster. It misreads text, makes erroneous grammatical corrections, and in fact misses simple misspellings. Recently, I was proofreading one of my own documents that contained the proper noun Bill. In my haste, I had spelled it Blill, but twice the spell-checker did not make the correction. Ironically, the 2003 Word spell-checker was much better, in fact, close to perfect.

CHAPTER TAKEAWAYS

- *Written documents must be perfect. You do not get a second chance.*

- *Don't trust the spelling-and-grammar checker. Before submitting any written document, read it aloud and then have an impartial third person do the same.*
- *Submitting a stand-alone resume for a job is risky. You need to submit your multi-document career profile to make your candidacy stand out from the rest of the pack.*

Chapter 16

A Sample Resume and Digital Profile

I have combined the sample resume and digital profile into one chapter because each must be a mirror image of the other for consistency. You need to have a resume and digital profile that talk the same language. Employers evaluating your candidacy will find every bit of information about you by conducting a Google search under your name. Everyone's life seems to be an open book these days. That's just the way it is, so we need to get into the game.

The first thing a human resources director and a hiring manger will do after reading your resume is to review social media to learn more about you. They will notice your Twitter images and tagline describing who you are. Next, they will look at Facebook, then LinkedIn, and after that, Indeed. The list goes on and will increase as time passes.

CONSISTENCY: PORTRAYING THE REAL YOU

If your Twitter picture was taken when you were a sophomore drinking beer on the beach, your Facebook picture is from your high school prom, and your LinkedIn picture is of you in business attire, the hiring manager might well ask, "Will the real Michael Hopkins please stand up?" Your profile must be consistent throughout if you want to advance through the hiring process.

I have noted that some online as well as print sources are saying that you no longer need a traditional resume. One source says, "Nowadays, you no longer need a multipage resume that includes lengthy, bullet-pointed lists of all your past working experiences. A paragraph-long summary is enough to get by in the modern job-search market." Nothing could be further from the truth, and I advise that you totally disregard such advice. It makes no sense whatsoever. The resume is still the document in chief, and you must get it right.

Let's review the major parts of your resume before looking at a sample that you can use for preparing your own. Please do not pay good money to a resume writing service to construct this document for you. Write your resume following the sample, and you will have a major part of your career profile completed.

THE MAJOR HEADINGS OF YOUR RESUME

All resumes are constructed using the same general format of major headings under which follow bullet points listing the particulars. Here are the major parts of your resume. For a full description of each major heading, refer to chapter 15.

1. Personal Identification
2. Objective or Summary
3. Work Experience
4. Awards, Recognition, Community Service
5. Technology Skills
6. Education

That's it, just those six major headings. Do not add "References on Request" or "Hobbies and Special Interests." If you want to discuss these add-ons, do so in the personal interview.

<u>The Sample Resume</u>

PAUL SILVESTRI
10124 South Komensky Ave.
Chicago, IL 60692
312-450-1200
psilvestri@saturn.com

OBJECTIVE

I am a *cum laude* college graduate with a major in Marketing Communications applying for the *Assistant Online Marketing Manager* position with Starbucks. My profile includes experience and training in online marketing, technology skills, and excellent verbal and written skills. Positive attributes include team player, technology savvy (including Web-programming languages), bottom-line oriented, basic proficiency in Spanish, working knowledge with social media, and self-starter. I'm ready and eager to begin work with Starbucks immediately to make a positive impact on your bottom line.

WORK EXPERIENCE

South Side City Bank. Summer Internship. May 2012–September 2012.

- Wrote 20 online customer service messages per week for late mortgage payments.
- Mentored by MarCom Director to handle live customer calls for interest rate quotes. Averaged 10 calls per week.
- Constructed risk management portfolios for 10 local small businesses.

City of Chicago. Interim Parking Meter Collector. June 2013–August 2013.

- Vacation-relief collector covering 20 square blocks in busy commercial area.
- Collections averaged $2,000 per day.
- Volunteered for overtime work. Averaged 10 extra hours per week at double-time pay.

DePaul University. Assistant to the Dean of Admissions. School years 2011, 2012, 2013.

- Reviewed incoming applications for admission using written department standards for evaluation. Averaged 50 scans per week for 6 months during each year.
- Acting Administrative Assistant to the Dean during vacation periods for full-time staff.

AWARDS, RECOGNITION, COMMUNITY SERVICE

- Lane High School. Senior Class Vice President.
- DePaul University. Dean's List for academic achievement, 2011, 2012, 2103.
- DePaul University. "Certificate of Accomplishment" for website design competition.
- Chicago School District 12. Volunteer Technology Skills Teacher. Weekends, 2011.

TECHNOLOGY SKILLS

- Proficiency with PowerPoint, Word, Excel, ACT/ SAGE.
- Working knowledge of social media, including

LinkedIn, Twitter, Facebook, Indeed, Simply Hired.
- Programming skills include basic-level JavaScript, HTML, Basic, MySQL, and PHP.

EDUCATION

- *DePaul University, Chicago, IL.* BS *cum laude*, Marketing Communications. 2013.
- *HigherNext.* Business and Technology Certification. 2013.
- *Rosetta Stone.* Online courses in basic and intermediate Spanish. 2012, 2013.

WRITING A DIGITAL PROFILE TO USE WITH SOCIAL MEDIA

This document is used with employment-focused social media like LinkedIn. You can think of it as a condensed version of your resume. You may need to make modifications required by the medium on which it will be posted. For example, Twitter allows only 140 words, which is not sufficient to tell your entire story, so you must be creative. (However, I do not recommend using Twitter as a main tool for your job search. Go back to chapter 9 if you still have questions.) The social media in question will define the format of your profile and even limit its length. When constructing your profile, have your written resume at your side and use it as a guide.

LinkedIn is the most frequently used social medium by human resources directors and hiring managers. I suggest that you complete the LinkedIn profile first and then move on to others. In my experience, LinkedIn has proved to be the go-to place for online job hunting, job-market networking, and establishing a digital presence. However, it is important to remember that LinkedIn is only a tool for taking you to the most important level in the job-hunting process, the personal interview. Everything else is secondary to that objective. Why? Because companies do not hire resumes, profiles, and tweets. They hire actual human beings who had the smarts to establish a personal relationship with key employees like hiring managers and human resources directors.

The LinkedIn Profile

To expand the productivity of my executive recruiting business, I have used LinkedIn extensively and find it valuable for locating key hiring managers and job candidates. This is a site for working professionals like college graduates seeking their first jobs. The LinkedIn profile for my recruiting company, Weiss & Associates, Executive Recruiting, is intentionally brief and bare bones. I have found that brevity is good. According to LinkedIn, my profile was the fifth most frequently visited site in 2012. You do not need to write more than is necessary to get the job done. There's more on LinkedIn in chapter 9.

I know that many of you are already on LinkedIn, but for the uninitiated, let me review the major parts of this popular medium. You might find it helpful to open LinkedIn as you read this material. The first place to go is to the help center, which you can access by clicking on the "Help Center" menu. You will find many suggestions for getting started and a list of useful free webinars and videos.

The Parts of a LinkedIn Profile

1. *Your Picture.* This is where some college-grad job hunters still insist on making fools of themselves by posting an image that is out of sync with the adult world of work. I will

not go into a litany of "do not's." Just look at a few dozen images of LinkedIn members and you will get the picture.

Your picture should be business professional, which means no rings in your nose, beads on your tongue or eyelashes, no tattoos, no orange or purple hair, no T-shirts, and no sunglasses. If you insist that the world of work has become informal, go ahead and post a ridiculous image. If this is your view of the world of work, expect calls only from circus hiring managers looking for people to work in a tent titled, "Freak Show." (I am not opposed to circus employment. One of the best is Ringling Brothers, Barnum & Bailey Circus, www.ringling.com.)

2. *Background.* Included under this heading are the summary, experience, skills and expertise, and education sections. Complete each section by condensing the major headings on your resume. View the background information for several other LinkedIn profiles and find one that you like. Notice that solid blocks are not in keeping with the overall format of LinkedIn profiles. They look tedious and time-consuming. Use bullet points as you did on your resume.

3. *Additional Information.* This section includes "Interests" and "Advice for Contacting." Under "interests," several bullet points will be sufficient. Under "Advice for Contacting," be very specific and list your primary choice. Be sure to include your email address. If you wish, include Twitter, Facebook, and your cell number. Also, preface your contact information with a sentence to direct the reader's attention, such as, "Seeking full-time employment in finance with large- or medium-size company."

Digital profile formats vary with the medium. I have used the LinkedIn format for the following sample.

A Sample Digital Profile
Background

Summary

Cum laude college graduate with a major in Marketing Communications seeking permanent employment. Profile includes experience and training in *online marketing, technology skills, excellent verbal and written skills.*

Positive attributes include: *team player; technology savvy (including Web-programming languages); bottom-line oriented; basic proficiency in Spanish; working knowledge with social media; self-starter.*

Ready and eager to begin work with a proven, profitable company to make a positive impact on the bottom line.

Experience

South Side City Bank. Summer Internship. May 2012–September 2012.

- Wrote 20 online customer service messages per week for late mortgage payments.
- Mentored by MarCom Director to take live customer calls for interest rate quotes. Averaged 10 calls per week.
- Constructed risk management portfolios for local small businesses.

City of Chicago. Interim Parking Meter Collector. June 2013–August 2013.

- Vacation-relief collector covering 20 square blocks in busy commercial area.
- Collections averaged $2,000 per day.

- Volunteered for overtime work. Averaged 10 extra hours per week at double-time pay.

DePaul University. Assistant to the Dean of Admissions. School years 2011, 2012, 2013.

- Reviewed incoming applications for admission using written department standards for evaluation. Averaged 50 scans per week for 6 months during each year.
- Acting Administrative Assistant to the Dean during vacation periods for full-time staff.

Skills and Expertise

- Proficiency in PowerPoint, Word, Excel, ACT/SAGE.
- Working knowledge of social media, including LinkedIn, Twitter, Facebook, Indeed, Simply Hired.
- Programming skills include basic-level JavaScript, HTML, Basic, MySQL, and PHP.
- Highly developed written and verbal communication skills.

Education

- ***DePaul University, Chicago, IL.*** BS ***cum laude***, Marketing Communications. 2014.
- ***HigherNext.*** Business and Technology Certification. 2014
- ***Rosetta Stone.*** Online courses in basic and intermediate Spanish. 2012, 2013

Interests

- Community Service

- Foreign Languages
- Active Sports

Advice for Contacting

Seeking permanent employment in digital marketing and digital communications.
    Contact Information: psilvestri@saturn.com

Digital profiles for media other than LinkedIn will be more closely defined and limit the number of words or headings. Review the details in chapter 9.

GOING FORWARD

It's important to remember that the resume and digital profile are only tools in the search process. They alone will not get you the job. However, they could eliminate your candidacy, as we saw in the example of poor Patti from St. Louis, who blew a $200,000 job because she made a spelling error on her resume.

The purpose of the resume and digital profile is to move your candidacy up a notch to the personal interview, which I will cover in part 5.

CHAPTER TAKEAWAYS

- *A resume for an entry-level candidate may be two pages long. There is nothing sacred about the one-page resume.*
- *The digital profile and the resume must be mirror images of each other.*
- *Quantify your job experience.*
- *Avoid the use of meaningless words such as "awesome."*

Chapter 17

Cover Letters and Follow-Up Letters

Formal cover letters should be written with the same care as resumes and digital profiles. They should be addressed to a living person with a title and company affiliation, not to Job Box #123 or Position #456, or Staffing Manager. (If you insist on doing that, save time and just address your cover letter to secondringofsaturn@outerspace.com. The result will be the same. Nothing.) A cover letter reflects your written communication skills, and frequently, it is the first document the reader will open in your career profile.

The online number of hits for "cover letters" is surprising. Much of what you read is redundant, esoteric, or too informal. A happy medium is the place to be. Length is important, too. I have read cover letters that are three pages in length summarizing the resume, and others that are only one sentence, like, "Enclosed is my resume in reference to the Marketing Manager position." There is a better way.

COVER LETTER FORMATTING

The cover letter is a business document and should be formatted as such. It should be written on digital letterhead, or print letterhead if you are submitting by mail. It should follow all of the rules for business communication, including an inside address and a date. Sending anything less will diminish your candidacy.

Submit the cover letter on your email communication page, or submit is as an attachment. There's some back-and-forth on which method to use, but I suggest that you submit it as an attachment. That way, it makes the cover letter part of your career profile, that impressive package of documents that will set you apart from the rest of the pack.

PURPOSE OF THE COVER LETTER

The cover letter serves as a summary and table of contents for your career profile. In addition, the cover letter should let the reader know that you have taken time to research the company and that you find it worthy of your candidacy.

CONTENTS OF THE COVER LETTER

All cover letters should include these five items:

1. The name of a person who referred you to the company, or your source of information about the open position, like a job posting on the company website.
2. The purpose of the communication, usually a response to a job posting.
3. A review of the items attached or enclosed.
4. A compliment about the company.
5. A postscript (PS) suggesting what you would like to happen next, a true action item. Do not disregard the impact of the PS. Always include one in your cover letter.

A Sample Cover Letter

Kristine Alston
125 Washington Ave.
Toledo, Ohio, 23678
213-476-9909

July 12, 2014

Mr. Howard Jones
Human Resources Director
Nike Inc.
25 Santa Maria Blvd.
Spokane, WA 45667

Dear Mr. Jones:

　　Edward Smith, your Associate Marketing Manager, referred me to you in reference to a position in his department. I'm submitting my candidacy for the position posted on your website titled Assistant Digital Marketing Manager. In support of my candidacy, I am submitting my Career Profile, which consists of the following documents:

- **Resume,** which highlights my work experience, education, technology skills, and awards for performance. Please note my community outreach initiatives.
- **Official college transcript,** as verification for my BA in Communications from Ohio State University. Note that while my overall GPA was 3.4, the GPA in my major was 3.9.
- **Letter of reference,** from Dr. Eugene Harris, my senior class advisor.

- **Technology Certification,** awarded by HigherNext Inc. upon passing a technology certification exam. It serves as verification that my technology skills are current and ready to be utilized to accomplish job objectives.
- **Article I authored,** titled, "The Green Revolution Is Changing Our Lives." It was published in the *Columbus Times* newspaper on May 3, 2013, and attests to my written communication skills.

My research has confirmed that Nike is the leader in the production and distribution of sports apparel for women and men, and that you have been profitable for the past twelve quarters. What I like best, however, is that your company has paid a quarterly dividend for the past fifteen years. This is my kind of company, and I would like to move my candidacy to the next step in your hiring process.

Sincerely,

Kristine

Kristine Alston

PS. I suggest that we meet for an interview on Tuesday, July 22 at 9 a.m. in your office. Alternatively, we could meet at a time more convenient for you, or we could continue the conversation by phone at any time. My contact information is on the resume. Thanks!

That is all you need in a cover letter. Don't spend hours or days raking the Internet for more information on cover letters. Spend that time seeking personal contacts at conferences and trade shows.

FOLLOW-UP EMAILS AND LETTERS

I never cease to be amazed at how candidates forget about an essential of business etiquette: the follow-up letter or email. Whenever you speak with a hiring manager or human resources director, correct business etiquette requires a follow-up with a written acknowledgement of your conversation and a thank you. Send this document by email or on a typed note sent by regular mail.

When I receive a follow-up note from a job candidate after an interview, I note that on the candidate's career profile. Hiring managers and human resources directors do the same.

The follow-up does not need to be lengthy and has a threefold purpose: to say thank you, to provide a brief recap of the heart of the conversation, and to suggest plans for going to the next step in the process.

GOING FORWARD

Always follow the rules and you will rise to the top of the pack. The cover letter and follow-up letter are tools, sales tools if you will, to move your candidacy to the next level. In this world of increasing informality, the rules of common courtesy still apply.

In part 5, I'll tell you how to manage the personal interview. Keep reading.

CHAPTER TAKEAWAYS

- *The cover letter and follow-up letter are documents that will enhance your candidacy.*
- *The cover letter and follow-up letter are always written in business format.*
- *Follow-up letters must be written promptly.*
- *Business etiquette is the rule when constructing a cover letter or follow-up letter.*

PART 5

VERBAL COMMUNICATION: SAY IT RIGHT!

Chapter 18

Personal Interviews at Offices, Trade Shows, and Restaurants

Before we get into the heart of the interview process, let's reconstruct the landscape. You are going to the interview because you need a job in order to become self-sufficient. You need to provide your own food, shelter, and clothing by working.

On the other side of the table or desk, the company exists to make money. It does this by hiring workers, like you, to make products or provide services, which the company sells to other people. The company makes money, which it uses to pay its workers. The objective of this game, called *business*, is to make more money than you spend. That enables the company to expand and hire more workers so it can produce more goods and services, hire more workers, and so on, ad infinitum.

This model has another benefit. It permits economists and business school professors to have fun constructing an esoteric vocabulary that includes words and acronyms like ROI, GDP, and EBITDA. Business can be fun once you learn how to play the game. The more you learn about business, the easier it will be to have an intelligent and meaningful conversation during the interview.

The *bottom line*, another business term, is this: the interview is a part of the process that enables both you and the company to make money. When the interview results in a job with the hiring manager saying, "You're hired!" everyone is happy and that includes parents of recent college graduates.

THE PERSONAL INTERVIEW AT THE CORPORATE OFFICE

The corporate office is a formal place, in fact, an unreal place because that is not where most work is accomplished. It is the playground for the human resources director or hiring manager, but for you it is unfamiliar territory and can be intimidating. The office environment places the interviewer at a distinct advantage. There is nothing you can do about this except to look at it objectively. The hiring manager needs a place to sit, work, and conduct interviews, but in all probability, he or she would like to be somewhere else, maybe on a golf course or tennis court. Who knows? The corporate office is here to stay, so we might as well get used to it. When you find yourself in the corporate office, just pretend it is the anteroom at your local Starbucks. Truth be known, that is probably where you and the interviewer would rather be.

A CHANGING LANDSCAPE

A recent phenomenon is the inclusion of parents in the interview process. You heard right. I will not go into detail, but this is something you should know and expect. Some companies are inviting parents to sit in on your interview. One such company is Northwestern Mutual, one of the best insurance companies in the business. Other companies are sending offer letters to both job candidates and their parents. Still others are inviting parents to company-sponsored open houses. Don't be surprised if you encounter this situation. Don't fight it. Go along with it, and it may reap benefits for you, like getting a job.

When you encounter this in your job search, make sure that your parents read this book before they become involved in the process.

INTERVIEWS ARE LOOKING FORWARD

An important thing to remember is this: during the interview with the hiring authority, the person sitting across the desk from you is forward-looking. That person has a good idea of what you have done in the past from your resume and other sources, but is really thinking about what you can do for the company going forward. The questions about what you have done and what you would like to do have one purpose: to determine how successfully you will perform if you are hired. Forget about all the pleasantries. The purpose of the personal interview is to give the hiring manager an idea of what you can do for the company going forward.

LISTEN AND LEARN

Many people do not really listen to what you have to say because they have other things on their mind. In his well-known book, *The 7 Habits of Highly Effective People*, Stephen Covey said that, "Most people do not listen with the intent to understand: they listen with the intent to reply. They are either speaking or preparing to speak."

A good example of Covey's theory is the TV interview. Interviewers are more concerned with presenting their own agendas instead of listening for responses to questions they asked. Why don't they let the person complete the answer? Before the response is even completed, the interviewer interrupts with her own statement. The same might happen in your interview, and if it does, you must deal with it to maintain the integrity of the interview and to make your point. If the interviewer interrupts before you have the last word out of your mouth, you need a response to keep the interview on an adult level, even though your gut reaction might be, "Shut up. Let me finish the answer to your question." Here is what you might say when this happens: "To complete my response to your first question, here is what I was going to say . . ."

That should keep the interview on the right track and make for a fruitful exchange of ideas and courteous discourse.

AFTER YOU SAY HELLO, IT'S SHOWTIME

After you exchange perfunctory hellos and pleasant greetings, it's show time. This is when the rubber meets the road, and after an hour or more, you will have a good idea if they're thumbs up or thumbs down.

Your first job is to establish a relationship of trust and friendship because hiring managers hire people they like. That's basic sociology and preempts every word that you might hear from online communication gurus telling you how to proceed through an interview. More words have been written about how to go through an interview than anything else written about the job-hunting process. Interview "experts" believe they can script an interview for you, which, if followed, will result in a job offer. That's not the way it happens. One never knows what the interviewer will ask or where the conversation will go, or if the interviewer will feel *simpatico* with you and vice versa.

The Golden Rules of Interviews

The two golden rules of interviewing are these: be courteous and be honest. These two rules build the foundation for all personal relationships. Once again, it is basic sociology.

Hi, Mom! Hi, Dad!

Do not be surprised if the person sitting across the desk from you is the same age as your parents or even grandparents. This person is probably at the manager, director, or vice president level, and to reach that point in the corporate hierarchy, it takes time. You might detect a note of condescension, but that's just the way it is.

The only way to deal with this is to be prepared to answer the questions in an adult manner and on your own terms. When you prepare for the interview, resolve that you are going to look at the hiring manager as a potential friend, not an authority figure like your high school principal. If you go in feeling that the hiring manager is an authority figure, the interview will degenerate into an adult-child exchange and will not have a good outcome.

Who Has the Aces?

Even though the hiring manager appears to hold all of the cards, it really is not so. While you are there for a job, the hiring manager is speaking with you because the company needs workers. The hiring manager needs someone like you to fill an important position. The hiring manager is under pressure, too, to find the right candidate as soon as possible.

While the hiring manager is evaluating the person across the desk, smart candidates are sizing up the hiring manager as well. It is important that the hiring manager is someone you respect, someone who shows courtesy and honesty. If you find any of these things lacking, erase this company from your list. You may need a job, but you do not want it at the expense of reporting to a fool or a jerk.

How the Interviewer Judges You

The two most important things on a potential employer's checklist seem so self-evident that they are often overlooked. However, if you fall short on either, your chances of moving ahead in the process will be greatly diminished.

1. ***Dress.*** Your appearance is the first thing a hiring manager notices. You may have submitted a world-class resume and impressive references, but if you walk into an interview dressed as if you're going to a homecoming party, you are history. Case closed. No second chance. In fact, this is such an important item that I have devoted an entire chapter to the subject (see chapter 20).

2. ***Appropriate Speech.*** After dress, the most important checklist item is verbal communication, which consists of three components: vocabulary, content, and delivery. Vocabulary and content are all-important and will tell the interviewer if you are in adult mode or if you are stuck in college-speak. At all costs, avoid common clichés like "awesome," "cool," or "dude."

To your friends, "awesome" might seem like a very descriptive word, but in business-speak, it means nothing, and you should avoid this word like the plague. Instead of saying a company is awesome, you could say something like this: "I want to work with Adobe because I'm impressed with your record of generating revenue. For example, in the last quarter your revenue was up 10 percent over a comparable quarter a year ago. This tells me that Adobe has a viable business model. I would like a chance to work for such a company and contribute my time and talents to help the company continue to grow."

I don't think you will have any trouble deciding that your business-speak answer is more meaningful than using "awesome." So what's the takeaway? The world of work is *business*, and appropriate speech is expected. Hiring authorities assume that you have the business savvy to use business-speak, and if you do not, you will be placed into the "not yet ready" box.

The content of your responses to questions will tell the interviewer if you are ready for a particular job. Couching your answers in quantitative terms will tell the interviewer that you understand business. To refresh your memory, review chapter 4.

The delivery part of your conversation reflects your level of confidence and maturity. Millions of words have been written on this subject, but it still comes down to a few basics. Sit straight, make eye contact, relax, smile, and display your personality. If you are not accustomed to using your hands to make a point, do not do this in an interview. You are having a conversation about how you can help the company going forward, not auditioning for a part in a movie.

If you want more on this general topic, conduct a Google search using the words "body language." If you want a quick overview of the topic, go to Wikipedia, where body language is defined as "a form of nonverbal communication consisting of body posture, eye contact, gestures, and facial expressions."

Body Language

To translate this into real life, here is an example of what I encountered recently while conducting a search for a vice president. This story indicates that delivery is just as important as content.

Fred from California. Fred had a personal two-hour interview with the CEO of a major company located in Los Angeles. The position required the candidate to live in the home office area, and Fred met that requirement. He did not need to relocate. On paper, he met every job requirement and more. So far, so good. However, something untoward happened during the interview process. The CEO rejected his candidacy citing these two reasons: first, Fred's answers "seemed shallow" (in other words, the CEO did not buy the content), and second, Fred "appeared insecure." In other words, Fred's body language told the CEO that there was a disconnect. For some reason, Fred was not buying into the conversation.

HOW THE INTERVIEW BEGINS

Trying to anticipate what the interviewer will ask can be a never-ending game. There seems to be one universal question, however, that all interviewers ask: "Would you tell me about yourself?" It appears to be a trivial question, but that's just the way it is, and you have to prepare yourself for it. If you are caught off guard, you might end up reciting your family history or give a chronological account of your life from birth to the present. What the hiring manager really wants to hear is what you might do for the company if you are hired.

To level the playing field and to keep this a true give-and-take rather than an interrogation, deflect the question and respond with an adult answer that includes some or all of five topics:

1. You are here because you have learned there is a specific employment opportunity.
2. You have researched the company and would like to work here for several reasons. State what they are. Some of these things could be your interest in the company's product,

company profitability, glowing reports from company workers, or the steady increase in the price of the company stock.
3. You would like an opportunity to increase the profitability
    of the company by using your talents, skills, intelligence,
    energy, and passion.
4. Highlight the successes and awards you received for achieve-
    ment. Verbalize the key points on your resume.
5. State your career goals and do not be shy. If you really would
    like to be the company president someday, say so. Tell your
    interviewer how you believe you could work your way up
    to that position.

All of this advice may be interesting and helpful, but how does
it translate into an answer for the question, "Would you tell me
about yourself?" Here's a script that you might use:

"I'm the kind of person who takes responsibility for my own
life, and that includes finding a position that will give me income
to provide for my own needs, including paying off my student
loan. I'm here because I believe that your company can provide that
opportunity. My research indicates that your last quarter generated
revenue that exceeded expectations and that your past three years
have been profitable. I want to be part of a company with that kind
of track record because it means that you are doing something right.
I want to build on that success by applying my intelligence, energy,
and passion to make this company even better and more profitable.
Also, my career vision includes a director-level position, and hopefully, I can find that here."

Read this aloud several times until you make it your own.
Modify it to include some hard numbers and specifics from your
resume. After you respond, ask the interviewer what he thought
of your resume and if there are any questions. You need to make
sure that your resume or your career profile was read and evaluated.
Remember that this is *your* interview, and you have every right to
ask questions as well. This might be a good place to begin evaluating the hiring manager. After you complete the answer to the first
question, ask the interviewer, "Could you tell me about your job

here, how long you have been here, what your responsibilities are, and what you did before taking this job? Oh, and by the way, I'm curious about where you went to college and what your major was." This question gives the hiring manager a chance to brag a little and tell you some success stories. Your expressed interest in the hiring manager's accomplishments helps build the relationship and provides valuable information to evaluate this person. Also, it makes the interview conversational rather than interrogative.

FREQUENTLY ASKED INTERVIEW QUESTIONS

The kinds of questions asked in an interview follow a somewhat standard format. Here are questions that may be asked regardless of the company or position:

1. Can you tell me something about yourself?
2. How did you find out about us?
3. Why do you want to work here?
4. What is your major qualification for this position?
5. Are there any areas where you think you need to improve?
6. What is your career goal?
7. Can you tell me about a work problem you encountered and how you resolved it?
8. What are your compensation requirements?
9. When could you begin work with us if we agree this is the right job for you?
10. Have you participated in community outreach programs?
11. What do you do with your spare time?
12. What is your main academic interest?
13. What books have you read recently?
14. Give me an example of how you use social media like Twitter?
15. What do you want to know about the company and the job?

You don't know how many of these questions the interviewer will ask, but be prepared to answer them. Conduct a rehearsal before the interview. Ask a trusted friend to ask you these questions and then deliver your responses. Practice until you feel comfortable with your answers. Remember to answer in business-speak and to quantify as much as possible.

INTERVIEWING THE INTERVIEWER

Remember, this is *your* interview, and you are entitled to ask as many questions as necessary to learn about the company and its people. Do not be intimidated by the interviewer even though that person may be older than your parents may be. You are now part of the adult world of work and you are communicating adult to adult. What questions should you ask?

Five Questions Job Candidates Should Ask

Most likely, you will come up with your own list of questions, but here are five you should ask according to Jeff Haden writing in April 2013 for *Inc.* online magazine.

1. *What are the few things that really drive results for the company?* Every profitable company has rubrics that account for its success. Learn what these are and you will know much about the company and what it expects from its workers. If you hear something like, "Everyone here works like crazy, even coming in on Saturdays and Sundays," consider it a yellow flag. You should not have to spend seven days a week to meet job expectations, and you should not be expected to be on call via texts and tweets 24/7, unless you are a medical professional.

2. *What do employees do in their spare time?* This might be a difficult question for the interviewer to answer, especially in a large company. However, the answer will tell you much about the kind of people the company hires, and if these are your kind of people. Do they spend off-work

hours at a sports bar? Do they volunteer their off-work hours for company-sponsored outreach programs? Do some of them take graduate level courses to improve their work skills?

3. *How do you plan to deal with . . . ?* The blank part of this question could be any number of items that you discovered while doing your research on the company and the industry. The question could be, "How do you plan to deal with lower margins for your technology products?" The answers to these questions will tell you if the company recognizes its problems going forward and has plans to deal with them.

4. *What do you expect me to accomplish in the first sixty to ninety days?* This question lets the interviewer know that you are no slouch. You want the company hiring manager to know that you are ready, willing, and able to be productive immediately.

5. *What are the common attributes of your top performers?* The answer to this question will tell you much about the corporate culture, the company expectations, and what workers are willing to do in order to be successful there.

PREPARING A WRITTEN INTERVIEW AGENDA

I am always impressed when a job candidate comes to an interview with a written agenda that includes questions about both the position and the company. I like it when the candidate hands me an agenda and requests a brief discussion of each topic if time permits. A written agenda sends a powerful message that you have carefully prepared for the interview, and that you are pursuing this particular opportunity, not just any job with any company. Here is a sample agenda that you can print on your letterhead and hand to the interviewer:

Sample Interview Agenda

Subject: Agenda for Interview with Adobe
Position: Assistant Inside Sales Manager
Candidate: Judith Hopkins
Human Resources Director: Joseph Kowalski
Date: June 7, 2015

I would appreciate the opportunity to discuss the following questions during my interview with Mr. Kowalski:

1. Why is this position open?
2. If someone else had this job, why did that person leave the company?
3. Why am I being considered for this position?
4. Would superior performance in this position lead to a promotion?
5. What are the three major expectations for the Assistant Inside Sales Manager?
6. To whom does this job report and what is that person's management style?
7. What is the background of the person to whom this position reports?
8. What is the company's revenue goal for this fiscal year? How much of an increase is that over the previous year's revenue?
9. What has made this company a leader in information technology?
10. Does the company participate in community outreach programs?
11. Does the company have an employment program for returning military personnel?
12. Why should I join Adobe?

I thank you for discussing these issues.

Sincerely,

Judy

Judith Hopkins

Answers to these questions are tools for evaluating the position and company. You need this information to decide if you want to continue the process. Answers to questions 10 and 11 will tell you much about the company culture.

The written agenda is another item that will distinguish you from the rest of the pack and take you to the next step, a job offer. Don't hesitate to use this technique for every interview.

ENDING THE INTERVIEW

Salespeople are trained to ask for the order after making their product presentation, instead of just saying, "Thank you for your time," and leaving. The same holds true for the interview. Close by saying thank you and asking, "What are the next steps in the process? I really would like to work here based on your answers to my questions and my research about the company. When can I start?"

If the interviewer gives a nebulous answer to your closing statements, counter with an action item like, "Thanks for your time. I'll follow up with you by email or phone to check on the status of my potential employment here. What else can I do for you at this time? By the way, what is your hiring deadline?"

INTERVIEWS WITH A PANEL OF HIRING AUTHORITIES

Occasionally, a panel instead of only one person will interview a candidate. The panel interview may sound intimidating, but it can work to your advantage.

The panel could consist of a hiring manager, the company human resources director, and a worker who might be your coworker if you are hired. For example, if you are interviewing for an assistant editor position with a publishing company, the worker may be an associate editor in that department.

The purpose of the panel interview is to save time, not to intimidate the candidate. When you walk in the door you really don't know if the interview will be with one person or with a panel, so be prepared mentally for both. Usually, a panel interview means that the company is seriously interested in your candidacy. It's a positive sign for you. Be reassured and confident that the interview is going to work to your advantage.

After the interview begins, determine the person who appears to be most friendly and supportive and build a relationship with him or her.

It really is better to be interviewing with a panel for a number of reasons. In the one-on-one interview, if you do not connect with the person across from you, there is nobody else you can turn to for help. In a panel interview, you have options for building strong relationships with more than one person.

PERSONAL INTERVIEWS AT CONFERENCES AND TRADE SHOWS

Many interviews take place on the floor of a conference hall or even in an exhibit booth. It is an informal atmosphere and there is a tendency to let down one's guard and fall into sloppy habits like "cool talk" or inappropriate dress. You will find many potential employers at convention centers. I suggest that you review chapter 12.

It's important to remember that you are here for business, which is finding a job. Do not be distracted by the informal environment. Even though many of the company representatives and customers are dressed informally, this is still a place where business is transacted and where candidates are interviewed and even hired. Always come prepared for business. Wear business attire, bring two dozen resumes, a hundred business cards, and a dozen written generic interview agendas.

FINDING THE HIRING MANAGER AT A CONFERENCE

Hiring managers frequently attend conferences and interview candidates there, sometimes in an exhibit booth or in a conference center restaurant or coffee shop. The setting is much less formal than an office, and the conversation is more relaxed. Frequently, you will meet hiring managers in their company exhibit booths, where they may be talking with customers. After introducing yourself and stating the purpose of your visit to the conference, ask for a brief interview. If the hiring manager is obviously involved with customers, ask when you could come back for a chat.

A conference center interview will be shorter in length because hiring managers are always watching the clock. They are there to meet with customers, sometimes by appointment, and to attend breakout sessions to learn about competitors' products and industry trends. Treat this situation as you would a cold call. (You can review information on cold calls in chapter 10.)

Always begin your interview by presenting the hiring manager with your resume and your calling card, and then following the rules for interviewing presented above.

BUSINESS ETIQUETTE AT CONFERENCES

As a rule of business etiquette, be respectful of the hiring manager's time. In fact, you might want to begin the conversation by saying, "I know this is a busy show and that your time is limited. I'll limit our time to fifteen minutes, and we can follow up at another time if necessary." Check your watch or smartphone, and at the end of fifteen minutes conclude the interview by saying, "I see that our fifteen minutes has passed. Maybe we can continue at another time if you wish. Thanks for taking time for this interview. I hope this is a productive show for you and your company. I'll check back with you after the show."

Do not be surprised if the hiring manager asks to continue the interview. If that happens, continue the conversation and present the hiring manager with a modified version of the interview agenda treated earlier in this chapter. For use at a convention center, prepare a generic agenda by deleting the name of a particular company.

Always get the hiring manager's business card, and when you are back at your home office, send a follow-up message by email or snail mail saying thanks and suggesting the next step.

PERSONAL INTERVIEWS IN RESTAURANTS

Occasionally, a hiring manager or human resources director will conduct an interview in a restaurant. The reason is not usually hunger; rather, it is because the hiring manager wants to see your level of maturity by observing your behavior in the community at large.

Interviews at restaurants can be tricky and sometimes fraught with danger. The hiring manager is placing you in this environment to determine how you handle yourself in a real-life setting. The informal ambiance can be deceiving, to say the least. The person across the table from you will be observing the way you interact with restaurant workers, your ability to stay focused despite the numerous distractions encountered at restaurants, your skill ordering from the menu, and your table manners. Here's an example of what can happen during a restaurant interview:

> ***Marc the Marine.*** I was interviewing a candidate for a sales manager position at the Marriott Hotel restaurant at the Newark, New Jersey, airport. It was a crowded morning and tables were close together. At the table next to us, there was a young couple with a screaming baby who was distracting me to the point where I was ready to ask the host to change our location. However, candidate Marc kept the conversation going as if there were no distractions. He did not even look at the unhappy baby. This caught my attention, and I gained a great deal of respect for Marc because of his discipline and understanding. We proceeded through the interview for

ninety minutes, and Marc won not only my respect, but also my recommendation for employment.

Before we parted, I complimented Mark for his control under trying circumstances. He told me that in the marines, you learn discipline and how to stay focused in difficult situations.

TABLE MANNERS

Why are table manners important? Because you represent the company when you are dining with customers, which some workers will do frequently.

Restaurant Interview Historymakers

The rules of restaurant etiquette are important, and violating them will make your candidacy a historical event. Here is my "history" checklist:

1. Lick your fingers at an interview, and you are history.
2. Dribble a drink or soup down the front of your shirt or top, and you are history.
3. Rest your arms on the table as you would at a bar, and you are history.
4. Slurp your coffee, soup, or iced tea so that it causes heads to turn your way, and you are history.
5. Spear your meat and veggies with your fork as though you are a Neanderthal, and you are history.
6. Chew with your mouth open, and you are history.
7. Order alcoholic drinks, and you are history.
8. Text or talk on your smartphone, and you are history.
9. Whine to the waitperson, and you are history.
10. Be demanding and disrespectful to restaurant personnel, and you are history.

Get the picture on table manners? Here's an example of how to lick yourself out of a job:

> ***Bob the Licker.*** I was interviewing Bob for a vice president of sales position over lunch in New York City, and from the beginning, I saw a red flag. It was Bob's demanding manner with the server, who was busy and trying to do a good job. Strike one! Next, I could not help but notice that Bob chewed with his mouth open, making nasty noises that were distracting. Strike two! Toward the end of our lunch, Bob gave three fingers on each hand a great, big lick. Strike three! You're out, Bob!

There are other dangers lurking at restaurant interviews that go beyond table manners and discipline. Let's look at a real-life example from the West Coast.

> ***Mrs. Pancakes.*** Recently, I was visiting with the vice president for human resources with a company in California. During the course of our conversation, we discovered that both of us believed in restaurant interviews because you could observe so much in a relatively brief amount of time in a real-life setting. She related that she disqualified a candidate recently because of a menu selection.
>
> It happened that she was having lunch with a candidate at approximately 2 p.m. The lunch menu included sandwiches, salads, light entrées, and a selection of desserts. The candidate asked the server if she could order pancakes with a side of bacon. The vice president perceived this as odd. A person ordering pancakes at two in the afternoon was not her idea of an ideal candidate, and she decided this was not the right person.

What's wrong with this picture? The only thing I could see was that the VP had a very rigid set of standards about what kind of food should be eaten for breakfast, lunch, or dinner. This true-life story may border on the absurd but illustrates an important point about interviews at restaurants: they are tricky and you just don't know what the person across from you is thinking.

Also, do not order the priciest thing on the menu as a matter of courtesy. My advice is to play it straight and be conservative. When it's breakfast time, do not order a filet with a baked potato and creamed spinach for $39.95. When it's lunchtime, do not order breakfast food. The company person sitting across from you could be Mrs. Pancakes! Careful!

WHAT CORPORATE EXECUTIVES EXPECT DURING INTERVIEWS

What do corporate executives advise candidates to do when they come to an interview? I have interviewed many corporate executives and hear the same themes repeated across the country. I'll cite two of these executives whose advice you should follow to the letter.

Susan Meell, CEO of MMS Education headquartered in Newtown, Pennsylvania, offers these four important suggestions for candidates interviewing personally with hiring managers and human resources directors:

1. Research the company. You must know something about the company to establish your credibility as a candidate interested in working for that company.
2. Be on time for the interview.
3. Dress appropriately. That means business attire, not jeans, a casual top, and sneakers.
4. Be ready to articulate and discuss how your previous experiences and accomplishments have prepared you for the position for which you are interviewing. Remember, the company wants to know how you are going to benefit the company.

Eric Gootkind, Director of Employment and Employee Relations at Measured Progress in Dover, New Hampshire, says there are four all-important requirements for all candidates in personal interviews:

1. Maintain eye contact with the interviewer.
2. Wear proper business attire.
3. Be prepared to give examples of your accomplishments.
4. Follow up with the interviewer promptly.

Thank you, Susan and Eric. This is good advice for all candidates interviewing for entry-level positions.

CHAPTER TAKEAWAYS

- *When interviewing, be courteous and be honest.*
- *Wear conservative business attire.*
- *Always present the interviewer with your written agenda.*
- *After an interview, send a follow-up message of thanks and ask for the next step.*
- *Turn off your smartphone before you begin the interview, no exceptions.*
- *Conclude the interview by asking for the job.*

JOB HUNTER'S LIBRARY

Marc Cosentino, *Case in Point*, Burgee Press, 2013. This is a very useful and popular book on case interviewing from an expert in the field.

Elizabeth Kuhnke, *Body Language for Dummies*, Wiley, 2012.

Shari Harley, *How to Say Anything to Anyone*, Greenleaf Book Group, 2012.

Chapter 19

Phone Interviews

The phone interview has become a regular part of the job-hunting process (unfortunately, I might add). The phone interview came about because of the great number of candidates applying for any single posted job. When a human resources director or hiring authority has a hundred applicants for one position, he or she makes the first cut using the candidate's resume and information from other sources like social media. After the list is narrowed to a handful of candidates, the next step is to evaluate them with a phone interview, or a "phone screening," as it is sometimes called.

Whenever you can, avoid the phone screening by volunteering to come in for a personal interview, even if this means driving three hours each way to the company location. Face-to-face communication is where you want to go, and the phone interview gets in the way.

THE PURPOSE OF THE PHONE INTERVIEW

For you, the candidate, there is only one purpose of the phone interview: to get you to the next step, the personal interview with the hiring manager. Nobody is ever hired as a result of a phone interview. It's just another step in the process.

For the interviewer, the purpose is to screen out the chaff and select finalists for personal interviews.

It does not seem fair because the hiring manager or human resources director is holding the cards, but that's the way it is. You can't change some things, so you must learn to live with them and do your best. The phone interview is one of them, and I'll help you do the best you can.

PHONE INTERVIEW PREPARATION

Prepare for the phone interview just as you would for a personal interview (see chapter 18). Use this checklist to make sure you are ready:

- Find a private location, preferably your home office, where there will be absolute quiet. Eliminate traffic noise, barking dogs, crying babies, and music playing in the background. If there are two phones in your location, turn off the one not being used. The last thing you want is your alternate phone ringing during an interview.
- Avoid holding the phone interview in a casual setting like a beach, restaurant, car, bar, or train. This is a business call, not a casual call. If there is a dog barking or clinking glasses in the background, surely the interviewer will hear the background noise and you will be history. There will be no second chances.
- Take the call at a table or desk where you can spread out documents for reference. You cannot do this if you are driving your car.
- Have your resume, the job description, company information, and a written interview agenda listing your questions in front of you during the call. Also, have a tablet or notebook and a pen for note-taking. Handwrite notes instead of entering them on your desktop or laptop computer. Keyboard noise can be heard on the other end of the line with today's sensitive audio technology.
- Stay focused. Write out an agenda listing the name of the

company, the name of the person with whom you will be talking (also include that person's title), the date, the time, and the location of the interviewer.

If the interviewer is located in another time zone, make the adjustment. If you are in New York and the interviewer is in Denver, there will be a two-hour time difference, so plan accordingly. If the call is scheduled for 9 a.m., Mountain Time, it will be 11 a.m. in New York. If you miscalculate the time difference and the caller gets your voice mail instead of your voice, you will be history. Not fair? Welcome to the real world!

- Dress for the phone interview, because the way you dress sets the stage for your behavior. Take the call dressed in business attire. If you are dressed in a yoga outfit, your conversation could easily become too casual. The same applies to your body language. If you take the call with your bare feet resting on the top of your desk, you could slip into casual mode and begin using vocabulary like "awesome." Go back to chapter 18 and review the section titled, "How You Are Judged by the Interviewer." The same rules apply to the phone interview.
- Prepare to answer the question, "Can you tell me something about yourself?" Once again, refer to chapter 18 for guidance. Remember, the interviewer is not interested in learning if you are a carnivore or a vegan, or where you were born, or if your favorite drink is a grande-size, skim milk decaf cappuccino with a dollop of whipped cream, and topped off with both nutmeg and cinnamon.
- Select only three questions from your written agenda. Usually, phone interviews are time sensitive, so you want to make sure you have covered what is important to you.
- Have your laptop or desktop computer running with company information on the screen.
- Smile during the phone interview. A smile on your face

will relax you and make the tone more conversational. Think of the phone smile as virtual body language.

HOW TO BEGIN THE PHONE INTERVIEW

Etiquette is everyone's concern. Should you address the interviewer by first or last name? Is it Mrs., Ms., Mr., Dr., or Mary? It's important to get it right. Here are some guidelines that follow the "listen first" rule.

How to Address the Interviewer

If the interviewer introduces herself as "Mrs. Niblick, Human Resources Director," then you address her as Mrs. Niblick throughout the interview. If she introduces herself as "Barbara Niblick," call her Barbara. Never, under any circumstances, address a person using a nickname like Barb if she introduces herself as Barbara.

If the interviewer introduces himself as "Dr. William Ford," call him Dr. Ford throughout the interview. If the interviewer introduces himself as "Bob Ford, Sales Manager," call him Bob. If the interviewer introduces himself as "John Cupcake," call him John, not Jack.

The most common error is to assume it is permissible to call a person by a shortened version of his or her name. I have found that the most frequently abused first name is Robert. Why does everyone revert to Bob?

After You Say "Hello"

The first thing to ask after you say hello is, "How much time do we have?" Knowing this will tell you how much time to spend answering questions, and how much time you can spend asking questions of the interviewer. Write the end time on a piece of paper and refer to it throughout the conversation.

After learning the amount of time you have, tell the interviewer that you have several questions you would like to ask and ask when it would be appropriate to do so. It could be the last thing on the agenda, or the first.

Now that the protocol and time period are settled, proceed through the interview using the guidelines for the personal interview in chapter 18.

Closing the Interview

The closing is the same for the phone interview and the personal interview. Get the interviewer's phone number and email address, say thank you for the interview, and ask for the job. Here's a script you might use:

"What are the next steps in the process? I really would like to work here based on your answers to my questions and my research on your company. When can I start?"

The same personal interview follow-up rules apply. Send a thank you note and ask for the next step.

SKYPE INTERVIEWS

You may be asked to commit to a Skype interview, but it does not happen frequently. The rules for a Skype interview are a combination of the rules for the personal and phone interviews. Before committing to a Skype interview, make sure that it really works in your location. There is nothing worse than a bad Skype connection. For more information on Skype, check out the website at www.skype.com.

GOING FORWARD

The phone interview can be a challenging hurdle in the process, but there is not much you can do about it except ask for a personal interview if both you and the interviewer are in the same location. Preparation is the key. Take the "dress up" rule seriously because it will guide your behavior and place the process in proper context.

In the next chapter, I'll talk about proper dress for a personal, phone, or Skype interview. Keep reading.

CHAPTER TAKEAWAYS

- *Wear business attire for a phone interview.*
- *Exercise business etiquette and protocol during a phone interview.*

Chapter 20

How to Dress for an Interview

How to dress for an interview is probably at the top of the list for job hunters new to the world of adult work. There are no hard-and-fast written rules for how one should dress for an interview, but there is a lot of tradition that needs to be followed. Companies do not tell you beforehand what to wear for an interview, and taking advice from a fellow job hunter new to the workplace may lead you in the wrong direction.

DRESS CODES FOR WORKING AND INTERVIEWING: THERE IS A DIFFERENCE

What you see on TV can be misleading. Frequently, the workplace portrayed on television shows workers in jeans, T-shirts, and sneakers. While this may be true in some companies, do not misinterpret the media-portrayed casual atmosphere to hold true for job interviews. The way you dress for an interview and the way you dress at work after you have been hired are two different things. Your first impression is a lasting one, and you do not get a second chance at making a first impression.

If you hate formal business attire, suffer through it during an interview. When you are hired, you can dress as the culture dictates.

Do Not Dress for Ping-Pong

In general, work environments are, by nature, relatively conservative places. They are designed to encourage maximum productivity, which results in a profitable operation. This is what companies need to do in order to make money to pay your salary and benefits package. Remember, you work in order to make money to provide your own food, shelter, and clothing. If the company does not make money, it cannot pay you, and you will be forced to dust off your spear and go hunting for antelope—not a good idea in an urban environment.

There is a good reason why the office at most companies is not a free-for-all environment filled with Ping-Pong tables, Frisbees flying through the air, workout rooms, and free pizza and soft drink kiosks liberally sprinkled throughout the building. This may be true for some tech companies like Facebook and Google, but for the remaining 99.9 percent of corporate America, this is not true.

Appropriate Dress for Interviews: Listen to Joyce

When you go to an interview at an employer's office, business attire is expected, even if the employer is a tech company noted for its "relaxed" culture. Joyce Boston, Human Resources Manager for Measured Progress, a K–12 testing and assessment company in Dover, New Hampshire, says, "Candidates appearing for an interview dressed in formal business attire stand out from the rest of the crowd. Candidates in business attire, both men and women, get my attention. That means a suit, tie, and leather shoes for men, and comparable business attire for women."

In addition, Joyce also recommends that you do not bring your phone to an interview, even if the ringer is on silent. Turn off the smartphone before you leave the car, *no exceptions*. There is nothing so important that it cannot wait until you complete the interview, usually sixty to ninety minutes for a first interview, and double that for succeeding interviews.

But what about those presidents and CEOs from the tech companies, like Mark Zuckerberg of Facebook, Bill Gates of Microsoft, or Meg Whitman, CEO of HP, you might ask? Sometimes they are dressed casually when you see them on a TV interview. Don't buy the TV image. When they have formal business meetings or meet with customers, they always dress in business attire. I'm sure that when Zuckerberg is meeting with the CEOs of JPMorgan Chase or Goldman Sachs, he isn't dressed in jeans and a T-shirt.

But, you might ask, "What about solid tech players like Twitter. Who wears a suit there?" Would you believe that the CEO does? When Twitter went public on November 7, 2013, the CEO, Dick Costolo, was interviewed on CNBC. He was dressed in a blue pin-striped suit, a white shirt with a spread collar, and a conservative tie. His hair was trimmed off the ears and shirt collar, and he wore stylish but conservative eyeglasses.

When you are hired, chances are that you will find a relaxed dress code, sometimes written, but most times not. My advice is to dress a cut above the crowd because how you dress will make a lasting impression on your managers and executives. When hiring managers and human resources directors are looking for internal candidates to promote, dress comes into play subconsciously. Do you want to be identified as a solid member of the "followers," or do you want to be viewed as a potential "leader"? Do not kid yourself. The way you dress creates a lasting impression on people in the company.

YOUR ATTIRE MAKES A LASTING FIRST IMPRESSION

When hiring managers interview candidates, the first thing they notice is appearance. Dress like a sophomore, and the human resources director will think of you, subconsciously, as a college kid not yet ready for the big-time. Dress in business attire, and the hiring manager will think of you as a serious candidate, one who is ready to work in the adult world of work. Company personnel charged with the responsibility of hiring the right candidates are looking down the road, too. If you are dressed properly, the hiring manager will see you as a potential director or vice president.

DRESS RIGHT FOR A SUCCESSFUL INTERVIEW

Selecting the right attire for an interview is a serious concern for all candidates seeking their first jobs. Realizing this is the real deal, not a part-time summer job, candidates spend much time tweeting back and forth about what to wear to an interview. I have some suggestions based on real time spent in the work environment.

Watch business programs on CNBC and Fox Business News, where you will see men and women from the business world. Note how show hosts and guests dress. All represent the business world. They may be people in their thirties to sixties, most in positions of authority and responsibility, like the hiring managers or human resources directors. These are the people who will be interviewing you.

Real World Faves   **Internet Sites for Proper Business Attire**
The Internet is loaded with useful information about dressing for interviews. Much of it is redundant because there is only so much you can say beyond "go conservative." Remember to distinguish between proper attire for a personal interview and attire for workers already hired. There is a world of difference, but this is sometimes overlooked on Internet advice columns. I particularly like the following sites for their helpful advice:

- *About.com,* www.jobsearch.about.com. I like this site because it goes into detail about appropriate dress for an interview for both men and women. While the importance for both men and women is equal, the topic presents a more serious challenge for women because there are more options available in clothing styles. This site sums it

up in a few sentences for women: "Solid color, conservative suit with coordinated blouse, moderate shoes, tan or
light pantyhose, limited jewelry, neat professional hair-
style, manicured nails, light makeup, little or no perfume,
portfolio or briefcase." I like the advice about wearing a
suit because a suit never goes out of style, for both women
and men.

- **Women in Business,** www.womeninbusiness.about.
com. This site has interesting and helpful suggestions for
women. Check it out for a quick review of what is proper
and what is not.
- **ECG Library for Men,** www.ecglink.com/library/ps/dress-
men.html. This is a good site for reviewing the general
topic of business attire for men. It includes good advice
for casual and business dress and grooming, and presents
some up-to-date observations on the difference between
casual and business.
- **ECG Library for Women,** www.ecglink.com/library/ps/
dress-women.html. This site provides up-to-date advice
for women in a friendly and caring way. Check it out
for an uncluttered look at the world of women's business attire. The section titled, Dress to Fit Your Audi-
ence is outstanding.
- **The Limited,** www.thelimited.com. This site provides much
good advice and pictures for women exclusively. Check it out
to see what is in style and what is not. Check it frequently.

The Best Stores to Purchase Business Attire . . . and Apply for a Job

There are many stores across the country where you
can buy appropriate business attire. While I can't know every
store in every town across the US, I can give you the names of
national chains that you can find in most large- and mid-size cities and towns.

Ann Taylor, www.anntaylor.com. This iconic retailer of women's clothing offers a wide selection of business and casual clothing. Go online and click on "Suits," and you will see pictures of knockout styles that will make the human resources director remember your name! Ann Taylor also sells separates, and you can coordinate a jacket and skirt or pantsuit for under $200, on sale. Ann Taylor holds sales periodically, so check the website frequently. Check out the career page as well for job opportunities. I saw both retail store and corporate job openings. Don't leave this website without looking at job opportunities!

Nordstrom, www.nordstrom.com. Nordstrom is noted for high-quality clothing for both men and women. Prices are high, but look for sales and you could walk away with stylish clothing at attractive prices. This company is noted for its wide selection of business and casual shoes for both women and men. Check its website for the dates of "half-yearly" (semiannual) sales. In addition, Nordstrom has outlet stores in some locations where you can find quality clothing at very attractive prices. Nordstrom has a website devoted exclusively to careers: www.careers.nordstrom.com. This company has a reputation for treating employees fairly and for providing good training. Buy your business attire at Nordstrom, and then march to the human resources director's office and request an interview. What a way to sell your candidacy!

Jos. A. Bank, www.josbank.com. This site gives tips for smart dressing, and you can view a wide variety of both casual and formal business attire. This nationwide chain caters primarily to men and has a very active TV and radio marketing campaign.

Brooks Brothers, www.brooksbrothers.com. Brooks produces high-quality clothing for both men and women. The company has retail stores located in shopping malls throughout the country. However, Brooks has outlet stores that sell traditional clothing at very attractive prices. For example, the traditional men's blue blazer, or sport coat, that retails for $500 in its regular stores sells for $200 at the outlet stores. Pure wool trousers sell for under $100. Shirts go for less than $50 and ties for under $30. You will not go wrong buying at Brooks Brothers outlet stores. By the way, most of Brooks's clothing is manufactured in the United States.

Macy's, www.macys.com. This national chain offers business attire for both men and women at very attractive everyday prices. Catch a sale day and you will be a happy job hunter. Macy's carries a number of famous designer labels for both men and women, and the sales reps are very knowledgeable. They will help you construct an entire outfit. Among its many labels for men are Michael Kors, Calvin Klein, Tommy Hilfiger, Ralph Lauren, Perry Ellis, Tasso Elba, Kenneth Cole, and others. Women will find a number of famous labels as well, such as INC International Concepts, Anne Klein, Alfani, and Ralph Lauren. If you like the idea of working for a celebrated department store with great clothing products, check out the career website at www.macysjobs.com. I saw hundreds of jobs spanning merchandising, sales, marketing, information technology, finance, and many others. I presume that employees receive discounts on products. Check it out!

Paul Fredrick, www.paulfredrick.com. This Pennsylvania-based clothier specializes in dress shirts for men. The company offers very attractive introductory prices for first-time customers (shirts, $19.95; silk ties, $19.95). Its products are high quality, its service is impeccable, and its prices cannot be beat. Don't mess with shirts and ties from traditional department stores and big-box retailers like Target. Go straight to Paul Fredrick to save time and money.

The Limited, www.thelimited.com. Women, check out the pictures and descriptions of this clothier's collection of jackets, blazers, and suits. The Limited produces conservative business apparel at reasonable, everyday prices, but look for its sales to save a bundle.

Talbots, www.talbots.com. This nationwide chain offers both casual and business attire for women. Its classic business suits are available as separates or as coordinated outfits. Prices are on the expensive side, so be sure to check out the many Talbots outlet stores. While you are checking out business apparel, go to the career page and see what's available. I noted both retail store manager positions and corporate positions listed on the website.

Bloomingdale's, www.bloomingdales.com. This reputable store carries designer clothing, shoes, handbags, and jewelry for women. On the website, view its suits, separates, and attractive business attire. Prices are high, so wait for sales, which are frequent. In addition, Bloomingdale's has an active Twitter marketing campaign to keep you abreast of sales and styles.

Lord & Taylor, www.lordandtaylor.com. You cannot go wrong with Lord & Taylor. It carries an impressive list of classic business clothing in a number of designer labels. Look online for the locations of outlet stores, and frequently check for online discount coupons. The store offers clothing for both men and women. Lord & Taylor has a separate website for job hunters. Its headquarters are in New York City, where many jobs are available. However, there are plenty of jobs with the company around the country as well. The last time I checked, there were information technology jobs open in St. Louis.

FAIL-SAFE DRESS FOR MEN

Men have an easier job selecting proper interview attire than do women. There are two choices that will get men through any interview, and they are available at a modest cost:

- **The Blue Blazer Outfit.** This casual outfit has been around for years, and it is something that you can wear for a personal office interview or when you go to a trade show.

It consists of the following: a blue blazer, dark gray or tan wool pants, a white or blue shirt (either button-down or traditional spread-collar), a conservative tie, black leather loafers or plain cap shoes, and black socks. This ensemble will cost about $300. By the way, patterned shirts can be worn instead of solid white or blue. However, do not go beyond small checks or stripes.

- **The Suit.** The dark blue or gray suit, solid or in pinstripe, will place you at the top of the pack. Select a blue or white shirt with a spread collar, and a red or dark blue tie. The tie is sometimes difficult because there are so many choices, but a good salesperson is always ready and willing to make helpful suggestions. Wear plain cap black leather shoes and black socks, and you will not go wrong. The cost of dressing in this ensemble will run between $400 and $500. However, it will last for at least three years, providing you do not put on any weight. When you are starting out after receiving your diploma, $300 to $500 may seem like a lot of money, but it's a good investment.

These two outfits will become part of your wardrobe not only for job interviews, but also for weddings, funerals, and attending trade shows and conferences. Hopefully, there will be more weddings than funerals.

FAIL-SAFE DRESS FOR WOMEN: LISTEN TO LINDA

Women have a greater challenge than men do because there are so many more options. The first and last rule is to select conservative outfits.

Linda Winter, Founder and CEO of the Winter Group, a Denver-based marketing and advertising company catering to the communications and education industries, is noted for her attractive appearance and for selecting the right attire for the right occasion. We asked Linda to provide guidance for women who are agonizing over what to wear for that all-important interview. Here is what Linda said:

> ***Listen to Linda*** Interview style should fit the organization you're talking to. For creative companies (publishing, advertising, design, technology, etc.), it's great to dress with a bit of individual "flair." Consider a scarf, a piece of "statement" jewelry, or a jacket with some memorable design elements. For conservative companies (banking, finance, real estate, health care, etc.), a skirt or pantsuit that's tasteful always works. Add a scarf, tasteful earrings, or a bracelet and a crisp blouse or sweater, and you should be dressed appropriately.
>
> Talbots, Ann Taylor, Banana Republic, Nordstrom, Macy's, and Dillard's all offer great options that you can put together in a variety of outfits. A white or oxford blue blouse with gray or navy slacks or skirt are great launching pads. From there you can accessorize with scarves, jewelry, shoes, and bags to showcase your own sense of style.
>
> If you're wearing a dress, add a complementary jacket or cardigan. And yes, either be sure your bag holds your files nicely or invest in an "on trend" tote to hold your resume, work samples, notebook, and other business essentials. Cookie-cutter? No! The goal is to look "meeting ready" and to show you understand the culture and style of the company you're visiting . . . and at the same time put your own unique personality and style into the mix!

GROOMING AND DRESS

Dress and proper grooming go together. You can dress like a celebrity, but if your hair looks like you just woke up after an all-nighter at the local pub, you are history. Rules for proper grooming apply equally to men and women. Remember them as you prepare for an interview or working a conference or trade show.

Hair

Wear your hair in a natural style. It can be reasonably long or short but never looking like you just came out of the shower or arrived home from a ten-day hiking trip. Your natural hair color is your best color. If you believe that dying your hair orange or light green is in style, then I advise you to look for a job in the circus, like at Ringling Brothers, www.ringling.com. Orange hair and business do not mix, unless you are in the entertainment business, where anything goes.

For men, hair applies not only to your head, but also to your face. A well-groomed beard is fine, but there is nothing better to turn off a hiring manager than a face covered in stubble. *Please*, men, shave before an interview, and don't cut your chin.

Nails

All of us know the importance of good nail grooming. One-inch claws, or nails bitten or filed to the nubs, are not interview-friendly. For some reason, men overlook this part of their grooming and often show up to interviews with dirt under their nails. It must be a throwback to Neanderthal times. Your hands are always in view, so groom your nails carefully.

Women, avoid the use of shocking or strangely colored nail polish. There is nothing wrong with clear polish. Nail art is not business appropriate, and excessively long nails might be a turn off as well.

Cosmetics

The excessive use of fragrances can be offensive to other people. Go very easy on the aftershave or perfume. The hiring manager at your interview may have an allergic reaction to strong-smelling fragrances.

Women, use common sense with facial cosmetics. Use lip gloss, eyeliner, foundation, and powder conservatively. Use these items for beautification purposes, not for attracting undue attention. If you just remember that an interview is a business deal and not a weekend party, you will pass the interview with flying colors.

DRESS FOR NONCORPORATE JOBS

I've given much attention to appropriate dress for corporate job interviews, but how does someone dress for a job that is performed in a more casual environment, like a garden center or a construction site? Once more, common sense rules. If you are interviewing for an apprentice electrician position with a job supervisor in a construction trailer, then you do not need to wear a suit. For this kind of job interview and others similar in nature, wear a pair of casual cotton khakis, a cotton or polyester knit shirt or top with a collar, conservative sneakers or loafers, and matching socks. Personal grooming should be the same for any type of job.

GOING FORWARD

In our appearance- and celebrity-conscious culture, it is easy to become preoccupied with how we look. It is important in the business world because first impressions are lasting impressions. Use the rules and guidelines in this chapter and you will be fine. Do not obsess over dressing for an interview. Use common sense, and if you want real-life models, observe how businesspeople dress for appearances on the TV business shows.

CHAPTER TAKEAWAYS

- *Always go to an interview in nothing less than fail-safe, conservative clothing.*
- *Purchase interview-appropriate clothing and it will be an investment for multipurpose use.*

- *When purchasing interview attire, always inquire about job opportunities. Get the name and contact information for hiring managers and human resources directors and follow up.*

PART 6

JOB DESCRIPTIONS, JOB OFFERS, AND COMPANY EVALUATIONS

Chapter 21

How to Interpret and Respond to a Job Description

Job descriptions are just that and nothing more. A posted job description *implies* that the position is open and the company is conducting a search for candidates, but that is not always true. Job descriptions are simply a concise rendering of the job title, job responsibilities, and job qualifications. Sometimes they include a description of the company. They rarely include compensation and benefits or names and titles of the hiring manager. A candidate should make a thorough evaluation before responding to them.

READING AND INTERPRETING THE JOB DESCRIPTION

A candidate's gut reaction after reading what appears to be an interesting job description is to respond with a resume and/or other requested information without a second thought. This is unfortunate because job descriptions are written for a number of reasons, and what you read can be easily misinterpreted. To begin, where do these job descriptions originate?

Who Writes Job Descriptions?

One of three sources writes a job description: the hiring manager, the human resources director, or a recruiter working collaboratively with both. Hiring managers write the most reliable job descriptions. Usually, they are realistic and portray the position and requirements honestly. It is in their best interests to fill an open position as soon as possible, and hiring managers are not out to play cat and mouse. For them, time is of the essence.

ARE JOB DESCRIPTIONS REALISTIC?

The job description is written with the *ideal* candidate in mind, and rarely, if ever, does that person exist. In all of my years recruiting for positions from entry-level to CEO, I have never found a job candidate who met every one of the requirements and qualifications on the job description. Companies always make compromises, and experienced candidates know this. If the hiring manager or human resources director did not make compromises, nobody would ever be hired. When you read a job description that says, "one to three years' experience required," do not disregard it even though you may be an entry-level candidate applying for your first job.

WHY ARE JOB DESCRIPTIONS WRITTEN?

Job descriptions are written to advertise a job opening within a company for a particular position or for an identical position in different locations. For example, one job description may be written for three sales representatives who would work in different parts of the country.

Also, job descriptions are written because the company wants to avoid the appearance of discrimination, or to meet OEO requirements. The Office of Economic Opportunity is a federal government agency that oversees fair employment hiring practices. Any company doing business with the federal government must sign an OEO document agreeing to meet rigid recruiting and hiring practices.

BEATING THE INTERNAL CANDIDATE

When a job comes open for any reason, the first place a company looks for a replacement is within its internal workforce. Frequently, a company knows the internal candidate who will be promoted into the open spot, but writes and posts the job description just the same to meet the OEO and/or other state and federal regulations. After a reasonable amount of time, during which the company gathers resumes from both internal and external applicants, the preselected internal candidate is promoted into the job. All of the candidates who applied for this position unknowingly submitted their candidacy in vain. The company will never admit to it, but rest assured that this happens every day. Unfortunately, there is nothing you can do about it.

WHERE ARE JOB DESCRIPTIONS POSTED?

A job description is posted in various places, not just on a company website. The job description you see on the website will be posted on various job boards like Monster, on social media sites like LinkedIn, and on websites of recruiters. It could easily find its way to a dozen or more places, which is why companies receive so many resumes in response to a posting.

WHAT JOB DESCRIPTIONS REALLY SAY

The typical job description will state the title of the position and where it is located. It will list the job responsibilities either in bullet-point format or in a text paragraph. Usually, these are broadly stated items. The job requirements and/or qualifications specify educational background, years of experience, and fields of expertise. The requirements are usually overstated, and nobody on Earth or Mars will ever have all of them. For example, some job descriptions may require ten years of experience in web design, but the company will hire someone with three to five years' experience when other factors are considered. There are always exceptions and compromises that companies will make for certain positions. However, some jobs require strict adherence to the specs in the job description, and I will discuss that later in this chapter.

A good job description should state when the job was posted, an important bit of information because it tells you how long the company has been looking for the "right" candidate. An active job search that has been going on for six months is a warning that something is not quite right.

The final item on most job descriptions is a request to send your resume to a particular place, or there may be a button that says, "Apply." A click here will take you into a list of procedural requirements for submitting your application and a request for much personal information.

Warning

If the job description or online application requests your age, driver's license number, or social security number, do not apply. This is your personal and confidential information.

JOB DESCRIPTIONS WITH STRICT REQUIREMENTS

Job descriptions for positions requiring certification and licensure leave little room for compromise by the company. Examples are jobs for medical personnel that by law require licensure and certification. The requirements stated on job descriptions written for physicians, certified nurse midwives, nurses, radiologists, physical therapists, and other medical personnel leave no room for compromise, and this is understandable. The performance of medical procedures and the prescription of medications are truly life-and-death matters.

Educators face strict requirements as well. All states require certification for classroom teachers. Most states require an advanced degree for school principals and superintendents. Most colleges and universities require a PhD for teaching and administrative positions. You cannot negotiate compromises on requirements of this kind.

Other positions dictate requirements by law, too. For example, lawyers must be licensed to practice in a certain state and must show proof of passing the bar examination. Other occupations involve certification and licensure as well.

WHAT JOB DESCRIPTIONS DO NOT SAY: THE BIG RED FLAGS

Frequently, postings on job boards, or even on LinkedIn, are tricky, to say the least. I've identified the big red flags of job descriptions. Note them well:

Red Flag #1. The job description does not disclose the name of the company or its location. The company could be a back-alley operation or a prominent company on Wall Street. You just don't know. The reason for this non-disclosure is known only to the entity writing and posting the job description, and you don't have time to play games. Do not send a resume or click on the "Apply" button if the name of the company is not listed. Doing so is equivalent to sending your resume into space and a waste of your precious job-hunting time. Always know the name of the company and the job location before submitting your resume or applying online. Make this one of your cardinal rules of job hunting.

Red Flag #2. The job description does not state the name of the company contact or that person's title. It might say, "Send your resume to Position #256 or Job #897." Sending your resume or answering online application questions in response to a job number is equivalent to sending your candidacy to the galaxy in Andromeda. There is no reason why the company should have all of your personal information, including name, address, email address, and phone numbers, while hiding the identity of a living person within the company. Once more, this is a game you do not want to play. If there is no name and title on the job description, but the position is something that you like, call the company customer service department and ask for the name and contact information for the human resources director. Then you can submit your candidacy to a living person. If the job description was posted on a board or by a recruiter and does not list a name, respond by email asking for the name of the person to whom you should send your credentials. When I write a job description under the name Weiss & Associates, Executive Recruiting, I always disclose my name and contact information. All reputable recruiters will do the same. I have noted lately that many company-posted job descriptions are not listing the name of a company person. That is an easy problem to fix. Just call customer service and ask. Legitimate companies always post their corporate and/or customer service numbers. If the company website has an online reply form, complete it and in the "Comment" or "Question" box, ask for the name and contact information of the human resources director, or the name of the hiring manager if you know the department where the position is located. For example, a job posted as "Assistant Marketing Manager" means the job is part of the marketing department. Ask for the name and contact information for the director of marketing.

Red Flag #3. Some job descriptions are nothing more than a general statement about a particular kind of job. Recently, I saw one of these on the LinkedIn site called "Recent College Grads." The job title was Virtual Executive Assistant to the CEO. It had several bullet points about responsibilities and qualifications, but did not include the name of the company, the name of the hiring manager, or the location of the company. In addition, it had a deceptive major heading titled, "Professional Chemistry," under which were three bullet points: upbeat demeanor, adaptable attitude, and composure under pressure. This could have been a bogus job description. It gave you nothing, but asked for much personal information after you hit the "Apply" button. Handing out your personal information to an unknown entity is a recipe for potential disaster. Never submit your resume or application for what appears to be a bogus job description, even if it comes from a reputable source like LinkedIn.

HOW TO RESPOND TO A JOB DESCRIPTION WITH A CAREER PROFILE PACKAGE

If you decide to pursue a position you found through any source, and it does not contain any red flags, what do you do next? Conventional wisdom says that you should submit your resume to a person with a name and a title and a company affiliation. But is that all one should do? Just send a resume?

Consider this. Hundreds or maybe thousands of other candidates probably saw the same job description that you saw on a company website. What happens next? Hundreds or thousands of candidates will, like sheep, send *only* their resumes. Why? Because that's what the job descriptions requested.

Just submitting a resume and maybe a cover letter means that you will be one of hundreds or thousands applying for that same position. To distinguish yourself from the rest of the crowd, you must submit a career profile, which I discussed in chapter 15. (You might want to review that material before moving on.) The career profile includes the following documents:

- Cover letter
- Resume
- College transcript
- Letters of reference
- Business and technology certifications
- Any articles or blogs you have authored as examples of your written skills

There are many candidates applying for one particular job, so you must use every means at your disposal to compete. Submitting the career profile is one of the tools in your job-hunting repertoire that will give you a distinct advantage. It takes time to assemble, but it is worth every minute because this is the real world, big time . . . looking for your first job to become an independent, self-sufficient human being. In addition, many of you have a student loan to repay as well. That is good enough reason to submit a career profile package.

SAMPLE JOB DESCRIPTIONS

Talking about good and not-so-good job descriptions is academic. There is nothing like a real-life example to distinguish one from the other. Here are two job descriptions to illustrate what I mean by a good job description versus a poor one.

A Good Job Description

Inside Sales Representative

Solberg Manufacturing, Inc., Itasca, IL (Greater Chicago Area)

Job Description

We are looking for a hustler at the start of his/her career to join our Inside Sales Department. The position is fast-paced and involves intensive customer contact, order management, and intra/interdepartmental coordination.

Our Inside Sales Representatives are responsible for fulfilling customer needs to ensure customer retention and satisfaction while supporting the outside sales effort. Our team members with well-developed organization skills and the ability to communicate effectively are top performers and eligible for opportunities for advancement. All excelling employees at Solberg are encouraged to set challenging personal and professional goals.

This is a great opportunity for those who have recently moved into a sales role or those looking to begin a career in sales and marketing. We will train the right candidates on all aspects of our business. Solberg invests in their employees and coaches those willing to be coachable.

As we continue to grow and expand our operations, advancement opportunities are available for the high achievers seeking continued professional challenges.

Desired Skills and Experience

- We welcome recent and upcoming college graduates.
- Previous sales and customer service experience is a plus (preferably in an industrial B2B setting).
- Any of the following experience is welcomed: project coordination, purchasing, use of design, and drafting CAD programs.

Requirements

- **A team player.** You work well with others, love high fives, and jump at opportunities to support your colleagues.
- **Driven.** You have superior follow-through and integrity, and you always meet deadlines. You don't get overwhelmed easily. A tough goal to reach? No problem!
- **Creative.** You're innovative, curious, and constantly looking for ways to improve upon things.
- **Communication wiz.** You have exceptional writing skills and natural grace under pressure, and are well-spoken on the phone and eloquent in emails.
- **Fun.** You're a charismatic people person who can talk to anyone; you're flexible, fearless, and excited to help build something awesome and share it with the world.

- **Smart.** You get mechanics (maybe tooled around with cars in your day), are an expert at Office Suite, and hold a bachelor's degree in business or something technical.

Bottom line? You're ready to hustle. You love people, are naturally motivated, and get a thrill from accomplishment. You must be excited to dig in and help a business reach the next level of success . . . Are you ready?

Company Description

Solberg is an exciting growth-focused organization with twelve facilities located throughout North America, South America, Europe, Asia, and Australia. Through our corporate headquarters just outside of Chicago, IL, Solberg provides filtration and separation solutions to customers ranging from original equipment manufacturers to resellers to end-users in highly diverse industrial markets. Our commitment to partner with customers creates a fun, energetic, focused, and fast-paced team environment that facilitates personal and professional growth. We have an excellent training and development program to ensure our employees are given the tools and knowledge to succeed.

Please visit www.solbergmfg.com to learn more about our company and culture.

Additional Information

Posted: June 14, 2013
Type: Full-time
Experience: Entry-level
Functions: Business Development, Sales, Customer Service
Industries: Machinery
Job ID: 6073491

This job description was posted on the Solberg Manufacturing Company website. It is well written and supplies all the information you need, and more, to make a decision about submitting your candidacy. There is one exception. It does not give the names of the sales manager or the human resources director. However, it does give the company website, so you can find the names of those individuals with a click on your mouse or iPad. If that does not work, call the customer service department to obtain that critical information. Once you have the name of the person and contact information, you can safely submit your career profile to Solberg.

Other job descriptions leave much to be desired, and the Internet is filled with them. Knowing how to distinguish the good from the bad from the ugly is a skill that all job candidates should cultivate. Reply only to those in the "good" category. To help you distinguish one from the other, read the following job description:

A Poor Job Description

Sales Representatives Needed!

New technology company has many job opportunities for sales reps nationwide. Sell game-changing software apps that can be described only as "awesome." Good starting salary and exciting bonuses and commissions for those who can cut it. You must be a self-starter and work with little or no supervision.

We want entry-level candidates with a college degree who have an intuitive sense of selling and who can hit the ground running with little or no training.

Join us and be part of a team that will make us a Fortune 500 company in the next three years. If this exciting opportunity is right for you, please respond by sending your resume to our job counselors at www.salesjobsforcollegegrads.com. Reference Job #297.

You can easily see the difference between the good and poor job descriptions. It would be a waste of time to respond to the latter posting, which does not even give the name of the company, much less the name of a person with a title. Never respond to job descriptions similar to this one.

GOING FORWARD

Let's assume you have submitted your candidacy for the Solberg Manufacturing position to the sales manager whose name you learned by calling customer service. You survived the phone screen, and then aced the personal interview. Three days later the sales manager says, "You're hired," and presents you with a written job offer. What's next?

Stay tuned because in chapter 23, I'll tell you how to negotiate your job offer from Solberg or any other company.

CHAPTER TAKEAWAYS

- *Never respond to a job description that does not provide the name of the company.*
- *Never respond to a job description that does not provide the name of a person with a title.*
- *Respond to a valid job description by submitting your career profile, not just a resume.*

Chapter 22

How to Evaluate and Negotiate a Job Offer

Your worth on the job market will fluctuate with the economic cycle and other factors. For example, the 2012 median salary for MBAs with one to three years of experience was $53,900, according to an article in the *Wall Street Journal* on January 7, 2013. That was down considerably from median salaries in the year 2001, almost twelve years earlier. Salaries for those holding bachelor's or master's degrees will vary, too, depending on the state of the economy, the geography, the industry, and the position. There is no accurate way to measure the going rate for entry-level candidates. However, by aggregating the data from a number of sources, one can make some educated guesses.

Contrary to current opinion, salaries are highly negotiable, even for entry-level candidates. I will tell you how that works and how to get the best offer possible.

THE JOB OFFER

Assume that you have made it through the interview process and are ready for a trip to the islands for some relaxation. But wait! You have been offered a real job paying real money and benefits with a profitable company in an industry you like. You have to postpone your trip and evaluate the offer, which came to you via email and stated the terms of employment: start date, salary, bonus possibilities, position title, responsibilities, benefits, and other things about which you know nothing, like passing a drug screening. Now what do you do?

The offer you received by email was written in very official terms and included these items:

- Annual Base Salary: $40,000
- Bonus for Meeting Objectives: 5 percent of base salary
- Benefits: shared-cost group medical and hospitalization; term life insurance at two times annual salary; company contributory IRA, eligible after twelve months of continuous employment; two weeks paid vacation; nine paid holidays and family leave days
- Start Date: August 1, 2015

In addition, there were three pages of solid type detailing the company's rights. One provision was a "termination at will" clause, which means that the company can fire you at any time, for any reason, without explanation, and you agree not to take legal action against the company.

Also, there was a "non-compete" clause, which stated that if you are terminated or leave the company voluntarily, you agree not to work for another firm within a fifty-mile radius considered to be a competitor for a certain period of time, maybe six months or one year.

Another provision caught you entirely off guard. It stated that your employment is contingent upon passing a drug-screening test and a credit check.

The fine print seemed never-ending. What's going on here?

EVALUATING THE OFFER

Although you might be pleased, thankful, and even flattered to receive this offer, it raises some questions, such as these:

"Don't I deserve more than $40,000 per year in base salary? Is that all I'm worth?"

"Can I pay all of my expenses after they take out federal, state, and city taxes, plus my share of medical insurance?"

"And what about this 'termination at will' clause? Can they fire me for no reason whatsoever?"

"What is this 'non-compete' clause? I've never heard of that."

"And how about the 5 percent bonus? Can I get any more?"

"The benefits seem okay, but can I do better, like more vacation time?"

"And what's all this I hear about the provisions of the Affordable Care Act (Obamacare) kicking in and costing employees a ton of money?"

You probably thought that the offer was the final step in the process. You just sign on the dotted line without reading the fine print and start work the following Monday. Now you are learning there's more to it than that. Once again . . . *Welcome to the Real World!*

Let's take a closer look at this offer point by point to discover what it really means and how much a "package" like the one above is really worth. As we learned in chapter 4, it's all about the numbers. The offer of employment is really a compensation package, and to determine the total dollar amount, we need to examine each component part. In our hypothetical offer, the real, bottom-line compensation is more than $40,000.

Base Salary

Every company offers a base salary in a language and style that implies it is final. The company wants you to believe the number in writing is final and non-negotiable, but that is not the case. In all my years as a retained recruiter, rarely has a company told me that a base salary offer for any job at any level is final, and that if the candidate does not like it the deal is off.

Base salary at any level in the corporate hierarchy is highly negotiable. An exception is a large company, like Microsoft, that has base salary linked to a grading level. For example, an associate marketing manager might carry a Level One designation, an assistant marketing director a Level Two, and a marketing manager a Level Three. Usually, it is the very large companies that have salary grading systems, making it difficult to negotiate upward.

Also, government jobs, city, state, and federal (and military, I might add), have grade-level designations, making it next to impossible to negotiate upward. Most private sector companies, however, are open to negotiation. They usually establish a base salary range for a particular position, say, $50,000 to $60,000 for an associate marketing director, and $35,000 to $45,000 for an assistant marketing manager, an entry-level position.

Another factor affecting the base salary could be location. For example, the base salary for an assistant marketing manager in New York City could go as high as $50,000, but in Casper, Wyoming, the base salary for a similar position would be in the $30,000 to $35,000 range. Considering the cost of living in New York City as opposed to that in Casper, the difference in base salary is understandable.

To make sure that any offer you receive is at market value, you must research what a particular job is paying in your local geography and not in the US generally. Frequently, certain job-rating agencies, including the US Department of Labor, quote average US base salaries, but these numbers are misleading. The only way to learn what the salary range is for a particular job is to research your own local area.

What Are You Really Worth?

Salary numbers fluctuate with the economic cycle, the workforce demand for a particular skill, and the geography. For example, in a very robust economy where annual GDP growth is near 5 percent, compensation in a high-demand field, like information technology, will be higher than it would be when the country is in a steep recession.

There are many online sources to help you determine what market value is. I recommend that you check out the following sites, remembering that the numbers you find are *estimates*, not firm and final numbers:

Occupational Outlook Handbook, 2013–2014, www.bls.gov

Salary.com, www.salary.com

PayScale, www.payscale.com

Bureau of Labor Statistics, www.bls.gov

Job Star, www.jobstar.org

Career Builder, www.careerbuilder.com

Continue to conduct online searches for salary information because the numbers change and more sources of information are always emerging.

Benefits

Workers often forget that benefits add to your compensation number. The entire benefits package must be monetized and added to base salary in order to determine the *true* value of your offer. Benefits cost the company approximately 30 percent of your base salary, and should be considered an important part of the package.

Traditional company benefits include health insurance, term life insurance, disability insurance, retirement plans such as an IRA, paid vacations, and paid holidays. A retirement program, such as a company-sponsored IRA (Individual Retirement Account) or Roth IRA, will most likely become effective after you work with the company for six to twelve months and usually cannot be negotiated. IRAs, holidays, life insurance, disability insurance, and medical insurance will not be negotiable. However, vacation time is negotiable, or it can be used as a trade-off for other benefits.

The most important benefits are medical insurance and disability insurance, because one never knows when illness or an accident will strike. Medical and disability benefits are as important as base salary. Remember what happened to Chicken Man in chapter 11, when an accident forced him to the sidelines for six months?

Bonus and Commission

Like base salary, bonus and commission can be negotiated, too. In fact, companies may be more flexible here than on base salary. In some companies, certain workers receive a fixed bonus based on total company performance; in other companies, bonus is based on individual or department performance.

Some workers, like sales representatives, receive a commission based on revenue goals. For example, an outside full-time sales representative selling into the school market for John Wiley & Sons publishing company might receive 5 percent on all sales revenue after reaching an established revenue quota of $2,000,000. If the sales rep delivers $2,800,000 ($800,000 over the revenue goal), the commission would be $40,000. If the sales representative had a base salary of $60,000, the total income from base salary and bonuses would be $100,000, plus the value of the benefits, usually 30 percent of base. In this situation, benefits would add another $18,000, making the total package $118,000.

There are as many different bonus and commission arrangements as there are companies. Rarely will you find two bonus and commission programs that are the same.

In small- to medium-size companies, the bonus and/or commission plans are sometimes negotiable. Large companies are usually not open to negotiation on these numbers. The bottom line is this: always try to negotiate a higher bonus or commission. If the offer says the bonus or commission plan is 5 percent, ask for

7 percent. The company can say no, and you can compromise by asking for 6 percent. There is nothing to lose by asking.

Profit Sharing

Some companies offer profit sharing in addition to, or in lieu of, bonus plans. The higher the company profits in any given fiscal year, the higher the profit sharing for each employee. For example, some companies, like Texas Instruments, have a profit sharing program based on total company revenue. Many Texas Instruments workers have become very wealthy working there over an extended period.

Stock Options

Another benefit in publicly traded companies is the stock option plan. (Stock options were not included in the sample job offer.) This benefit permits workers to purchase shares of company stock at a price that is far below market price. The number of shares of stock an employee receives is directly proportional to rank. Presidents get more that vice presidents, who get more than directors, who get more than managers, and so on.

Companies offering attractive stock option or profit sharing plans usually have a workforce that is stable and long lasting. I have noted that workers in companies with profit sharing plans or stock purchase plans, like Apple, retain workers for longer periods. For example, Apple provides a discounted stock purchase plan for its workers, which has created many millionaires. I know Apple employees who joined the company in 1980 and are still there, primarily because of the stock purchase plan. Consider the Apple worker who purchased Apple stock on a regular basis at a discount of 15 percent of market price over a period of thirty years. In 1980, Apple stock was selling for well under $50 per share. At the end of 2013, the stock was selling at approximately $550 per share. You can do the math yourself. That person's wealth today is measured in the millions of dollars.

Negotiating stock option plans is easier with a smaller company than it is with an established company like Google. The risk of continued long-term employment with a start-up or small company is greater than that with an established company. These companies will be more generous with stock options to compensate workers for risk and to attract qualified employees.

COMPANY COMPENSATION PARAMETERS

An important thing to remember when negotiating base salary is that the company must work within established parameters in order to keep peace in its workforce. Let's assume that a company has a staff of twenty customer service representatives working from its offices in Scottsdale, Arizona, all making a base salary in the $35,000 to $45,000 range, depending upon length of service, competence, and educational background. In that situation, it will be impossible to negotiate beyond $45,000. There would be a breakdown of trust if a customer service rep with two years of experience making $37,000 learns that an entry-level candidate is making more. How will you learn the salary range for a particular position? Ask the director of human resources or the hiring authority with whom you are negotiating.

There are other parts of the compensation package where the company may have more flexibility, like paying tuition for a graduate level degree, or even paying off your student loan.

Base salary is usually negotiable to a certain point. If the base salary offered is $30,000, ask for $40,000. The company can say no or counteroffer at $35,000 or at a number in between. You have nothing to lose by asking. That's how the business world, the real world, works.

The basic rule for negotiating base salary and benefits is this: *be reasonable; do not be greedy.*

DETERMINING THE TRUE VALUE OF A JOB OFFER

A job is worth much more than base salary. As an example, add to a base salary offer of $40,000 the value of the benefits it provides.

This is usually 30 percent of the base salary. Multiply $40,000 by 30 percent and you get $12,000. Add that to your base salary and your compensation number grows to $52,000. Sound better? Add to that any form of bonus money, say, $3,000, and your *real* compensation number is $55,000, not bad for an entry-level position. In business, it's all about the numbers.

When your parents, spouse, or partner asks, "How much is Costco paying you for your entry-level job?" just respond, "$55,000." Tell that to Uncle Bill in Biloxi, and of course, tell that to Grandma, too. All will be proud that their recent college graduate is making more than $50,000 per year straight out of school!

THE SMALL-PRINT CLAUSES

Job offers may contain a number of provisions or clauses that are frequently overlooked because they are written in small print and in legal jargon. They just don't seem that important, but you should know what they mean.

Termination-at-Will Clause

This clause is found in many job offers. It means that the company, for no reason whatsoever, can terminate your employment. It can happen at closing time any day of the week when your boss or the human resources manager calls you into the office and says this is your last day working there. The explanation for your dismissal may include any number of euphemisms, like downsizing, rightsizing, or reorganizing. It means that there is no statutory right to your job and there is nothing you can do about it. However, there are exceptions and you can research the issue by Googling "termination at will."

State law governs termination-at-will. For example, Iowa is a termination-at-will state, meaning that an employer or employee may terminate the relationship at any time and for any reason. Click for more information at www.iowaworkforce.org/labor/wagefaqs.pdf.

Any prospective employee can refuse to sign a job offer containing this clause. However, entry-level workers have little bargaining power. I advise you to sign the offer agreeing to this clause.

Non-Compete Clause

Like the termination-at-will clause, state law governs the non-compete agreement. For example, in California it is enforceable only under strictly defined circumstances. It means that you agree not to take a job that would be in competition with your company or to disclose proprietary company information after separation. Usually, this is time sensitive. In most situations, it is limited to one year after separation from the company. There is a geographical component to this clause as well. In many companies, the prohibition against working for a competitor is limited to those within a certain number of miles from the former place of employment.

There is an entire body of law governing the non-compete agreement. Google "non-compete agreement" for your particular state for the details.

An entry-level worker has little negotiating power to remove this clause. I advise you to sign it and get on with the job.

Drug Testing and Credit Check Clause

There is a growing trend for companies to require a drug screening and credit check as a condition of employment. Employers usually outsource these pre-employment tests and checks to companies specializing in this type of activity. The potential employer always pays the bill for these screenings.

Refusing to submit to the pre-employment drug screening, or refusing to give permission to the company to conduct a pre-employment credit check will jeopardize your chances of employment. If you have nothing to hide, agree to the drug screening and credit check. If you try to negotiate these items, you will not be hired.

There is a body of law surrounding pre-employment background checks. Conduct your own online research if you would like to know more.

The Relocation Clause

If a company offers you a job based in another location, the job offer will contain a relocation clause. The terms vary widely from company to company, but usually, they state how much the company will pay to relocate you, your dependents, your spouse or partner, and your household goods. There is much flexibility here, and companies are willing to negotiate the terms of relocation. This is a highly negotiable item, and later in this chapter, I will give you a vivid example to illustrate that anything is negotiable when it comes to relocation. You will not believe what happened to Peggy from Phoenix!

STOP! YOU ARE NOT YET READY TO SIGN!

Are you ready to take the path of least resistance and sign on the dotted line without negotiating? Stop right there. There are many ways to negotiate a better employment package in a friendly way. Negotiating need not be hostile. You still have a way to go before celebrating, and I will tell you how it works.

YOU *CAN* NEGOTIATE A JOB OFFER

Dr. Chester Karrass, author of four books on negotiating, tells how you can negotiate a job offer in his book, *In Business as in Life, You Don't Get What You Deserve, You Get What You Negotiate*. I suggest that you take time to read this book and two others by Karrass titled, *Give and Take* and *The Negotiating Game*. These are classics and will provide a realistic appraisal of what can be negotiated, how much can be negotiated, and how it is done.

Negotiating may sound intimidating for the uninitiated, but the concept is easy and the implementation can be fun and profitable. Basically, it means that when someone makes you an offer, you say thank you and make a counteroffer. For example, when a store clerk at Dunkin' Donuts tells you that munchkins are three for sixty cents, you might counter with, "Hey, that seems like a lot of money for just three little munchkins. How about giving me six for seventy-five cents?" Does that work? You bet. I have used that negotiation tactic a number of times, and it always works. Try it and you will walk away with six instead of three munchkins. (Try the sugar-coated. They're the best.)

The reason that Dunkin' Donuts is willing to give you six instead of three is that it does not want munchkins hanging around for more than a day because they are small and have a tendency to dry out quickly. It's a win-win situation and everyone is happy. Maybe Dunkin's flexibility is the reason why it is the number one purveyor of coffee in the world. Sorry, Starbucks!

All of us have had fun negotiating with street vendors, whether in San Francisco, in Chicago, in New York City, or in Delhi, India. In most cultures, negotiating is an accepted, and expected, way of conducting business. The seller always starts with a high price and the buyer always counters with a lowball offer. The final price is usually somewhere in between. In the USA, the most highly negotiable products are automobiles, housing, including purchases and rentals, furniture, clothing, food, job salaries, and benefits. There is nothing wrong with negotiating. It violates no ethical principles or laws.

THE PROCESS OF NEGOTIATING A JOB OFFER

The first principle to remember is that the corporate office is nothing more than a gussied-up street vendor cart where everything is negotiable. A carpeted floor, a wood desk, a two-story window overlooking Central Park, and other trappings are just that, trappings. This is just a place to transact business, including negotiating compensation packages. It can be an intimidating environment, but remember that job offer negotiations can take place just as well on a bench in Central Park in New York City, or at a Starbucks in New Orleans, or on the River Walk in San Antonio. The corporate office is just a convenient place for the hiring manager and human resources director to conduct business.

Hostility Does Not Work. Be Nice!

Negotiating need not be hostile. Go about it with a sense of adventure, a smile, and good intentions, and you will always come away with more than what was offered. The process breaks down when one of the two parties becomes greedy. The key to successful negotiating is to make sure that everyone is a winner. Let's consider a real-life story that I encountered when placing a director-level candidate with a large company in the education industry.

Peggy and Her Goose. Peggy lived in Phoenix, Arizona, and was seeking a director-level position with a company that published testing and assessment products for high school students. She had much to offer by way of experience and accomplishment, and was willing to relocate. This New York-based company found Peggy to be the ideal candidate and made her an offer that consisted of a generous salary, bonuses, and benefits, which included health, life, and disability insurance, an IRA, and a relocation package.

The relocation package included reimbursement for moving household items and transporting a spouse and dependents . . . and pets. Peggy astutely negotiated a higher base salary and told the company she needed a relocation package that was more generous. The company balked, and this is where my recruiting firm stepped in to salvage the deal.

Peggy said she needed the relocation package to include reimbursement for transporting her aging parents and several of her pets. I convinced the company that the additional cost was worth the price because Peggy was a one-of-a-kind candidate. In the end, the company agreed, and this is what Peggy's relocation package included: reimbursement for moving all household goods, transportation for her aging and infirm parents, two house-hunting trips to New York, and transportation for her pets, which included a cat, a dog, *and her pet goose.*

Is this insane or what? Not really, because the company found a good employee for a responsible position, and Peggy was happy because she negotiated a higher base salary and a better relocation package. Her parents were happy because they were coming with Peggy to New York. In addition, the goose was happy because its life was spared and it was starting a new life with Peggy on the East Coast. In the end, everyone was happy. I believe this is the only time in recorded history that a company paid for the relocation of a pet goose for job purposes.

This true story illustrates that everything in the job offer is negotiable, even relocation expenses for a . . . goose. By the way, the company refused to pay for goose maintenance while in transit. Peggy had to pay for goose food from her own pocket. Still, everyone was happy.

NEGOTIATING BEYOND THE PACKAGE

As an entry-level candidate, you can negotiate the base salary within reason, but it may be more difficult or impossible to negotiate certain items. Some benefits are highly negotiable, but others are cast in stone.

Creativity is one of the keys to successful negotiation. Let's assume that you and the human resources director negotiate the base salary offer of $40,000 up to $42,000, and she tells you that is all that can be done. Is that the end of the line? Do not be fooled by her statement, "That's the best we can do." Remember, everything is negotiable, even when the transaction is taking place in a corporate office rather than on the street. This deal is not yet done, and here's what you do next.

Going Beyond "That's the Best We Can Do"

Before you begin negotiating a job offer, make a plan, and then work your plan. Write down those items of the job offer that you would like to negotiate, like tuition for continuing education, and a higher base salary. Select one area of your education that needs upgrading, like digital marketing, and make that an item for negotiation. Your skill set will need to be upgraded going forward, particularly your technology skills, and that costs money whether you are taking courses online or in a brick-and-mortar environment.

The same applies to learning a second language like Spanish. Strengthening your technology skills or learning a foreign language will be considered a benefit to the company.

After you get that intimidating "that's the best we can do" counteroffer here's how to respond:

"I'm really flattered that you have made me an offer to work here, and I'd like to share something with you. In order to make my employment more beneficial to your bottom line, I would like to continue my education by taking two courses in digital marketing at Florida Tech. Tuition is $1,200, and I would appreciate that cost becoming one of my benefits. Would you consider that?"

The hiring authority will most likely respond in one of three ways:

- "Yes, we will pay the entire cost for these courses."
- "No, we just cannot afford to pay these costs."
- "We can pay half of the tuition cost."

If you don't ask, you get nothing. A simple question, courteously put, can result in significant benefits for you, like tuition reimbursement or something even bigger . . . *like your student loan.*

NEGOTIATING REPAYMENT OF YOUR STUDENT LOAN

Let's assume you are carrying the monkey on your back called a student loan, and your monthly payments for the next ten years will be $300 per month. I'm talking about real money for a recent college graduate, so let's see what could be done to reduce your debt load.

Before entering into negotiations for repayment of your student loan, contact your private loan company or Sallie Mae and ask for the most lenient terms available. These numbers change frequently, and you want to be sure that you are getting the best deal. Right now, most lenders are offering borrowers like you an opportunity to make interest-only monthly payments for a stipulated amount of time.

An income-based repayment program dates back to 2007 and you should take advantage of it. Your repayments are limited to 15 percent of your income and continue for twenty-five years, after which time the remaining balance is forgiven. Remember, however, that student loan repayment provisions are politically driven, particularly in national election years, when promises made by political candidates for public office have just one objective: to get your vote.

The most important thing you can do as you enter the adult world of work is to get out of debt and remain out of debt. If you are carrying a student loan, get rid of it as soon as possible. Debt will cloud your judgment and be a constant worry.

HOW TO MAKE A PROPOSAL FOR PAYMENT OF YOUR STUDENT LOAN

Do everything possible to have the company pay off your student loan in whole or in part, and be prepared to make major concessions for that benefit. Do not hesitate to pursue the loan issue vigorously. It's worth the effort, and here is a script you might use to begin negotiating with the hiring authority or human resources director:

"I'm really flattered that you have made me an offer. I would like to work here because your company is on my A list. However, I would appreciate your considering this: I have an outstanding student loan of $30,000. My monthly payments are $300. With my salary of $40,000, I will need to work on weekends at a part-time job to make the required monthly payments. I don't like that idea for a number of reasons, and here is what I propose. If the company will assume my monthly payments, I will give back my two weeks' paid vacation for the next two years. Alternatively, I will work every Saturday for the next two years if that works better for you."

Possible Company Responses

Here are three possible answers to your proposal:

- "Yes, we consider your proposal to be reasonable. We will assume payments of your student loan."
- "No, we just can't do that."
- "We're willing to pay a portion of the loan for you. Let us determine what is fair and get back to you."

YOU CAN'T LOSE BY NEGOTIATING

There is always more to negotiate beyond the "final" package. No matter what happens, you win. If the company says no, you can rest easy having the satisfaction that you stepped up to the plate and tried your best to negotiate additional salary and benefits and repayment of your student loan. If the company says, "Yes, we can pay some or all of your student loan," you have hit the jackpot. Congratulations! Blast tweets and texts across the country to let your friends know of your success, and do not forget to include Grandma in Chicago and Aunt Holly in Hartford.

AFTER YOU ACCEPT THE OFFER, WHAT'S NEXT?

The biggest mistake a worker can make after starting a new job, whether it's an entry-level position or a presidency, is to assume the job is going to last throughout the work cycle. That is not the way it works. After you celebrate your well-deserved success and are on the payroll, what do you do next? Rest on the laurels of victory and assume this job is forever? If you do that you have forgotten what I said about the work cycle in chapter 7. You have no idea how long this job will last. It could be six days, six weeks, six months, or six years.

The world of work is a cruel taskmaster, and you must prepare for your next job because you never know when that first job will end.

FIVE ACTION ITEMS TO IMPLEMENT AFTER YOU'RE HIRED

So what's next? Here are five action items that will keep you in the ball game called *W-O-R-K*:

1. Update your resume and your career profile. Be ready to begin another job search when this one comes to an end, which it can on any given day. How so? Something entirely out of your control could happen. Your company could be sold, resulting in your being cut along with hundreds of your colleagues. Alternatively, your company could miss its quarterly number by a wide margin, and your boss will be given orders to slash the department workforce by 30 percent.

2. Continue adding new contacts to your network through LinkedIn and through personal networking.

3. To remain current on what is happening in the economy generally and the job market specifically, review financial programs on TV like CNBC and read financial magazines like *Forbes*. Review job boards and websites. Continue attending conferences and trade shows in your area, even if you have to give up a weekend to do it. This is where you meet people face-to-face and develop personal relationships that result in jobs, if not now, then a year or so down the road.

4. Maintain your home office to continue your research on the job market.
5. Do the best you can in your new job. The best preparation for a promotion is to excel in your present position.

A SPECIAL NOTE ABOUT THE AFFORDABLE CARE ACT HEALTH BENEFITS

The Affordable Care Act goes by many names. It is frequently called Obamacare or the health care act, and by the abbreviation ACA. All mean the same thing, but you need to be familiar with these terms so you are not caught off guard during an interview with a hiring manager or human resources director. This important piece of legislation is the law of the land, and its many provisions have been upheld by the Supreme Court.

Prior to October 1, 2013, when the Affordable Care Act became effective, a company would say, "Here is our medical and hospital plan. The plan is through Aetna, and here are your benefits and your costs." That is no longer the case. The implementation of the Affordable Care Act has changed all of that. Multiple rules and regulations have been imposed on companies depending on their legal status, revenue, number of employees, and other factors. It's no longer one size fits all. Also, employees have certain options, like buying insurance directly through the Health Insurance Marketplace provision, which permits employees to purchase health insurance individually through several "approved" insurance companies. The companies could be different from one state to the next. Costs vary and so do the benefits.

Health benefits are now a matter for serious discussion with potential employers, so do not hesitate to ask for explanations and options. The human resources director will be familiar with the new provisions and will share them with you.

A prudent thing to do now, however, would be to go online and research this important topic yourself, because new information is becoming available every day through a number of different sources. Do that by going to the official website at www.healthcare.gov or by Googling "Obamacare" and "Affordable Care Act."

GOING FORWARD

Debt can be the most debilitating issue in your personal life. It sucks money out of your pocket like nothing else, and it plays upon your psyche like a never-ending nightmare. If you have a student loan to repay going into your first job, or your second or your third job, do everything you can to negotiate repayment into your job benefits program. Also, do everything you can to negotiate a higher base salary and benefits. You will not be sorry.

CHAPTER TAKEAWAYS

- *You get what you negotiate.*
- *Do not settle for the first offer. Base salary, bonuses, and some benefits are always negotiable.*
- *You cannot afford to rest on the laurels of victory. Your present job will not last forever. It is subject to a sudden ending, so you must be prepared to begin another job search immediately.*
- *Personal debt stifles creativity and career aspirations. Freedom from personal debt will set you free to discover your niche in the real world of work.*
- *When negotiating compensation, do not be greedy. Be reasonable.*
- *If relocation is part of your first job, or second or third, remember that relocation expenses are negotiable. Do not hesitate to ask for expenses to relocate your pets, even a pet goose.*
- *Do everything possible to negotiate repayment of your student loan by the company.*

JOB HUNTER'S LIBRARY

Chester Karrass, *In Business as in Life, You Don't Get What You Deserve, You Get What You Negotiate*, Stanford Street Press, 1996 (the Kindle edition was published in 2013).

Suze Orman, *The 9 Steps to Financial Freedom*, Three Rivers Press, 2012.

Chapter 23

How to Evaluate a Company

Learning the names of potential employers is a relatively simple matter with the technology we have at our disposal. However, learning about the company itself, its finances, its culture, and its practices is quite another story. It requires research to see what is behind the name.

Company evaluations usually focus solely on finances. While finances are critically important, there are other criteria we need to explore to determine if a company is a good place to work.

As you proceed through the job-hunting process, you will learn that potential employers can be divided into several categories, like Fortune 500 companies, mid-size companies, small capitalization companies, and start-ups.

While the following checklist applies to evaluating all companies, there are special criteria that apply to each. For example, start-ups are frequently exciting places to work because of the enthusiasm and sense of mission by the executive staff and founders. Check out the many websites for information about how to evaluate a start-up company by conducting a Google search and entering, "How to evaluate a job at a start-up." Do the same for companies that fall into other categories.

THE COMPANY EVALUATION CHECKLIST

Many times companies are judged solely by word of mouth, a dangerous practice because unsubstantiated information can be misleading. Take for example a situation where a guy I'll call "Anthony" has been fired from XYZ Corporation. After word circulates through his circle of friends, you might believe that he was unjustly fired and that XYZ Corporation is a nasty place to work. The truth, however, could be that Anthony was fired because he was not able to fulfill his job responsibilities after repeated warnings.

You need more than hearsay to evaluate a company. What's needed is a company profile based on verifiable information. The following checklist should be a part of your research:

1. **Company Finances**

   A history of profitability is the most important thing you want to know about a company. A consistent record of growth and profitability means that a company has a viable business model that its employees know how to execute. For example, a company such as Procter & Gamble, the producer of household consumer products like Crest toothpaste, Head & Shoulders shampoo, and Duracell batteries, has an impressive record of consistent growth and profitability over the past *175 years*. The company employs more than 126,000 workers and generates more than $83 billion in annual revenue. That's impressive.

   Research every company that you find interesting by using any number of online resources. For starters, just look at the company website and you will find the financial information you need. For example, look at P&G at www.pg.com. For a quick summary of any company, go to Wikipedia and Hoover's (www.hoovers.com), which is a Dun & Bradstreet business research and evaluation firm.

   Also, read books that tell you in everyday language how to evaluate a company in financial terms. I recommend that you read these two books by Jim Cramer: *Stay Mad for Life* and *Jim Cramer's Real Money*.

2. **Company Mentors**

Many companies assign a mentor for every employee regardless of rank. Some companies even provide a mentor for their presidents and vice presidents. The *Business Dictionary* (www.businessdictionary.com) definition of mentoring is, "An employee training system under which a senior or more experienced individual is assigned to act as an advisor, counselor, or guide to a junior or trainee worker. The mentor is responsible for providing support to and feedback on the individual in his or her charge."

The person providing the counseling is called the mentor, and the person on the receiving end is called the protégé. Companies with a formal mentoring program have found the process to result in increased productivity, worker satisfaction, and long-term employment. As a worker new to a company, and as a first-jobber in addition, you will find mentors to be of inestimable value. They will help you learn not only how to fulfill your job responsibilities, but also how to work within the company culture. Having this information will contribute to your success and job satisfaction.

When you research a company of interest, check its website to learn if it has a mentoring program. If it is not mentioned, send an email to customer service or human resources inquiring about such a program. If you cannot find this information before an interview, make sure it is on your written agenda for the interviewer.

How Many Companies Have Mentoring Programs?

It is difficult to say how many companies have formal mentoring programs. Some sources estimate that 70 percent of the Fortune 500 companies have mentoring programs, but the quality of each program has not been determined. Large companies that have formal mentoring programs are

Citigroup, Nationwide Mutual Insurance, McGraw-Hill, and Texas Instruments.

3. **Company Benefits**

Most large- and medium-size companies offer the usual array of benefits: medical and dental insurance, life insurance, long-term disability insurance, paid holidays and sick days, vacation time, and Individual Retirement Accounts (IRAs). All of these benefits are important, but what distinguishes one company from another are the following:

- Retirement plans like an IRA or a Roth IRA, where the company makes a monthly contribution to your account
- Company-paid pension plans, which are fast disappearing from the corporate landscape—if the company does have a pension plan in addition to an IRA program, it is a check in the plus column
- Tuition reimbursement for graduate work like an executive MBA
- Professional development courses that focus on your job responsibilities
- Flexible working hours for workers with family responsibilities
- Student loan repayment programs
- Programs for returning military personnel

When you interview for any position, learn the extent of the company benefits. Most companies will honor your request by furnishing you with a brochure detailing the specific benefits.

4. **Company Litigation Record**

The last thing you want to do is to work for a company that has been involved in numerous lawsuits filed by employees, customers, or both. This is a matter of public record, but finding this information may be time-consuming. It is appropriate to ask the hiring authority during your first interview about the company's record of litigation. Inquire about the number of lawsuits filed against the company over the past five years and the issues that caused the litigation. Ask if there are any *pending* lawsuits, and about the issues behind them. Here's a recent real-life example:

Where Merck Went Wrong. Let's review a case involving Merck, a large pharmaceutical company manufacturing numerous prescription drugs. One of its products was the anti-arthritis drug, Vioxx. The market for anti-arthritis drugs is huge and the company reaped billions of dollars from the sale of Vioxx.

Beginning in the year 2000, users claimed they were suffering severe side effects. Vioxx was named in a number of wrongful death claims as well. The company said these side effects and deaths were just coincidental. However, after thousands of lawsuits were filed against Merck, the courts determined that the company had misrepresented the potential harm that Vioxx might cause to regular users. Merck fought back hard but in the end pulled Vioxx from the market. In a 2011 lawsuit filed by the US Department of Justice, Merck pleaded guilty to criminal charges and paid a $950 million fine.

Would anyone want to work for a company that had lied about the efficacy of its product, a prescription drug that caused death or severe side effects for thousands of people?

Other companies have been sued by their employees for many reasons, including harassment by a boss, favoritism, and gender, racial, or religious discrimination. However, one must be judicious in determining culpability. The filing of a lawsuit always makes headlines, but the result of the lawsuit, which could be acquittal two years later, often goes unreported.

5. **Reputation**

Some companies are considered American icons; others are thought of in dubious terms. One must be careful when making a judgment based on hearsay. Consider the source and conduct your own research using all of the digital sources at your disposal like Facebook, Twitter, LinkedIn, Google, and both online and print resources focused exclusively on business. Even then, it is difficult to make an honest assessment of a company to determine if it is worthy of your time and talents.

Take, for example, what was a true American icon in the financial industry, Merrill Lynch, founded in 1914. Millions of customers had placed their financial interests in Merrill's hands over the decades and were happy. Its employees were happy, too, until something went amiss in 2008 because of mismanagement by the CEO and other executives. Thousands of employees lost their jobs and the company was sold to Bank of America. Relying on the long-term outstanding reputation of the company, employees just trusted the CEO despite evidence that something was wrong.

6. **Your Immediate Boss**

Your supervisor is the person who can make the difference between loving your job and hating to report to work each day. In fact, worker dissatisfaction with the boss is the number one reason why workers quit their jobs. Therefore, it is important to learn who your boss will be *before* you start working for the company. Here's how you might proceed:

The human resources director handles the hiring process for most entry-level jobs and does all the up-front work like searching for qualified candidates, conducting phone screenings, and conducting personal interviews. If you are one of the finalists, the human resources director will arrange an interview with the hiring manager, the person to whom you will report. That person will be your boss.

In your initial interview with the human resources director, learn the name of your potential boss and ask about his or her background and qualifications. Learn how long this person has been with the company and how many jobs this person has had over the last ten years. Ask if any lawsuits were ever filed against this person by subordinates. Ask about the boss's management style. After you learn that person's name, and before your interview, conduct a Google search to see what you can find. Also, go to LinkedIn and read the hiring manager's profile.

If there is something that you do not like or understand, contact the human resources director and express your concerns. Do not accept any job, no matter how good it appears to be, if you observe something questionable in the boss's background. Learn all you can about your potential future boss. The last thing you need in your first job, or any job, is a boss who does not meet your standards for leadership and ethical behavior. In short, you do not want to report to a fool or a jerk.

The Big Boss, the CEO
There is another boss whom you should consider when evaluating any company—that is, the person running the entire show. Use the same investigative procedures described above to learn about that person.

The Good Big Boss. An example of a good and competent "big boss" is Marc Benioff, CEO of the world's largest cloud-computing company, Salesforce.com, www.salesforce.com.

Another is Gary Kelly, CEO of Southwest Airlines, www.southwest.com. This is the only American airline with a consistent record of profitability.

Another is Meg Whitman, CEO of Hewlett-Packard, www.hp.com. She is in the process of restoring HP's reputation and operations. It will take time to fix this dysfunctional company, but we are confident that Meg Whitman will do it.

All of these CEOs have a verifiable reputation for fair play, a concern for company workers, a record of proactive outreach to the community, and a record of donating a portion of company profits to charitable causes.

7. **Corporate Environment**

You can learn much about a company from its work environment. When you are there for a personal interview, observe the physical work space, the décor, the location, and the behavior of its employees. Also, ask the human resources director or the hiring manager where your future work space would be. If it is in a cubicle near an elevator that is constantly buzzing, or next to a restroom where the only music you hear is the constant flush of toilets, you may want to consider another company. You do not want to work in a depressing environment. Ever.

You may find that the *real* office environment is much different from that depicted in TV ads. Most companies do not provide recreational facilities like Ping-Pong tables and workout rooms. They have a regular work schedule and rules to follow, and give little time to recreational pursuits during work hours. If you find general mayhem, consider it a big red flag. Here's an example of a dysfunctional work environment that I found in New York City:

Yo-Yos in Manhattan. I was once visiting a tech company in SoHo. When I walked through the door to see the CEO, I found empty boxes piled high in a large open space with desks scattered here and there. There were young workers sitting on desks and walking around in circles while talking on cell phones, and many were playing with yo-yos. *Yes, many were playing with yo-yos.* Immediately, I surmised that something was wrong, drastically wrong.

I entered the CEO's office, which had a large window overlooking the yo-yo playground. I was not startled when he said, "Look at that. These are all smart, young people, but they can't focus. They all have good tech minds, and many have dropped out from places like Yale, Columbia, NYU, and the like. They are more interested in playing with those damn promotional yo-yos than they are with connecting with customers." My first thought, which went unspoken, was, *Well, you're the CEO. Why not do something about it?* This was a dysfunctional office environment and a dysfunctional corporate culture. What I observed reflected a total lack of training and discipline. This company went out of business nine months later.

You *can* judge a book by its cover, so observe carefully what you see happening in the corporate work space. Yo-yos and good business practices do not mix. Be careful and use common sense when evaluating a company.

8. **Anecdotal Information**

   One can learn much about a company and a potential boss by conducting a survey among friends and acquaintances. Veteran workers are good sources of information. Social media, like Twitter, are excellent sources for gathering information about a company, too. Some scoff at using anecdotal information, but often this research method yields accurate results.

   The best method to learn about a company is to find current employees and ask for their opinions. Use social media, like Twitter, Facebook, and LinkedIn to locate current employees.

9. **Community Outreach**

   Companies, like individuals, have an obligation to participate in community affairs to make this a better world in which to live. Outreach programs involve proactive participation in the community. Other programs include outright monetary grants for any number of programs designed to help those in need, or to foster participation in the fine and performing arts. Company donations for scholarships reflect good executive leadership and management. For more on this topic, read chapter 24.

10. **Company Etiquette**

   Observe the behavior of company employees from the moment you walk in the door for a personal interview or connect for a phone interview. Did the receptionist treat you with courtesy and respect? Did the person on the other end of the line put you on hold for ten minutes? Did the interview take place at the appointed time or did you have to wait an hour to see the hiring manager? Did the hiring manager read your resume before you began the interview? Did the interviewer answer all of your questions and concerns? Did the interviewer interrupt the phone interview to take another call?

You can tell much by observing the little things. If you see yellow flags during the hiring process, surely there will be red flags when you begin working there.

Real World Faves — Three Quality Companies

There are many great companies across the US. One can identify them using a number of criteria. Here are three companies that I've selected based on the quality of their products and services, their attention to the welfare of their employees, and their community outreach initiatives.

Safeway Foods, www.safeway.com. This food company employs thousands of workers in a variety of different positions. The common misperception of large food companies, like Safeway or Acme, is that their jobs are what you see on the supermarket floor. However, most of the jobs are behind the scenes. This company believes that workers should be health-conscious and practice healthy living, particularly as it applies to weight control. As a result, Safeway has state-of-the-art workout facilities and coaching, which has resulted in a healthy workforce. Healthy workers are happy and productive workers, and their insurance costs are much lower. The last time I checked the company's website, there were many job openings in a variety of locations.

Cleveland Clinic, www.my.clevelandclinic.org. This major hospital, located in Cleveland, Ohio, is noted for its high-quality care. All professional staff members are on salary and are trained to treat healthy people as well as care for those who are ill. The Cleveland Clinic is noted for programs designed to keep healthy people healthy. Its philosophy is brilliant in its simplicity: keep people healthy and you will have fewer sick people. The hospital's program includes education relating to lifestyle, nutrition, exercise, and weight control. Also, jobs are available for medical professionals and nonprofessional workers at the Cleveland Clinic, the latter spanning a variety of positions in marketing, finance, and human resources.

Northwestern Mutual, www.northwesternmutual.com. This outstanding life insurance company, with home offices in Milwaukee, Wisconsin, and regional offices throughout the country, has been in business since 1907. Yes, this company has been in business for more than a century, which means it is doing something right for its customers and its employees. Northwestern employs close to 6,000 workers in a wide variety of positions covering sales, marketing, finance, underwriting, and human resources. The total life insurance in effect for policyholders was $1.4 trillion at the end of 2012. In addition, 2012 revenues were $24 billion. At the end of 2012, total company assets were $115 billion, including $31 billion in cash equivalents. However, the Northwestern story does not end here. Northwestern funds a childhood cancer foundation to help find a cure for this terrible disease that affects millions of children each year. It's called the Northwestern Mutual Foundation. Here is what the CEO, John Schlifske, said in the 2012 annual report: "I want to tell you about a new battle we've joined. In 2012 we launched a philanthropic program to help fight childhood cancer. The aims of this program are twofold: 1. We will support families affected by this terrible disease. 2. We hope to accelerate a cure for childhood cancer itself. We believe that by investing in the communities in which we work, we can make a difference in people's lives." Northwestern is a good example of how workers and companies can use the large amounts of money they make to do something good for the community. Northwestern is a company you should explore for job opportunities. The last time I checked its website, there was an opening for an entry-level salesperson in Boston, among many others.

THE INTERVIEW CHECKLIST

When you interview with a company, try to learn as much as possible about its culture and operations. Remember that this is a two-way street. You are entitled to as much information about the company as the company is entitled to learn about you. The interviewer will pepper you with questions, and it is your prerogative to do the same. This is your life. You need to know about the company and people to whom you will give your time, intelligence, and passion. You will spend eight to ten hours a day working there, and you want to make sure that you are not working on a ship of fools.

Prepare a checklist and present it to the interviewer during the course of your conversation. Tell the interviewer you are evaluating the company and would like to discuss the items on your checklist. I discussed the interview written agenda in chapter 18 and presented a sample, but here is an alternative to consider:

Sample Company Evaluation Checklist

Company: Safeway Foods
Interview: June 1, 2015
Candidate: Mary Jones
Interviewer: Marshall Blakemore, Human Resources Director
Subject: Company Information

1. What were company revenues for the past three years?
2. What was the company profitability after taxes over the last three years?
3. How long has the CEO been with the company?
4. What is the annual rate of employee turnover?
5. Does the company have any community outreach programs?
6. Is there litigation pending against the company, and if so, what are the issues?
7. Does the company have a mentoring program?
8. Tell me something about the person to whom I would be reporting.
9. Please describe the company culture.

10. Please tell me something about your own career with this company.
11. Why is this job open?
12. When you have a job opening, do you recruit internal candidates or do you always go outside to find candidates?

Real World Faves

Sources for Company Information

There are many online and print sources for information about companies and the individuals who work there. Here are six that I have found most useful:

CNBC Business News. On TV and online, www.cnbc.com

FOX Business News. On TV and online, www.foxbusiness.com

Forbes Magazine. In print and online, www.forbes.com

Hoover's. www.hoovers.com

LinkedIn. www.linkedin.com

Wall Street Journal. www.wsj.com

CHAPTER TAKEAWAYS

* *Learn about the company and your potential boss before accepting a job.*
* *Do not work for a company that refuses to disclose information you request.*
* *When you are on the job, you work for your boss, not the company name.*

JOB HUNTER'S LIBRARY

Jim Cramer, *Stay Mad for Life*, Penguin, 2014.

Jim Cramer, *Jim Cramer's Real Money*, Simon & Schuster, 2009.

Troy Adair, PhD, *Corporate Finance Demystified*, McGraw-Hill, 2011.

PART 7

GIVING BACK WHILE MOVING FORWARD IN YOUR NEW JOB

Chapter 24

Work and Money: Make It Big and Give It Away Big

When you are a college graduate and haven't found a job nine months after graduating, you might find yourself falling into a state of self-pity. Perhaps it will cheer you up to look at your world objectively, through the numbers, to see just how fortunate you are.

First, you have worked hard for the past four or more years to earn a diploma. You have spent a considerable amount of money, anywhere from $75,000 to more than $250,000 for that piece of paper declaring you are a college graduate, something attained by only 35 percent of the US population. That places you in an elite group of human beings who will be qualified for more jobs and who will make more money than the other 65 percent of the population without a college degree. Feel better about yourself and your chances for success?

Next, you are fortunate to be a citizen of the United States either through birth or immigration. This is a blessing coveted by millions around the globe who have been dealt a different set of cards. On a relative basis, you are holding most of the aces. Holding a college degree in America is like being preordained for success. Here is an example of how workers in foreign countires view the United States:

Janusz from Krakow, Poland. On a recent visit to Poland, I was having a buffet breakfast in a hotel restaurant in Krakow, a beautiful city where the Jagiellonian University, founded in 1364 and the second oldest university in Central Europe, is located. You know the kind of buffet we're speaking about; eat as much as you want from a table that only your grandmother could fix. In a Polish restaurant, this is the next thing to heaven. I went to the carving table and asked the young man tending it for a thick slice of Polish ham. Noting my American accent, he began to tell me how he was saving his money for immigration to the United States. His destination was New York City. When I asked him why he wanted to come to America, he responded enthusiastically, "In America you have access to the best colleges in the world and the best jobs, too. I look forward to coming to America someday!"

So what is this business of work in America all about? Is the acquisition of wealth the only thing that matters? And what about those upper income folks that the media and politicians like to demonize?

AMERICA THE GREEDY?

Throughout your college years, most likely you have heard that making a lot of money is just not right and that those who do so should be highly taxed. After all, those who make millions year after year and have net worth in the millions and billions of dollars are just plain greedy. Nobody should make a lot of money. We need to level the playing field. "Tax the wealthy!" is the rallying cry you will hear throughout political campaigns. In academia, the cry is similar: "Let's tax the rich and give more handouts to the needy. Let's level the playing field." What's wrong with this picture?

In reality, only 2 percent of the US population makes in excess of $250,000 per year, and most of these people own small businesses, the major engine for creating jobs. The owner of a local retail store making this amount of money can barely stay afloat after paying federal, state, and local taxes, operating expenses, and medical, dental, life, disability, and unemployment insurance for his employees. In addition, small business owners are faced with many new costly rules and regulations stemming from the Affordable Care Act (sometimes called Obamacare). The owner of a small business lives from day to day, and there is nothing "rich" about making $250,000 per year.

However, there are some very wealthy people who make a million dollars per year and some who make a billion a year. If you listen to the media and some politicians, you will hear these workers vilified for being greedy. What they do not tell you is that the upper 2 percent of the workers in the US pay 70 percent of collected federal taxes, the money that keeps the country going day to day. The same media gurus will not tell you that 48 percent of the people in the US pay no taxes, and that most of those receive food stamps, which are paid for by the rest of workers in America. But what they do not tell you is the reason behind the numbers. For example, according to the United States Census Bureau (www.census.gov), the 2012 poverty rate for children ages one through eighteen was 21.8 percent, and for the country as a whole it was 15 percent.

Of course, there's nothing wrong with helping out people who have a temporary need for basic necessities. Used properly, entitlement programs are a useful and necessary safety net for those who come upon unfortunate times. I myself once needed to tap into an entitlement program (unemployment compensation) after I was fired along with the entire staff of 150 workers when our educational technology company was sold. The money I received in monthly unemployment compensation took care of my monthly mortgage payments while I was looking for another job.

TWELVE WEALTHY AMERICANS AND THEIR NET WORTH

Who are some of the wealthiest Americans and what do they do with their money? A 2012 special issue of *Forbes*, the weekly business magazine founded in 1917, profiled the wealthiest 400 people in America. Ninety-five percent of these people made it on their own rather than inheriting their wealth.

The front cover of the 2012 issue was titled, *The Richest People in America. Making It Big. Giving It Big. The Titans of American Philanthropy.* I urge you to read this article, which can be found on the *Forbes* website at www.forbes.com. (This material was updated by *Forbes* in a special edition published in October 2013. There is no material change in the numbers.) Here are twelve of America's most wealthy people, along with their net worth:

1. ***Bill Gates,*** founder of Microsoft, $72 billion
2. ***Charles and David Koch,*** Koch Industries, $72 billion
3. ***Warren Buffet,*** CEO, Berkshire Hathaway, $58.5 billion
4. ***Larry Ellison,*** CEO, Oracle, $41 billion
5. ***Michael Bloomberg,*** Mayor of New York City and CEO, Bloomberg LLC, $31 billion
6. ***Jeff Bezos,*** CEO, Amazon, $27.2 billion.
7. ***Larry Page,*** Google cofounder, $24.9 billion
8. ***Mark Zuckerberg,*** founder and CEO of Facebook, $19 billion
9. ***Diane Hendricks,*** owner, ABC Supply, $4.4 billion
10. ***Oprah Winfrey,*** talk show host, actress, author, producer, philanthropist, $2.9 billion
11. ***Mark Benioff,*** CEO, Salesforce.com, $2.6 billion
12. ***Meg Whitman,*** CEO, Hewlett-Packard, $1.9 billion

What do these people do with their money? Buy yachts? Live in multimillion-dollar houses? Own airplanes? Drive expensive and prestigious cars? It may be all of the above, but why does it matter if

Meg Whitman lives in a multimillion-dollar house, and who cares if Larry Ellison bought one of the Hawaiian Islands? Does that imply they have done something "wrong"? Here is the rest of the story about wealthy Americans.

Many Americans have made a lot of money, and they have contributed in abundance to charitable causes in America and across the globe. The amount of their contributions is startling, and this story needs to be told.

CHARITABLE CONTRIBUTIONS OF TEN WEALTHY AMERICANS

Wealthy Americans make a lot but give it away as well, in large amounts. The same *Forbes* article detailed the charitable giving of America's most wealthy individuals. The total amount of money given away by our most wealthy individuals is nothing short of startling and sets the record straight about how the wealthy spend their money. Here are ten examples:

1. *Marc Benioff.* He has given away more than $30 million and counting. In addition to money from his pocket that he donates to charitable causes, his company, Salesforce. com, donates 1 percent of corporate revenue to charity each year.

2. *Michael Bloomberg.* He has donated $1.1 billion to Johns Hopkins University. This is a remarkable story of a true outlier and a model to emulate. Michael Bloomberg was a C student at a Medford, Massachusetts, high school, but Johns Hopkins University took a chance on his candidacy and accepted him. There he learned leadership and financial skills that enabled him to create businesses. In the process, he made a lot of money.

   His contributions to Johns Hopkins University in Baltimore have funded construction of a physics building, a school of public health, a children's hospital, a stem-cell research institute, a malaria institute, a library, and many works of art as well. Mr. Bloomberg has stated that he plans to give away all of his $25 billion before he dies. This is a noteworthy example of what you can do when you make a lot of money. Thank you, Mr. Bloomberg.

3. *Warren Buffet.* His $17.5 billion in donations to a variety of causes, mostly to education, is almost hard to believe. Mr. Buffet has no problem sharing his wealth with others.

4. *Steve Case.* The former CEO and chairman of AOL, and former CEO of Time Warner, is not stingy when it comes to philanthropy. His charitable contributions through the Case Foundation have exceeded hundreds of millions of dollars.

5. *Larry Ellison.* He has given away $444 million to the Ellison Medical Foundation for research on aging.

6. *Chuck Feeney.* Have you ever heard of duty-free shops? Feeney founded that and other businesses as well and accumulated billions in the process. Today, however, he is worth a paltry $2 million. What happened to the rest of his money? He donated the billions he made to a variety of charities across the globe. Bill Gates said, "This is the ultimate example of giving while living. Chuck Feeney is a remarkable role model."

7. *Bill Gates.* The founder of Microsoft has donated $28 billion, most of it for education and health initiatives in America and Africa. One of his favorite targets for donations is the United Negro College Fund, which he supports through the Bill & Melinda Gates Foundation.

8. *T. Boone Pickens.* This titan of the oil and gas industry has donated $625 million to education, mostly to Oklahoma State University.

9. *Stephen Schwarzman.* Steve is cofounder of Blackstone, a hedge fund and private equity firm based in New York

City. He has made billions but has given much of it away to a variety of charitable causes. He provides several hundred scholarships for New York City children each year, and his best-known gift was to the New York City Library. The amount? $100 million.

10. *Oprah Winfrey.* She has given away over $400 million, most of which goes to education and scholarships for students in America and Africa.

WHAT ABOUT THOSE WEALTHY POLITICIANS?

Politicians, too, are subject to vilification along with successful business people. It is totally unjustified. Here's an example very close to home:

President Barack Obama. The 2012 tax return for President Obama, a matter of public record, listed an adjusted gross income of $608,611. However, he donated $150,034 to thirty-three different charities, almost 25 percent of his income. That's a lot of money to give away in one year! This is another example for all of us to follow.

AND HOW ABOUT THE RICH ENTERTAINERS?

In addition to contributing their money, many wealthy Americans in the entertainment business donate their time as well. Here's a good example:

Jon Bon Jovi. He makes millions annually from his entertainment feats, not bad for a song-and-dance routine. However, he has not only donated millions of dollars to charity, but also contributes hundreds of hours of his own time each year to help the unfortunate in New Jersey's most needy areas like Newark. Contributing both your money and time to help those in need is about as charitable as it gets.

HOW DO THE WEALTHY GET THEIR MONEY?

These wealthy Americans did not inherit their wealth, they earned it. While Joe Six-Pack was drinking Buds in a sports bar arguing about who was the American League MVP in 1995, these people were working toward their graduate degrees and working sixteen-hour days. To learn how to make it in America, follow the example of these individuals. Also, study the list of the 400 wealthy Americans listed in the *Forbes* article to learn how these people accumulated such wealth.

Their contributions have provided much for those in need here in America and across the globe. Make a million, make a billion, and contribute in proportion to your success.

HOW YOU CAN GET INTO THE GAME OF GIVING

I strongly advocate setting aside a portion of your income, regardless of the amount you make, for charitable giving. The more you make, the more you should give. There is nothing wrong with making a lot of money. There is something very right about giving some of it away. Where you give your charity dollars is up to you. In addition to donating money, consider donating your time as well. It could be as basic as teaching kids who are handicapped or behind the curve to read or learn basic math concepts. Whatever you donate will come back to you in different ways and provide that feeling of fulfillment all of us desire. It's not all about making money.

To help the uninitiated, I've prepared a list of nonprofit organizations where your money will be well spent helping those less fortunate. The list of organizations deserving of your support could fill dozens of pages, but here are some that I'm happy to recommend based on personal experience and research. As you review each website, remember to look at the job section. Your research into where to donate your money may be a step to finding a job as well.

Real World
Faves

Where to Donate Your Money

The American Red Cross, www.redcross.org. This icon of charitable works has a long and storied history. Donating money on a regular schedule to this organization will help those less fortunate overcome obstacles to leading a quality life. This is a huge organization, and its administration requires significant dollars to support its infrastructure, especially salaries for its executive staff. For example, the CEO has an annual salary that exceeds $500,000. Less than 78 percent of your charitable contributions will get to those in need, but the Red Cross is worthy of your support.

Catholic Charities USA, www.catholiccharitiesusa.org. Ninety-three percent of donations to Catholic Charities goes directly to a particular charitable cause. The remaining 7 percent is used for infrastructure costs. This organization is considered one of the best among charitable organizations. Catholic Charities supports all people in need, not just those of the Catholic faith. If you want to see ninety-three cents of every dollar you donate go to those in need, donate to Catholic Charities regularly. How about $20 per paycheck? Heck, that's only the cost of a pizza and a Coke.

Robert Wood Johnson Foundation, www.rwjf.org. This New Jersey-based charity is the country's largest philanthropic organization devoted exclusively to health-related initiatives. Programs include solving problems of childhood obesity, substance abuse, alcoholism, and age-related problems. The RWJF was founded in 1972 and is based in Princeton, New Jersey. It has been reported that this organization spends more than $400 million per year on these programs. You cannot go wrong donating to the RWJF on a regular basis. When you review the website, remember to check out the jobs page. The RWJF is considered a first-rate employer.

United Way, www.unitedway.org. In 1887, a Denver woman, a priest, a rabbi, and two ministers came together to found the United Way. Its initiatives include improving the quality of general education, health education, and health care for the needy, and helping people find jobs to become self-sufficient. If you donate $35 per month, you can go to sleep knowing that your job is doing more than providing your own food, shelter, and clothing. It's a good feeling. Give generously.

Your Local Church, You do not have to be a church member to contribute to local church-sponsored charitable programs. And it does not make any difference if your local church is Catholic, Protestant, Jewish, or nonsectarian. All churches provide food, shelter, clothing, and career support for those in need. You can be assured that most of your contributions, say, 99 percent, will go to the needy because infrastructure costs are almost nonexistent. Church members contribute their time to make it work.

If your base salary is $35,000, you will never feel pinched if you contribute just $25 per month to your local church. Go online or make a call to your church to learn where to send your contributions. When you are making $100,000 per year, you can donate even more!

The Kosciuszko Foundation, www.thekf.org. The Kosciuszko Foundation is dedicated to promoting educational and cultural exchanges between the United States and Poland and to increasing American understanding of Polish culture and history. Founded in 1925, on the eve of the 150th anniversary of Thaddeus Kosciuszko's enlistment in the American revolutionary cause, the Foundation is a national nonprofit, nonpartisan, and nonsectarian organization.

Contributions to the foundation are used to support higher education initiatives and provide scholarships (over $100,000 per year) for deserving students with leadership skills who are pursuing graduate level and professional degrees. You cannot go wrong making contributions to this worthy organization.

My firm, Weiss & Associates, Executive Recruiting, funds an annual scholarship for candidates applying for graduate level assistance through The Kosciuszko Foundation.

Doctors Without Borders, www.doctorswithoutborders.org. This organization is staffed by medical professionals and provides medical assistance to needy people in more than sixty countries in the developing world. Its services prevent and cure diseases and save the lives of people who do not have access to regular medical care. Give generously to this organization. Its professional staff is dedicated to humanitarian ventures and needs your help.

Susan G. Komen, www.komen.org. This well-known nonprofit organization is the premier foundation dedicated to finding a cure for breast cancer and for providing education and support to women afflicted with this disease. It is active in more than fifty countries and is highly ranked for its effective services. You can donate your time as well as money to Komen. Breast cancer kills thousands of women around the world annually, and Komen is dedicated to reducing those numbers. Your donations could not go for a better cause. If you make $50,000 per year, donating $50 per month to Komen is not going to send you to the poorhouse. Your annual $600 donation will be greatly appreciated by women in treatment for breast cancer.

Wounded Warrior Project, www.woundedwarriorproject.org. This nonprofit organization has one mission: to support our military veterans who suffered physical and mental injuries while serving our country. The organization assists wounded military veterans in regaining their health so they might participate in an active and productive post-service life. In addition, Wounded Warriors provides career counseling and recruiting services for military veterans seeking their first civilian jobs. In addition to donating some of your income to this program, consider donating some of your free time to make this organization work. You will find much satisfaction providing assistance to wounded veterans returning to civilian life.

Goodwill Industries International, www.goodwill.org. Goodwill is a nonprofit worldwide organization that provides assistance to needy individuals on a number of different levels. It provides clothing, food, housing, job training, career guidance, and a number of other services. One of its most ardent supporters is the talented and prominent entertainer Beyoncé Knowles. She donates not only large sums of money but also her time to support Goodwill programs. There is a Goodwill location in almost every city across the US.

COMMUNITY OUTREACH

Giving up part of your entry-level compensation could be difficult during the first few years of your adult work life. If you are really pressed against the wall to pay for your basics (and repaying that nasty student loan), consider donating a portion of your spare time to community outreach projects instead. Every community, from a large city like Chicago to a small town like Dover, New Hampshire, has a number of outreach programs. To find these opportunities, Google "community outreach projects" for your hometown. Alternatively, contact one of the organizations listed above.

A complete life is one that includes giving to those in need. You were given an opportunity to earn a college degree. Give back generously to the community. Make it big, and give back . . . big. You will not be sorry.

CHAPTER TAKEAWAYS

- *Be generous with the fruits of your labor.*

- *Do good works for those in need by contributing your time and expertise.*
- *Share what you earn with others who are less fortunate than you are.*

JOB HUNTER'S LIBRARY

Jim Cramer, *Stay Mad for Life*, Simon & Schuster, 2007.

Suze Orman, *The Money Book for the Young, Fabulous & Broke*, Riverhead Books, 2007.

Editors, *Standard & Poor's 500 Guide 2013*, McGraw-Hill, 2013.

Robert Kiyosaki, *Rich Dad Poor Dad*, Plata Publishing, 2011.

Chapter 25

Using What You Have Learned from This Book as You Move Forward

It is my hope that *Welcome to the Real World* has taught you that finding a job is a full-time job in itself and that you must use your intelligence, energy, and passion to find potential employers in the flesh. Your entire work effort must be centered on one thing: to reach potential employers personally, to press the flesh, to establish a relationship. The reason is that employers do not hire resumes, tweets, or videos. They hire living, walking, talking, texting, breathing human beings. That's basic sociology. It's your job to locate hiring authorities and communicate to them what you can do for their companies going forward.

If you do not find working for someone else your idea of a good time, you can start your own business. It need not be another Apple, Microsoft, or Facebook. It could be something more commonplace. You might recall that Gary from Pennsylvania started a window-washing business, which yields a handsome six-figure income and gives him enough time to be active in the community as well. We know from Gary's experience that all work has dignity. You do not have to be a manager, director, vice president, president, or CEO because you have a college degree. All work has value. All work has dignity.

Also, I hope the book has been helpful in teaching you not only how to locate employers, but also how to communicate with them on a variety of levels. I encourage you to rehearse the scripts for getting past the gatekeepers and your responses to the usual questions asked during interviews. You now know how to approach company workers at trade shows, conferences, and job fairs, and that even in a digital world, the good, old Yellow Pages are still a good place to find potential employers.

As for communication skills, you have learned the critical importance of submitting perfect written documents to potential employers. We saw how tragic it was for poor Patti from St. Louis to lose a $200,000 job because of a spelling error on her resume. I still feel for her, but I want *you* to learn from her mistakes. And it goes without saying that verbal skills are necessary to communicate your ideas and plan for the future.

In chapter 4, I provided a refresher course in basic work economics to learn what the numbers mean. I hope you'll no longer be intimidated when you hear a talking head on CNBC wax eloquently about the so-called "underemployment rate." Now that you know the numbers game, you can hold your head up high and be thankful that you live in America, the number one destination for people from foreign countries seeking employment opportunities. You and I know that even with an unemployment rate of 7 percent, there is still an abundance of jobs on the market because on any given day, workers die and need to be replaced, workers quit their jobs for alternate opportunities, workers retire, and workers are fired. Also, we know that the politicians and "experts" on TV and Twitter are plain nuts when they whine, "There's nothing out there."

Welcome to the Real World taught you that you must first plan your work and then work your plan. Following this simple rule, John from Minneapolis created one of the largest automobile dealerships in his hometown. If you do not plan your job search, chances are good that you will wind up somewhere else, like sitting in a dark corner of a coffeehouse with a tablet on your lap, firing off messages to your friends, bemoaning the lack of job opportunities, and sending resumes to Job #364 on the planet Jupiter.

I've stressed over and over again that the primary purpose of working is to become self-sufficient—that is, to be able to pay for your own food, shelter, clothing, and other twenty-first-century necessities like insurance, transportation, entertainment, charitable giving, and technology products.

The chapter takeaways are the modern-day rules of work. Learn them well and you will never again go to bed wondering why you cannot find a job. Begin developing a job hunter's library using the books listed at the end of each chapter. After all, you will be working for the next forty or more years, so why not make the most of this time by learning all you can about how to make your work life and personal life live together in harmony? Finally, congratulations college grad! You can be the master of the universe! Now, leave the house and find that first job!

ACKNOWLEDGMENTS

I have many people to thank for making this book a successful venture. The prize goes to my wife, Marilyn Baker, who, despite coming home utterly fatigued after seeing twenty-five patients or more each day at the Robert Wood Johnson Hospital in Hamilton, New Jersey, went the extra mile to read and critique the manuscript.

My thanks go out to my literary agent, Gene Brissie, for placing *Welcome to the Real World* in the good hands of Skyhorse Publishing. The connection with Gene was made by a colleague in the publishing business, Neal Goff, president of Egremont Associates and former president of the Weekly Reader publishing company and Prentice Hall Direct. Thanks, Neal.

Several manuscript readers deserve my thanks, too. First is John Meeker, founder and president of Meeker & Associates, Executive Search and Consulting, who took time away from his own book, *Encore Careers*, to read the manuscript and offer helpful suggestions for improvement. Next are Susan Meell, CEO of MMS Education, and Ed Meell, founder of the same company, former editorial director of McGraw-Hill Films, and member of the board of trustees of Cedar Crest College.

Chapter 20, *How to Dress for an Interview*, was critiqued by Linda Winter, founder and CEO of the Winter Group, a technology marketing and consulting firm in Denver, Colorado. Her insight and suggestions will prove helpful for newly minted job candidates seeking their first jobs. If job candidates want to get it right, they should . . . *listen to Linda*. Also, Melissa Jaivin, former vice president for sales and marketing at several prominent school technology publishing firms contributed to this chapter.

My thanks, too, go to Alice Miller, Kelsey Bair, and Laura Bair for sharing their first job experiences in detail. I hope that first-jobbers will profit from their stories. And we cannot forget Marshall Weiss, a student at the University of Wisconsin who is bilingual in English and Spanish. Marshall reviewed all of the Spanish vocabulary and cultural references and offered helpful advice. Thanks, Marshall!

A number of corporate executives I interviewed gave their suggestions for improving *Welcome to the Real World* and provided rules for candidates in the job-hunting process. They are Eric Gootkind, director of employment and employee relations with Measured Progress; Joyce Boston, human resources manager with Measured Progress; Christine Willig, senior vice president of product development with McGraw-Hill School Education; Kiel King, a West Point graduate and founder/owner of Kings of Fitness; and Gary Schultz, founder and owner of GCS Window Washing.

Welcome to the Real World would not have become a reality without the insight, patience, and direction of Holly Rubino, senior editor at Skyhorse Publishing. She is the best. Thank you, Holly!

INDEX

About.com, 314–315
Acronyms, in resumes, 231–232
Adair, Troy, 74, 374
Adidas, 156
Adler, Carlye, 111
Adobe Creative Suite, 75, 158
ADP (Automatic Data Processing), 72
Adult-age children, living with parents, xi–xii
The Affluent Investor (DeMuth), 96
Affordable Care Act (2013), 355–356, 379
Agilent Technologies, 210
Agriculture and food companies, 154–156
Alabama, convention centers in, 189
Alaska, convention centers in, 189
Albaugh, Jim, 241
Albuquerque Convention Center, 193
Alcoa, 236
Alcoholic beverages, at trade shows, 187
Alison (online company), 77
Amazon, 7, 380
American Association of School Administrators
    (AASA), 202
American Booksellers Association (ABA), 201
American Library Association (ALA), 202
American Red Cross, 385
Americans for Democratic Action, 21
American Society for Training and Development
    (ASTD), 77–78, 202–203
American workforce
    goods producing industries in, 151–158
    job sectors in, 150–151
    services providing sector in, 158
    size of, 62–63, 149–150
America's Center Convention Complex, 192
Anchorage Convention Centers, 189
Angel funding sources, 223
Ann Taylor, 316
AOL, 382
Apple (company), 22, 108, 215, 345
Apps
    business and technology, 75–76
    checking for new, 108
Arizona, convention centers in, 189
Arkansas, convention centers in, 189
Articles published, in career profile, 261–263
Artificial intelligence, 105
Arts and humanities majors, job opportunities
    and, 6–9
Association for Supervision and Curriculum
    Development (ASCD), 202

Association of American Publishers (AAP), 202
Association of American Railroads (AAR), 236
Association of Educational Publishers (AEP),
    202
Association of Education Publishers (AEP), 15
Atlanta Convention Center, 198
Atlantic City Convention Center, 193
Attire
    best stores to purchase business, 315–318
    first impressions and, 313–314
    for interviews, 289, 311–314
    for men, 318–319
    need for dressing in business, 134–135
    for noncorporate jobs, 322
    for phone interview, 307
    social media and, 116–117
    teaching positions and, 13
    for trade shows, 184
    websites on proper business, 314–315
    for women, 319–320
Aulet, Bill, 213, 224
Austin Convention Center, 195
Austin, Texas, 176–177
Automatic Data Processing (ADP), 72
Auto shows, 207–208
Awards, in resume, 256, 270

Background checks, pre-employment, 348–349
Bacteriology, technology and, 105
Bain & Company, 157
Baltimore Convention Center, 191
Banking and financial institutions, 10–12
Bank loans, 223
Bank of America, 10, 158, 366
Barclays, 10
Barnes & Noble, 7, 31
Barnouin, Kim, 180
Bartiromo, Maria, 32
Base salary, 341–342
Beijing International Book Fair (BIBF), 206
Being fired, 89–92
Being hired, 89
Being laid off, 89–94
Belcan TechServices, 37
Benefits, job, 343–344, 364
Benioff, Marc, 167, 368, 380, 381
Berlitz, 23
Bezos, Jeff, 380
Biden, Joseph, 241

Bill & Melinda Gates Foundation, 105, 162, 382
Bing, 118–119
Birmingham-Jefferson Convention Complex, 189
Blackstone Group, 240–241, 382–383
Blogs, in career profile, 261–263
Bloomberg, 32
Bloomberg, Michael, 380, 381–382
Bloomingdale's, 318
Body Language (Kuhnke), 304
Body Language for Dummies (Kuhnke), 304
Body language, in interviews, 290–291
Boeing, 17, 152, 153, 210, 236, 239–240
Boise Center, 190
Bolles, Richard, 137
Bologna Children's Book Fair, 206
Bonus plans, in job offer, 344–345
BookExpo America (BEA), 136, 203
Booz Allen Hamilton, 237
Bosses, 366–368
Boston Convention and Exhibition Center, 191
Boston, Joyce, 312
Branson, Richard, 214, 224
Briefcases, 54–55
Brooks Brothers, 316–317
Buchan, Carl, 237
Buffalo Niagra Convention Center, 193
Buffet, Warren, 380, 382
Built in Chicago, 222
Bureau of Labor Statistics (BLS), 18, 63, 72, 151, 155, 158, 161, 343
Burlington Northern Santa Fe, 237
Bush, George W., 15
Business and technology certification, 24, 75–79, 261
Business as in Life, You Don't Get What You Deserve, You Get What You Negotiate (Karrass), 349
Business attire, 134–135
Business Brilliant (Schiff), 224
Business calling cards, 55–56
The Business Directory, 363
Business etiquette, 81–85
Business majors, job opportunities with, 9–12
Business publications, 31–32
Business, starting your own, 21–22, 213–224, 391
  doing it your way and, 215–216
  famous entrepreneurs and, 214–215
  with a franchise, 220–222
  with a partner, 219–220
  resources for, 29–37
  as sole proprietor, 216–218
  sources of money for, 222–224
  tips for, 214
  types of businesses for, 218–219
  by veterans, 230
Butte Silver Bow Civic Center, 192

California, convention centers in, 189
Calling cards, 55–56
CalWest Educators Placement, 13
Career Builder, 33, 343
Career Confidential, 37, 43, 250
Career profile package, 248–249. *see also* Resumes
  articles/blogs published/posted, 261–262
  business and technology certifications, 261
  college transcripts, 259–260
  cover letters, 259
  letters of reference, 260–261
  responding to a job description with, 333–334
Career publications, 31–32
Cargill, 210
Carney, Sandoe & Associates, 14
Case in Point (Cosentino), 304
Case, Steve, 382
Casone, Cheryl, 32
Casper Events Center, 196
Cassell, Jay, 203
Caterpillar, 17, 153, 247
Catholic Charities USA, 385
Caveon, 166
Cell phone, in home office, 53
Centex Homes, 210
CenturyLink Center, 192
CEOs (chief executive officers), 367–368
Certified Business Laureate Program (CBL), 24, 76
Certified Professional in Learning and Performance Certification (CPLP), 78
Charitable contributions, 381–383
Charitable giving
  by entertainers, 383
  places to donate for, 384–388
  by politicians, 383
  by ten wealthy Americans, 381–383
Charitable organizations, 161
Charleston Civic Center, 196
Charleston Convention Center, 194
Charleston, South Carolina, 178
Charlotte Convention Center, 193
Checkers Drive-In restaurant, 221
Chevron, 152
Chicago Tribune, 8
Chief executive officer (CEO), 367–368
China, Twitter version in, 120
Chrysler, 17, 153
Church, giving to your local, 386
Cisco Systems, 100
Clark, Wesley, 230
CL Center, 190
Cleveland Clinic, 237, 371
Cleveland Convention Center, 194
Clothing. *See* Attire
Clothing companies, 156–157

CNBC Business News, 374
CNBC channel, 32, 72
Cobo Conference/Exhibition Center, 191
Coca-Cola Company, 170, 229–230
Cohen, Jared, 111, 128
Cold calls, 143–145, 178–179, 211
College Board, 161–162, 163
College diploma, percentage of population
    receiving, 87–88
College graduates
    hope for recent, 71–72
    technology and, 109–110
    Welcome to the Real World's guidance for, 3–4
    working in white-collar jobs, myth of, 4–5
College graduates, options for newly, 5–6
    continuing education, 22–24
    employment with large company or small
        business, 6–18
    firing off resumes, 26
    government employment, 18–21
    military service, 25–26
    Peace Corps, 24–25
    starting your own business, 21–22
College majors
    arts and humanities, 6–9
    business, 9–12
    education, 12–16
    finding your passion and, 17–18
    job opportunities and, 6–17
    STEM (science, technology, engineering, and
        mathematics), 16–17
Colleges, miitary-friendly, 241–242
College transcripts, 259–260
Colorado Convention Center, 190
Colorado, convention centers in, 190
Colorado Women's Hall of Fame, 21
Columbia Bank, 11
Columbia Law School, 242
Columbia University for Career Education, 85
Combined Insurance Company of America, 237
Commission plan, in job offer, 344–345
Common Core Standards, 15–16
Communication skills. *See* Interviews; Written
    communication
Community outreach/service
    by companies, 370
    included on resumes, 256–257, 270
    by yourself, 388
Commuting time to work, 45
Companies. *see also* Employers
    best conservative growth, 172–173
    best to work for, 166–172
    evaluating, 361–374
    for-profit, 162–173
    military-friendly, 237–241
    specializing in your passion, finding, 42
Company finances, 362
Company mentors, 363–364
Compensation. *See* Job compensation

Computational systems, 105
Conferences
    business etiquette at, 299–300
    finding employers at, 146
    personal interviews at, 298–300
Connecticut, convention centers in, 190
ConocoPhillips, 152
Consortium for School Networking (CoSN),
    203–204
Constant rate of unemployment, 65–66
Consumer Electronics Show (CES), 181
Continuing education
    Certified Business Laureate Program (CBL),
        24
    graduate level courses, 22–23
    negotiating company paying for, 353
    for returning military personnel, 225–226
    Spanish language courses, 23
Convention centers
    finding location of, 187–188
    job opportunities with, 187, 188
    Real World Faves, 197–201
    state locations, 189–196
Coolidge, Calvin, 29
Corporate Alliance, 222
Corporate environment, 368–369
Corporate etiquette, 81–85
Corporate Finance Demystified (Adair), 74, 374
Corporate jobs
    for education majors, 14–15
    resources for finding, 29–37
Cosentino, Marc, 304
Cosmetics, for interviews, 321–322
Costco, 169–170, 241
Costolo, Dick, 122, 313
Coursera, 77
Cover letters, 277–281
    contents of, 278
    formatting, 277–278
    purpose of, 259, 278
    sample, 279–280
Covey, Stephen, 50, 287
Cox Business Center, 194
Cox Convention Center, 194
Craigslist, 34, 124–125
Cramer, Jim, 32, 362, 374, 389
Credit check clause, in job offer, 348–349
Cumberland County Civil Center, 191
Curriculum vitae (CV), 250
Customer service representatives, job
    opportunities as, 7–8

Daily/monthly planning book, 54
Day, Christine, 156
Dayton Convention Center, 194
Delaware, convention centers in, 190
Deloitte, 237
DelPo, Amy, 79

Delta, 153–154
Democratic National Committee (DNC), 159
DeMuth, Phil, 96
Denver Tech Center, 209–210
Department of Defense, 25
Department of Education (DOE), 16
Detroit Free Press, 8
DeVry Institute of Technology, 163
Diamandis, Peter, 104–105
Digital manufacturing, 106
Digital profile, 127–128, 263
    consistency in, 267–268
    sample, 274–276
    writing, 263, 269–271
Disciplined Entrepreneurship (Aulet), 224
Disney, 239
District of Columbia, convention centers in, 190
Dixie Convention Center, 195
Doctors Without Borders, 387
Dow Chemical, 153, 154
Dow Chemical Company, 170
Dress. *See* Attire
Drug screenings, 348
Duke Energy Convention Center, 193
Duke University School of Law, 242
Duluth Entertainment Convention Center, 192
Dunkin' Donuts, 350

ECG Library for Men, 315
ECG Library for Women, 315
Edison Conference Center, 193
Editorial positions, 8
EdNET Conference, 204
Education
    as heading in resume, 258–259, 271
    international book fairs for, 205–206
    work cycle and level of, 87–88
Educational Directions Incorporated, 14
Educational Testing Services (ETS), 161–162,
        163
Education conferences, 202–205
The Education Group, 14
Education industry, 163
Education majors, job opportunities for, 12–16
Educator's Ally, 14
EdWeb, 14
Elig, Marc, 238
Ellison, Larry, 215, 380, 382
Ellison Medical Foundation, 382
Emails, follow-up, 281
Employers
    calling on potential, 70
    making a target list of potential, 42–43
    top 100 military-friendly, 235–236
Employers, how to find, 131–148
    being proactive and, 132–134
    cold-calls and, 143–145
    conferences and trade shows and, 146

contacting hiring authorities and, 132
    corporate websites and, 147
    internships and, 138–140
    job boards and, 147
    networking and, 140–143
    newspapers and, 137–138
    social media and, 147
    Yellow Pages used for, 135–137
Employers, where to find, 149–180
    American job sectors and, 150–151
    American workforce size and, 149–150
    best geographic locations, 176–178
    cold-calling and, 178–179
    convention centers, 187–208
    for-profit companies and, 162–173
    in goods producing sector, 152–158
    nonprofit companies and, 161–162
    at office, business, and industrial parks,
        209–210
    in the public sector, 159–161
    Real World way for, 174–176
    in services providing sector, 158
    small businesses and, 173
    trade shows, 181–187, 201–208
Employment, full, 64
Encore careers, 94–95
Entitlement programs, 379
Entrepreneurs
    famous, 214–215
    resources for, 221–222
Entrepreneurs Organization, 222
Ernest N. Morial Convention Center, 191
Ethan Allen, 157
Etiquette
    business, 81–85
    company, 370
    at conferences, 299–300
    restaurant, 301–302
Evaluations, company, 361–374
ExecutiveNet, 36
ExxonMobil, 152

Facebook, 22, 76, 113, 119, 122–123, 215
Fact *vs.* fiction on job market, 61–62
Family and Medical Leave Act (FMLA), 20–21
Farr, Michael, 211
Fastweb, 121
Federal government jobs, 18–21, 160–161
Feeney, Chuck, 382
Fiction *vs.* fact on job market, 61–62
Fifth Third Bank, 11
Finances, company, 362
Financial institutions, 10–12
FirstJob, 34
First Niagara Bank, 11
Fishman, Stephen, 224
Florida, convention centers in, 190, 197–198
Florida Educational Technology Conference

(FETC), 204
Follow-up letters and emails, 281281
Food and agriculture industry, 154–156
Forbes, 8, 32, 221, 374, 380
Ford, 17, 153
Ford Foundation, 162
Fordham Law School, 242
Formatting
    cover letter, 277–278
    resume, 252
For-profit companies, 162–173
Fort Lauderdale/Broward County Convention
        Center, 190
Foundations, 162
FoundersCard, 222
FOX Business News, 374
Fox Business News (FBN), 32
Fox Jobs Reports, 32
Franchises, 220–221
Frankfurt Book Fair, 205
Franklin, Benjamin, 164
Freedman, Rory, 180
Frost Bank, 11–12
Full employment, 64

Garden State Convention and Exhibit Center,
        193
Gates, Bill, 22, 105, 214–215, 313, 380, 382
Gaylord National Resort and Conference Center,
        208
GDP (gross domestic product), 64, 74, 151
General Electric (GE), 69–70, 152, 171, 235,
        236, 237, 240
General Mills, 239
General Motors (GM), 17, 152
The Generals (Ricks), 243
George R. Brown Convention Center, 195
Georgia, convention centers in, 190, 198
Georgia World Congress Center, 190
GI Jobs, 234
Give and Take (Karrass), 349
Gladwell, Malcolm, 38
GOALS! (Tracy), 224
Goldman Sachs, 10
Goods producing industries, 151–158
Goodwill Industries International, 388
Google, 102, 118–119, 158, 247, 248
Gootkind, Eric, 304
Government jobs, 18–21
Graduate level courses, 22–23
Grammar mistakes, in resumes, 251
Grilled Cheese Truck, Inc., 230
Grooming, 320–322
Guerin, Lisa, 79

Haden, Jeff, 294
Hair, for interviews, 321

Half, Robert, 85
Harden, Jeff, 32
Harley-Davidson, 125–126
Harley, Shari, 304
Harvard Law School, 242
Hawaii Convention Center, 190, 199
Hawaii, convention centers in, 190, 199
Health benefits, 357–358
Heidrick & Struggles, 36, 72
Helena Civic Center, 192
Help for Wounded Veterans, 233–234
Hendricks, Diane, 380
Henry B. Gonzalez Convention Center, 195
Hewlett-Packard, 235, 368
HigherNext, 10, 24, 76
Highlights for Children, 163, 172
Hiring managers
    attire of, 134–135
    business etiquette with at conferences,
        299–300
    finding at a conference, 299
    found in the Yellow Pages, 135–13
    in interviews, 288–289, 292–293
    job descriptions and, 328
    at trade shows, 186
Hirsch, John, 44
H.J. Heinz, 155
Home-based workers, 100–101
Homebuilding and improvement industry
        conventions, 206–207
Home Depot, 157, 171
Home office, 40–41
    amount of time spent in, 58
    discipline by using a, 52
    record-keeping template in, 57–58
    seven steps for establishing a, 52–56
    unplugged in, 56
Hoover's, 374
Housing companies, 157–158
Houston, Texas, 210
How To Say Anything to Anyone (Harley), 304
Human resources director, job descriptions and,
        328
Human work cycle. *See* Work cycle

Idaho, convention centers in, 190
Identification, in resume, 254
IHG (Intercontinental Hotels Group), 238–239
Ikea, 157
Illinois, convention centers in, 190–191, 199
Immigrants, 150
Immigrants, coming to the U.S. for jobs, 71,
        150
*In Business as in Life, You Don't Get What You
        Deserve, You Get What You Negotiate*
        (Karrass), 359
Inc. Magazine, 32, 173
Indeed, 123

Indiana Convention Center, 191
Indiana, convention centers in, 191, 200
Indianapolis Convention Center, 200
Information sources, for job hunters, 72–74
Institute for Veterans and Military Families
    (IVMF), 236
Insurance industry, 45, 164–165, 208
Insurance Journal, 208
Intercontinental Hotels Group (IHG), 238–239
International book fairs, 205–206
International Reading Association (IRA), 204
International Society for Technology Education
    (ISTE), 126, 198, 204–205
Internet. *see also* Websites
    recruiters found on, 36
    as source for job searching, 43
    used to find business parks, 209–210
The Internship (film), 102
Internships, 138–140
Interviews, 285–304
    attire for, 289
    body language in, 290–291
    closing/ending, 309
    company evaluation and, 372–374
    at conferences and trade shows, 298–300
    corporate executive expectations during,
        303–304
    at the corporate office, 286
    dressing for, 311–323
    ending, 297
    frequently asked questions in, 293–294
    golden rules of, 288
    grooming for, 320–322
    hiring manager role and, 288–289
    listening during, 287
    as looking forward, 287
    overview, 285–286
    with a panel of hiring authorities, 297–298
    parents included in, 286
    phone, 305–310
    preparing a written agenda for, 295–297
    questions asked of interviewer in, 294–295
    at restaurants, 300–303
    "tell me about yourself" question in,
        291–293
    verbal communication in, 289–290
Investments, retirement, 95
Iowa, convention centers in, 191, 200–201
Iowa Events Center, 191, 200–201
IPad, 108
IRAs (Individual Retirement Accounts), 364
It Worked for Me (Powell), 243
IWork, 108
IX Center, 194

Jacob K. Javits Convention Center, 193
Javits Center, New York City, 146, 201, 203
J.B. Hunt, 237

Jim Cramer's Real Money (Cramer), 362, 374
JIST Publishing, 7, 31, 73
Job boards, 33–34, 42
    finding employers through, 137
    social media and, 113–114
Job compensation. *see also* Salaries
    fluctuations in, 68–69
    in work cycle, 67–68
Job descriptions, 327–338
    contents of, 329–330
    location of posting of, 329
    people who write, 328
    purposes of, 328
    red flags of, 331–333
    samples of good *vs.* poor, 334–338
    with strict requirements, 330–331
    written with ideal candidate in mind, 328
Job fairs, 146
Job market, fact *vs.* fiction on, 61–62
Job offers, 339–359
    benefits in, 343–344
    bonus/commission plan in, 344–345
    company compensation parameters and, 346
    determining true value of, 346–347
    evaluating, 340–346
    example of, 339–340
    negotiating, 349–354, 355
    profit sharing plan in, 345
    salary in, 341–343
    small-print clauses in, 347–349
    stock options in, 345–346
Job opportunities, college major and, 6–17
Job rank, fluctuations in, 67–69
Jobs
    follower role in, 27–28
    leader role in, 28
    Occupational Outlook's rating of, 30–31
    technology, 110
    top, in industry, 35
    top, leading to executive-level jobs, 35
Job search, 392. *see also* Employers, how to find;
        Employers, where to find; Job offers
    beginning your, 39–40
    best locations for, 176–178
    calling on potential employers, 70
    company evaluation and, 361–374
    finding out who is hiring, 69–70
    internal candidates and, 329
    personal meetings and, 49–50
    plan for, 45–49
    planning your, 392–393
    preparation for, 40–44
    resources for, 29–37
    responding to job description with career
        profile package, 333–334
    social media and, 113, 118–128
    summary of advice on, 391–393
Jobs, Steve, 22, 215

Job Star website, 343
John B. Hynes Veterans Memorial Convention
    Center, 191
John Deere, 17, 153
John Hirsch Cambridge Motors, 44
John Hopkins University, 381–382
Johnson and Johnson, 173
John Wiley & Sons, 31
Jos. A. Bank, 316
Jovi, Jon Bon, 383
JPMorgan Chase, 10, 210
Juneau Centennial Hall Convention Center, 189
J. Weston Walch Publishing, 209

Kansas City Convention Center, 201
Kansas City Convention & Entertainment
    Centers, 192
Kaplan, Robert, 180
Karrass, Chester, 349, 359
Kay Baily Hutchinson Convention Center, 195
Kellogg, 153
Kelly, Gary, 168, 368
Kennedy, Edward, 15–16
Kentucky, convention centers in, 191
Kentucky International Convention Center, 191
Kernan, Joe, 32
King, Captain Kiel, 228–230
Kings of Fitness, 230
Kitchen Table Entrepreneurs (Shirk/Wadia), 224
Kiyosaki, Robert, 38, 389
Knoxville, Tennessee, 177–178
Koch, Charles, 380
Koch, David, 380
Kodiak Petroleum, 210
Koller, Daphne, 77
Korkki, Phyllis, 127
Korn Ferry, 36
Kosciuszko Foundation, 386–387
Krispy Kreme franchise, 27

Ladders, 33–34
LaHood, Ray, 236
Landline phone, for home office, 53
Langhorne, Pennsylvania, 209
Las Vegas Convention and Visitors Authority,
    192
Lawrence Convention Center, 194
Law schools, military-friendly, 241–242
Layoffs, 89–94
Lean In (Sandberg), 148
Letters of reference, 260–261
LifeBound, 73–74
Lifehack.org, 85
Like a Virgin (Branson), 224
The Limited, 317
The Limited website, 315
LinkedIn, 113, 147, 247, 263, 367, 370, 374

contact information found on, 132
digital profile for, 272–276
employers looking at your profile on, 117–
    118, 119, 267
explained, 34–35
job searching on, 125–127
needing to know, 76
networking with, 143, 147
red flag job description on, 332–333
technology jobs found on, 110
Litigation records, company, 364–366
Local government jobs, 18–21, 159–160
Lockheed Martin, 153, 236, 240
London Book Fair (LBF), 205–206
Long Beach Convention and Entertainment
    Center, 189
Lord & Taylor, 318
Los Angeles Convention Center, 189
Los Angeles Times, 8
Losing My Virginity (Branson), 224
Louisiana, convention centers in, 191
Lowe's, 157, 235, 237–238
Lululemon, 156–157

Macy's, 317
Mad Money (television program), 32
Maine, convention centers in, 191
Making a Difference (Sullenberger), 243
Mangelsen, Tom, 5
Mansfield Convention Center, 192
ManTech International Corporation, 237
Manufacturing jobs, 153–154, 236
MarketPro, 36
Marshall, George, 243
Martin Trust Center for MIT Entrepreneurship,
    213
Maryland, convention centers in, 191
Massachusetts, convention centers in, 191
MassMutual Financial Group, 172
May Civil Center, 192
Mayer, Marissa, 104
MBA (Masters in Business Administration),
    9–10
McCormick Place, 188, 190–191, 199
McDonald, Kirk, 109
McDonald's, 171, 235
McGraw-Hill, 8, 31, 158
McGraw-Hill Education, 163
McKee, Peggy, 250
Meadowlands Exposition Center, 193
Measured Progress, 163, 172
Medicine, technology and, 106
Medtronic, 171
Menendez, Robert, 227
Men, fail-safe dress for, 318–319
Mentoring programs, 363–364
Merck, 365
Merrill Lynch, 366

Metrics, resume, 253
Metrolina Expo Center, 193
Meydenbauer center, 196
Miami Beach Convention Center, 190, 198
Michigan, convention centers in, 191
Microsoft, 22, 138, 158, 214–215, 247, 382
Microsoft Office Suite, 75
Microsoft Outlook, 54
Military Family Act (1985), 20
Military personnel, returning, 225–247
    civilian jobs for, 227–228
    continuing education for, 225–226
    employment advantages for, 228–230
    government benefit delays for, 226–227
    help from organizations for, 232–235
    military-friendly colleges and law schools for,
        241–242
    resume writing for, 231–232
    starting their own business, 230
    top 100 employers for, 235–236
Military service, 25–26
MIND Research Institute, 163, 172
Minneapolis Convention Center, 192
Minnesota, convention centers in, 192
Mississippi Coast Convention Center, 192
Mississippi, convention centers in, 192
Missouri, convention centers in, 192
The Money Book for the Young, Fabulous & Broke
    (Orman), 389
Monster.com, 33, 247
Montana, convention centers in, 192
Morgan Stanley, 210
Moscone Center, 189
Myth on college grads, 4–5

NAHB International Builders Show, 207
Nails, for interviews, 321
Nanotechnology, 106
Nashville Convention Center, 195
National Academy of Recording Arts and
    Sciences, 42
National Association of Biology Teachers
    (NABT), 205
National Association of Home Builders
    (NAHB), 207
National Association of Manufacturers, 236
National Association of Mutual Insurance
    Companies (NAMIC), 208
National Bureau of Economic Research (NBER),
    64
National Council for the Social Studies (NCSS),
    205
National Council of Teachers of Mathematics
    (NCTM), 43, 205
National Institutes of Health Revitalization Act
    (1993), 20
National Labor Relations Board, 72
National Science Teachers Association (NSTA),

205
National Women's Hall of Fame, 21
Navy Pier, 191
Nebraska, convention centers in, 192
The Negotiating Game (Karrass), 349
Negotiation
    of job offer, 349–354, 355
    of repayment of student loan, 354–355
Networking
    after you are hired, 356
    for educators, 14
    with LinkedIn, 143
    LinkedIn used for, 143, 147
    at lunchtime, 187
    online *vs.* in-person, 127
    sources of, 140–143
Networks, 105
Nevada, convention centers in, 192
New Balance, 156
The New Digital Age (Schmidt/Cohen), 110–
    111, 128
The New Geography of Jobs (Noretti), 180
New Hampshire, convention centers in, 193
New Jersey, convention centers in, 193
New Mexico, convention centers in, 193
Newspapers, job searching through, 137–138
New York City Library, 383
New York, convention centers in, 193
New York International Auto Show, 208
New York Times, 8
New York University School of Law, 242
Ng, Andrew, 77
Nike, 153, 156
The 9 Steps to Financial Freedom (Orman), 359
Nissan Motor, 210
No Child Left Behind Act (NCLB), 15–16
Non-compete clause, in job offer, 340, 348
Nonprofit companies, 161–162
Nonprofit organizations, 384–388
Nordstrom, 316
Noretti, Enrico, 180
North Carolina, convention centers in, 193
North Dakota, convention centers in, 193
Northwestern Mutual Fund, 372
Northwestern University Law School, 242

Obama, Barack, 241, 383
Obamacare, 355–356, 357–358, 379
Obama, Michelle, 241
Objective
    for job search, 40
    in resumes, 254–255, 269
Occupational Outlook Handbook, 2013-2014,
    151
    access to, 7
    finding your passion by exploring, 18, 41
    as information source, 73
    job opportunities found in, 7

researching salaries in, 343
as resource for job hunting, 30–31
Office environment, 101–104
Ohio, convention centers in, 193–194
Oklahoma City, Oklahoma, 177
Oklahoma, convention centers in, 194
Omaha, Nebraska, 177
100 Fastest-Growing Careers (Farr), 211
O'Neill, Tip, 159
Online job boards, 33–34
Online resources, 43
Operation Enduring Care, 233
Oracle, 215
Orange County Convention Center, 190, 197
Oregon Convention Center, 194
Oregon, convention centers in, 194
Organizations
    charitable, 161
    nonprofit, 384–388
    professional, 43
    veterans, 232–235
Orman, Suze, 38, 359, 389
Outliers (Gladwell), 38

Page, Larry, 380
Palmetto International Exposition Center, 194
Parents
    adult-age children living with, xi–xii
    included in the interview, 286
Passion, finding your, 17–18, 41–42
Paul Frederick, 317
PayScale website, 343
Peace Corps, 24–25
Pearson, 8, 158
Pennsylvania Convention Center, 194
Pennsylvania, convention centers in, 194
"People kennels," 101–104
Personal identification, in resume, 254
Personal interviews. *See* Interviews
Personal meetings, 49–50
Personal networking. *See* Networking
Petroleum industry, 152–153
Pew Research Center, 23, 72, 95, 119
Pfizer, 173
Philadelphia Home Show, 207
Philanthropy. *See* Charitable giving
Phoenix Convention Center, 189
Phone interviews, 305–310
Pickens, T. Boone, 382
Pinterest, 113, 119, 125
Pittsburgh, Pennsylvania, 177
Plan, job search, 45–49
Portland Business Journal, 174
Powell, Colin, 243
PowerPoint, 75
Print sources, job hunting, 38
Private sector. *see also* Companies
    fastest-growing companies in, 174

home-based workers in, 100
Procter & Gamble, 153, 362
Professional Healthcare Recruiters, 36
Professional organizations, 43
Professional resume writers, 250
Profit sharing, in job offers, 345
Publications, for job hunting, 31–32
Public sector
    federal government, 160–161
    foundations, 162
    home-based workers in, 100
    local government, 159–160
    nonprofit companies, 161–162
    state government, 160
Published articles, in career profile, 261–263
Publishing conventions, 203, 205–206

Qualcomm, 239
Quick, Becky, 32

Radio-Frequency Identification (RFID)
        technology, 107
Railroad companies, 236
Raytheon, 166, 171–172
Real World Faves
    best companies to work for, 166–172
    best conservative growth companies,
        172–173
    best industries in for-profit sector, 162–166
    best stores to purchase business attire, 315
    best trade shows, 201–205
    charitable organizations, 385–388
    clothing company, 156
    convention centers, 197–201
    explained, xiv
    financial institutions, 10
    information sources for job hunting, 71–74
    Internet sites for business attire, 314–315
    Lululemon, 156
    military-friendly companies, 237–241
    military-friendly employers, 235–236
    quality companies, 371–372
    sources for company information, 374
    television programs, 32
    trade shows by industry, 201–205
Rebooting Work (Webb/Adler), 111
Recession
    hiring and layoffs during, 69–70
    unemployment rate and, 63–64
Recruiters
    for education majors, 13–14
    list of suggested, 36–37
    overview, 34–36
Referrals, 143
Regions Financial Corporation, 11
Relocation clause, in job offer, 349
Republican National Committee (RNC), 159

Reputation, company, 366
Resources. *see also Occupational Outlook Handbook, 2013-2014*
  business and career publications, 31–32
  for entrepreneurs, 221–222
  on finding corporate jobs, 29–37
  franchise, 221
  information sources for job hunters, 72–74
  job boards, 33–34
  recruiters, 34–37
  television programs, 32
  Venture for America, 29–30
Restaurants, interviews at, 300–303
Resumes
  acronyms in, 231–232
  amount received by companies, 247–248
  curriculum vitae (CV) and, 250
  major headings of, 268
  in personal career profile package, 43
  purpose of, 251
  sample, 269–271
  sent as part of a career profile, 248–249
  sent directly to human resources director, 7
Resume writing, 249–259
  file name for, 252
  five common mistakes in, 251
  formatting for, 252
  general rules for, 250–251
  length and, 252, 268
  major headings and, 253–259
  neat appearance of, 252
  by professional resume writers, 250
  spelling for, 253
  style for, 253
  for veterans entering civilian workforce, 231–232
Retirement, 94–95
RFID technology, 107
Rhode Island Convention Center, 194
Rhode Island, convention centers in, 194
Rich Dad Poor Dad (Kiyosaki), 389
Ricks, Thomas, 243
Robert Half, 37
Robert Wood Johnson Foundation, 162, 385
Robotics, 105
Robots, 106–107
Romney, Mitt, 9
Rosetta Stone, 23
Ryan Homes, 157

Safeway Foods, 371, 373–374
Sage ACT, 54
Salaries
  grading levels and, 341–342
  in job offer, 341–343
  median, 339
  negotiating, 346
  researching market value of, 342–343

taxing the wealthy and, 378–379
Salary.com, 343
Salesforce.com, 100, 101, 158, 167, 368, 381
Salt Lake City, Utah, 177
Salt Palace Convention Center, 195
Sample digital profile, 274–276
Sample interview agenda, 296–297
Sample job descriptions, 334–338
Sample resume, 269–271
Sandberg, Sheryl, 148
San Diego Convention Center, 189
San Jose, California, 177
Schiff, Lewis, 224
Schlifske, John, 372
Schmidt, Eric, 110–111, 128
Scholastic, 163
Schroeder, Patricia, 19–21
Schultz, Gary, 22, 216–218
Schultz, Howard, 168–169
Schwarzman, Stephen, 241, 382–383
Scuderi, Royale, 85
Seagate Convention Centre, 194
Seasonal unemployment, 65
Security industry, 165–166
Sensors, 105
Services providing sector, 158
ServPro, 221
The 7 Habits of Highly Effective People (Covey), 50, 287
Shellenbarger, Sue, 103
Shelter companies, 157–158
Shirk, Martha, 224
Simply Hired, 124
Sina Weibo, 120
Sioux Empire Fairgrounds, 195
Sixty Minutes, 40
Skinny Bitch (Freedman/Barnouin), 180
Skyhorse Publishing, 8, 203
Skype interviews, 309
Small Business Administration, 173
Small businesses, 173
Small Giants, 222
Smith, Brad, 138
Social media, 113–128
  cleaning up self-images of yourself on, 116–117
  company use in hiring process, 114
  digital profile used with, 127–128, 267–268, 271–276
  first step in using, 117–118
  hiring managers reviewing your, 267–268
  job leads through, 113–114
  job searching through, 137
  needed tech skills with, 76
  not using exclusively for job search, 127
  personal networking used in addition to, 115–116
  sites for job searches, 118–127
Social networking. *See* Networking

Social Networking for Educators, 14
Society for Industrial and Organizational
    Psychology (SIOP), 199
Software and Information Industry Association
    (SIIA), 205
Solberg Manufacturing Inc., 334–337
Sole proprietorship, 216–218
Sorkin, Andrew Ross, 32
South Carolina, convention centers in, 194
South Dakota, convention centers in, 195
Southern Company, 237
Southwest Airlines, 168, 247, 368
Spanish language, learning, 23
Spell-checkers, 263–264
Spelling, resume, 253
Spokane Center, 196
Sports Illustrated, 8
Squawk Box (television program), 32
Standard & Poor's 500 Guide 2013, 148
Stanford Law School, 242
Starbucks, 168–169
The Start Your Own Business Bible (Walsh), 38
State Farm, 172
State government jobs, 18–21, 160
Statehouse Convention Center, 189
Stay Mad for Life (Cramer), 362, 374, 389
STEM (science, technology, engineering, and
    math) majors, job opportunities with,
    16–17
Stock options, 345–346
Structural unemployment, 65
Student loans, negotiating repayment of,
    354–355
Sullenberger, Chesley "Sully," 243
Summary, in resumes, 254–255
Sun Trust Banks, 11
Susan G. Komen organization, 387
Syracuse University, 236

Table manners, at restaurants, 301
Talbots, 318
Tampa Convention Center, 190, 198
Taxation of the wealthy, 378–379
Teavana Holdings, 169
Technology, 99–111. *see also* Social media
    college graduates updating skills in, 109–110
    constant changes in, 99–100
    explosive innovation in, 104–106
    game changers in, 106–108
    home-based work and, 100–101
    job openings in, 110
    work location and, 100–104
The Technology Council of Greater Kansas City,
    222
Technology skills
    listed in resume, 257–258, 270–271
    needed, 75–76
Television programs, for seeking employment, 32

Tennessee, convention centers in, 195
Ten Speed Press, 32
Termination-at-will clause, in job offer, 347–348
Texas, 176–177, 195
Texas Computer Education Association (TCEA),
    205
Texas Instruments, 167, 345
3-D barcodes, 107
Tiffany & Company, 168
Time Warner Cable, 210, 382
Toyota, 175–176
Tracy, Brian, 224
Trade shows, 146, 181–187. *see also* Convention
    centers
    alcoholic beverages at, 187
    establishing contacts at, 185–186
    by industry, 201–208
    lunchtime at, 187
    personal interviews at, 298
    preparation for attending, 182–184
    recognizing hiring managers/executives at,
        186
    what to do at, 184–185
Transportation industry conventions, 207–208
Travel and Leisure, 8
Travelers, 158
Trump, Donald, 157
Trump Organization, 157
Tuition assistance programs, for veterans, 226
Twitter, 76, 113, 119–120, 263
Typos, in resumes, 251

UC Berkeley School of Law, 242
Underemployment, 66–67
Unemployment
    avoiding, 26–27
    constant rate of, 65–66
    GDP and, 64, 74
    seasonal, 65
    structural, 65
Unemployment compensation, 379
Unemployment rate, 63–64
    finding a job with an above 6 percent, 70–71
United Negro College Fund, 382
United Rentals, 238
United Services Automobile Association
    (USAA), 237, 238
United States Steel Corporation, 237
United Way, 386
University of Phoenix, 163
Upper Midwest, 178
USAA (United Services Automobile
    Association), 238
US Bancorp, 11
U.S. Census Bureau, 18, 45, 379
U.S. Department of Defense, 234
U.S. Department of Education, 19
U.S. Department of Health and Human

Services, 19
U.S. Department of Labor, 19. *see also*
   Occupational Outlook Handbook, 2013-
   2014
USO, 232–233, 232–234
US Office of Personnel Management, 161
US Steel, 153
Utah, convention centers in, 195

Venture for America, 29–30
Verbal communication. *See* Interviews
Verizon, 235, 238
Vermont, convention centers in, 195
Veterans. *See* Military personnel, returning
VFW, 234
Virgin Airlines, 214
Virginia Beach Convention Center, 195
Virginia, convention centers in, 195
Vistage, 222
Vistaprint, 55
Voice mail message, 53–54

Waco Convention Center, 195
Wadia, Anna, 224
Wakefern, 155
Wall Street Journal, 8, 32, 72, 105, 109, 113,
   127, 137–138, 154, 213, 339, 374
Walmart, 171, 227–228, 240, 247
Walsh, Richard, 38
Walter E. Washington Convention Center, 190
Washington, convention centers in, 196
Washington D.C. convention centers, 197
Washington State Convention and Trade Center,
   196
Wealthy, America's
   charitable contributions of, 381–383
   donations by, in entertainment business, 383
   net worth of twelve wealthy Americans,
      380–381
   taxing, 378–379
Webb, Maynard, 111
Websites
   education major recruiters, 13–14
   financial institutions, 11
   government, 18
   military opportunity, 25–26
   on proper business attire, 314–315
   for researching salaries, 343
   reviewing corporate, 137
   Spanish language learning, 23
   on using Twitter, 121
Wells Fargo, 10, 158
Western Union, 210
West Virginia, convention centers in, 196
Weyerhaeuser, 157–158
What Color is Your Parachute? (Bolles), 137

What You Really Meant to Do (Kaplan), 180
White-collar employment, myth of having to
   obtain, 4–5
Whitman, Meg, 313, 368, 380, 381
Whole Foods Market, 170
Wildwoods Convention Center, 193
Window Business Start-Up Kit, 217–218
Winfrey, Oprah, 380, 383
Winn Newman Lifetime Achievement Award, 21
Winter, Linda, 319–320
Wisconsin Center, 196
Wisconsin, convention centers in, 196
Women, fail-safe dress for, 319–320
Women in Business website, 315
Women & Money (Orman), 38
Work cycle, 87–96
   assuming job will last throughout the,
      355–356
   being fired or laid off phases of, 89–94
   being hired phase of, 89
   being retired phase of, 94–95
   education level and, 87–88
   job rank and compensation in, 67–68
   three phases of, 88
Work environment, 100–104, 368–369
Work experience, in resume, 255–256, 269–270
Workforce, American. *See* American workforce
Working for Yourself (Fishman), 224
Workplace
   dress code at, 311–312
   home-based, 100–101
Work plan, 45–49
Wounded Warrior Project (WWP), 234–235,
   387–388
Wozniak, Steve, 22, 215
Written communication, 263. *see also* Career
      profile; Resume writing
   cover letters, 277–280
   digital profile, 271–276
   follow-up emails and letters, 281
Written work plan, 45–49
Wyoming, convention centers in, 196

X PRIZE Foundation, 105

Yahoo, 104
Yellow Pages, 135–137
Yellow Pages, 8
Yellow Ribbon Program, 235
Young Entrepreneur Council, 222
Young Presidents' Organization, 222
YouTube, 119, 122

Zuckerberg, Mark, 22, 215, 313, 380